W9-ASB-023

POPULAR PLAYS
for
CLASSROOM READING

Popular Plays

for

Classroom Reading

edited by

A. S. Burack, 1908- comp.

Editor, PLAYS, *the Drama Magazine for Young People*

and

B. ALICE CROSSLEY

Professor of Elementary Education
Boston University

Publishers   PLAYS, INC.   *Boston*

Library of Congress Cataloging in Publication Data

Burack, Abraham Saul, 1908–   comp.
  Popular plays for classroom reading.

  CONTENTS: Miller, H. L. Ghost in the house.—
Boiko, C. Take me to your marshal.—Whitworth, V. P.
The mechanical maid. [etc.]

  1. College and school drama. 2. Oral reading.
[1. Plays. 2. Oral interpretation] I. Crossley, B.
Alice, joint comp. II. Title.
PN6120.A4B8487   808.82′41   74–998
ISBN 0–8238–0151–9

POPULAR PLAYS
for
CLASSROOM READING

TABLE OF

CONTENTS

Introduction

Reading plays aloud in the classroom is a popular and valuable part of school reading programs. For teachers, it is an ideal way to introduce a new dimension into the reading program to help young people master basic oral reading skills. For students, taking part in the production of a play is an enjoyable way to increase their reading proficiency, sharpen their awareness of language in use, develop their social skills, enhance their self-confidence. It will also serve as a spur to further reading on their own.

Because young people today spend many hours each day watching television, they take special pleasure in applying their imitative talents to acting out stories and dramatizing everyday situations. The dramatic material in Popular Plays for Classroom Reading was selected to provide the teaching tools particularly suited to this heightened awareness of dramatic presentation on the part of modern middle-graders. There is a rich mixture here of high-interest dramatic material which will immediately engage the attention and interest of young people: comedies with lively, natural-sounding dialogue to which they can quickly relate, and mysteries with exciting plots and intriguing solutions. Even those who are unresponsive to traditional reading programs will respond with enthusiasm to taking part in a tense mystery or adventure play or an hilarious comedy.

The original versions of many of these plays were published in PLAYS, *The Drama Magazine for Young People,* and all have been produced hundreds of times by students in elementary and high schools. They were chosen because of their proven popularity, high dramatic interest, and fast pace. Familiar and unfamiliar vocabulary is found in all of the plays, and as children practice reading aloud for the class, they will learn the meaning and proper usage of the new words. The dramatized excerpts from the classics are included not only because young people enjoy them, but because they often stimulate interest in reading the original book or story.

How to use this book in the classroom

POPULAR PLAYS FOR CLASSROOM READING can be used regularly as a supplementary part of the reading program. For the average classroom, a set of seven or eight copies of this book will be adequate, since children may share copies when plays with large casts are produced, and may often take more than one part. Many of the roles that are now assigned to boys can also be taken by girls, and vice versa.

As presented here, the oral reading plays may be undertaken as a group project by children working on their own, with minimum assistance from the teacher. After they choose the play, they may select a student chairman, assign the parts, practice reading aloud, and then rehearse the production for presentation to the entire class or several classes combined in an open classroom situation.

Each play is preceded by suggestions to the students on proper ways and methods of expression in reading the plays—voice, pitch, tone, etc. —and step-by-step procedures to follow in rehearsing. With help from the teacher, the group can easily be ready to present their play to the class after only two or three practice sessions. An inexpensive cassette tape recorder can be used by the children as they practice their parts, giving them a chance to listen to themselves read. They and other members of their group, with the guidance of the student director or chairman, can criticize each other and suggest ways to improve the reading (pronunciation, tone, diction, voice, pitch, pace, appropriateness of emotional quality, etc.) to make the final classroom production most effective. Tape recorders may also be used to record the final rehearsal so that it may be played back at a later time for the rest of the class, or cassettes can be saved to compare early readings with later ones.

Improving reading skills

Reading a play aloud with a group of classmates requires each player's close participation because of the immediacy of the drama itself. If the player's attention wanders, he may lose his place, or miss his cue, throwing off the rest of the cast and breaking the entire mood and movement of the play. The attention of the group and their excitement in wanting to find out what happens next—rather than prodding from the teacher —are the best incentives for members of the group to stay alert.

Such required attention to the script leads quite naturally to increased comprehension of the material. Following the flow of dialogue from one reader to the next, as all members of the group must to keep their places and not miss their cues, makes it easier for students (especially reluctant readers) to understand what is being said—as in the flow of normal conversation—than it would be for them to grasp the meaning of page after page of silent reading.

In the course of oral reading, the student cannot skip over or ignore unfamiliar words or phrases in the text, as children often do in silent reading. And in the informal group setting, young people working with one another find it less difficult to ask the meaning of an unfamiliar word in their own lines or the lines of other readers. Reading or hearing a new word in the play, and then possibly discussing it in the group, clarifies and reinforces the student's comprehension of its meaning. In this way, the new word or phrase becomes a part of the student's and the group's reading and speaking vocabulary. As many adults will testify, it is possible through silent reading to develop a fairly large vocabulary which the reader recognizes and comprehends but is not able to use in everyday conversation and may not even be able to pronounce correctly. Reading plays aloud greatly enhances and enlarges one's speaking or oral vocabulary, making for greater precision and color in speech.

Reading comprehension is also developed through oral play reading because of the attention given to proper phrasing to convey tone and meaning and to the importance of observing punctuation marks for clarity. Practice in play reading, accompanied by such direction and interplay among the members of the group, is an important step toward helping students become expressive oral readers.

Other advantages

Learning to read expressively before an audience is extremely valuable experience, since it develops in the reader a feeling and sense for the flow and cadence and rhythm of language and stimulates his appreciation of the spoken and written word. This ear for language and heightened awareness of the meaning, nuances and possibilities of words and phrases in writing and speech will increase the student's enjoyment of literature and will help him write precisely and effectively.

There are a number of careers and professions in which skill in expressive reading will be helpful and often essential—television and radio, films, teaching, lecturing, law, public relations, politics. And those who do not go on to these professions will find the carry-over from oral reading training helpful in their everyday lives, whether in presenting a report or paper, making a persuasive sales presentation, or as a parent reading aloud to a child.

Personal values in play reading

All children love to "make believe"—often to pretend they are someone else—and taking part in a play is a natural progression from their informal play-making. Teachers often observe a shy or withdrawn child take on an entirely different personality, acting like a changed person as he takes the part of an outgoing character in a play, for example. There is something about pretending to be someone else, even for the duration of a short play, that frees the inhibited person and enables him to throw himself completely into a role and act out feelings and needs he may have felt but was reluctant to display.

In addition to being a wonderful outlet for children's imagination, reading plays aloud—which often takes place with nothing more than a circle of chairs at the front of the classroom—brings out the child's creativity and resourcefulness.

The student also feels great personal satisfaction from the successful reading of a part in a play, an attainable goal which can be measured by the response of his peers in the group and his classmates. Meeting this type of challenge can give the player self-confidence, and a sense of personal esteem that is enjoyable and almost immediately perceptible, as other school achievements may not be. And his sense of responsibility to others in the group enhances his self-image.

Social values

Of course the show cannot go on without the cooperation of the whole cast, and participants in a play-reading group quickly feel the need for mutual respect and tolerance—and they respond to it. To make this kind of cooperative effort work, each player must exercise self-discipline. Pressure from others in the play-reading group and the interaction among them as each waits for a cue and the response required—these are factors that encourage discipline, restraint, cooperation, and response to the social situation.

Built into the dramatic format is a degree of competition, self-criticism and self-analysis which requires understanding from the students involved. Assigning parts can be an exercise in self-evaluation for the group. This process calls for a sense of fairness to make sure that the most suitable person is given the proper role, based on his or her reading skills and expressiveness. The need for tolerance of those who may not read as easily or as fluently or convincingly as the others is particularly great when the group is working without the direction of a teacher. In selecting the right players for star roles or bit parts, members of the group exert a kind of pressure on each other toward objective judgment so that none of them will play favorites. Undertaking a joint task like the oral reading of a play will, moreover, tend to unite a group, and lead to new friendships as the group members come to appreciate one another. Needless to say, the social and personal values taught by such experiences have long-range effects on the individuals' growth and development and total personality.

Themes and ideas

The situations in the plays in this collection, most of which take place in familiar settings, are wholesome, with lifelike and believable characters involved in activities close to the children's everyday or fantasy lives. The motivation for the characters' behavior logically follows the plot of the play. Not only do the plays make good reading, but they present ethical and sometimes moral conflicts and challenges which young people will readily discuss.

Each of the plays is a dramatic work of high quality, which will enrich the children's general reading of books and magazines. And plays, which by their very nature must be exciting to hold the attention of the audience from beginning to end, provide some of the most enjoyable hours of reading for children.

Stimulating other reading

The adaptations from favorite classics found in POPULAR PLAYS FOR CLASSROOM READING add another important dimension to the reading program for children. These dramatizations are complete in themselves, faithful to the original works, and wherever possible use the language of the originals. The most exciting and essentially dramatic sections of the original books or stories make up the plays, and classroom tests have revealed oral reading productions often draw the children irresistibly to reading the whole book.

Thus, the plays included here can become the jumping-off place and focus of class discussions, or the basis of an entire unit in literature (*Tom Sawyer, Oliver Twist*) or history (*The Scarlet Pimpernel, How Much Land Does a Man Need?*). Also, these classics of literature can be assigned as special book reports, or research projects for individuals or committees.

Remedial reading

The plays in this book are designed to encourage slow readers to become active participants in small play-reading groups. Role-playing and interaction within such a group help reduce the reluctant reader's sensitivity to suggestion and correction, and with help from the teacher, it is possible for the slow reader to take part in these plays with others in the class who read at the regular level.

The highly plotted material in dialogue form is particularly inviting to those often discouraged by masses of unbroken narration on a page. To use these plays with slow readers, special help in preparation from the teacher is suggested, and extra practice sessions will be required, often preceding the regular meetings of the entire play-reading group. In this way, the slower readers will be secure from the outset and therefore make faster progress not only in developing oral reading skills, but in relationships with other members of the group.

With guidance and special attention by the teacher, problem readers can perform satisfactorily in the production of the play, sharing the experience with the entire class when the play is finally performed for an audience. Gaining such satisfaction from successful oral reading as part of the group may be a new and exhilarating experience for these readers which will enable them to approach further reading with anticipation and pleasure.

In particular, work in expressive oral reading will show the reluctant reader or the student who reads a year or two below his grade level the importance of knowing the meaning and sense of words. Reading plays in particular demands the concentration of the participants who must follow the give-and-take of dialogue, and understand what is being said to be ready to read on cue.

And finally, the plays in POPULAR PLAYS FOR CLASSROOM READING were selected for their high plot interest, strong story lines, and interesting characters and situations—all factors which will encourage the slow readers to take part in oral play reading. The fast pace and action of the plays are likely to be more satisfying and exciting than the standard books for silent reading.

Oral play reading as a vital part of the classroom reading program can not only teach the mastery of expressive oral reading skills, but also add immeasurably to the development of the personal and social values of the participants.

Suggestions for Teachers

Successful use of plays in the reading program depends in the final analysis on the teacher. Her delight, enthusiasm, and interest will be shared by the children.

Ultimate enjoyment for the listener is dependent on the skill of the performers. Such skill is hard-earned, and the result of intelligent practice. Only the teacher can help the children to see the need for following the directions outlined for each play.

In the beginning it is suggested that the children work with the teacher in order to develop an understanding of the procedures and a recognition of the level of reading required for a good performance. In a short time it should be possible to have a group of children work alone. When the chairman of the group is chosen, the teacher should emphasize the need for him to follow the directions preceding each play.

The remainder of this section is organized under three major headings: *Use of Voice, Characteristics of Plays,* and *Techniques of Evaluation.* Sample materials are given under each of the three headings. It is suggested that teachers prepare multiple materials of this type for *Articulation, Pitch, Stress,* and *Pause,* based on excerpts from the plays which the children are going to read. These exercises should be so constructed that children can practice them alone.

If some of the plays seem very long for a single performance, do not hesitate to break them into two acts. This can be done by choosing a natural break just before the entrance of the Narrator.

Use of Voice

Formal training in use of voice is an intricate and scientific procedure which does not fit the purposes of this book. There are, however, a few simple techniques to which children can be introduced, that will prove both interesting and effective.

Articulation

A clear and distinct utterance of the syllables within words is very important to good reading. It has often been said that good articulation is to the ear what clear open type is to the eye.

Rapid and slovenly speech coupled with lack of opportunities for

Because of the excellence of these "Suggestions for Teachers," this chapter has been adapted and reprinted from *Favorite Plays for Classroom Reading,* by Donald D. Durrell and B. Alice Crossley (© Plays, Inc., Publishers).

oral practice often result in a monotonous, slurred, inarticulate oral performance in reading.

The following is a short list of tongue-twisters which can be practiced to advantage by most youngsters. Use of the teeth, tongue and lips is essential to keep the articulation clear and clean-cut.

He sawed six, sleek, slim saplings for sale.
The slim, strong masts stood still in the midst of the stays.
I thrust three thousand thistles through the thick of my thumb.

"And the flung spray and the blown spume, and sea gulls crying." (*Sea Fever* by John Masefield)
"To the gull's way and the whale's way, where the wind's like a whetted knife." (*Sea Fever*)

Pitch

Children associate pitch with music more than with reading and speaking. Essentially it deals with the highness or lowness of a tone.

All good reading and speaking utilize variety of pitch. Nothing is more deadly or conducive to sleep than a complete monotone from speaker or reader.

Change of pitch is often very natural when one is speaking with emotion. Excitement or anger not only make the voice louder but they also make the pitch rise. In contrast, as one feels sadness, deep seriousness, or fatigue, the voice is apt to lower in pitch and become softer.

Many exercises in pitch can be done in a choral situation.

Place the voice on a comfortable low middle range and call the tone low *do*. Practice the scale ascending and descending using the speaking voice. Do not attempt accurate scale tones. Use the scale as an approximation to move the pitch up or down.

```
                                                        do
                                                ti
                                        la
                                sol
                        fa
                mi
            re
do
```

When the children can use their voices in unison to speak a scale, try varying the pitch of a sentence. Repeat "May I go to a movie?" for every single note of the scale, starting with low *do*. Then use the same sentence for a *do-mi-sol-do* sequence.

Vary your sentences and practice in like manner at different times. This type of exercise will help to vary the pitch of the reading voice and result in a more effective interpretation of the play.

Stress

Increasing the force or accent on a word in a sentence can bring about changes in meaning both subtle and obvious. Children enjoy choral reading of simple sentences, placing the stress on different words.

Try the following with your class or a small group:

Will you ride to town today? (Merely asking)
Will *you* ride to town today? (Designating a person)
Will you *ride* to town today? (Ride, not walk)
Will you ride to *town* today? (Place is now important)
Will you ride to town *today?* (Time is now important)

or

You sound as if you didn't believe in magic.
You sound as if *you* didn't believe in magic.
You *sound* as if you didn't believe in magic.
You sound as if you didn't *believe* in magic.
You sound as if you didn't believe in *magic.*
You *sound* as if you didn't believe in *magic.*

Try a combination of pitch and stress:

Mary is going to the party tomorrow.

<pre>
                                          w?
                                       o
                                     r
                                   r
                                 o
                           m
                        o
Mary is going to the party t
                          y
                        t
                      r
                    a
Mary is going to the p   tomorrow?
</pre>

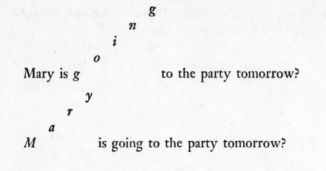

Mary is g   to the party tomorrow?

M   is going to the party tomorrow?

Pause

If children could be taught to understand the value of the pause there would be less unintelligible reading and fewer incorrect pauses which obscure meaning.

Good oral reading is in part dependent on knowing when to pause and take a breath. Reading over to oneself to understand the meaning is essential in deciding where one should pause.

The following practices are taken from plays presented in this book:

"My passenger is angry beyond belief; / he has stalked off to the Blake farm / calling down curses on my head."

"Elijah is beside himself with worry / and perhaps doesn't mean / what he says."

"We have called you here / to relay a special message / from His Majesty / the King."

"Word has reached him / that there is talk in the palace / that the Prince has gone mad."

Practices of this type can be made from speeches within the various plays.

Emphasis

Emphasis can be gained by employing any one or a combination of the following.

1. Change of pitch.
2. Change of stress.
3. Use of the pause.

In the final analysis good oral reading is dependent on a clear understanding of the material to be shared with the listener. Given this, the children can employ any of the uses of voice described above to the mutual satisfaction of both reader and listener.

Characteristics of Plays

The following points should be clarified in connection with play practice and reading.

Comparison of Stories and Plays

Stories are written to be read aloud or silently. Plays are written to be acted and spoken. Stories have the opportunity to make detailed descriptions of places and action. Plays depend upon the scenery and the limited action possible on the stage. Everything else is brought out in the conversation.

Dialogue

The conversation among those who are characters in the play makes the listener aware of what is happening. This conversation is supported by some action. The dialogue may also bring out things that have happened previously or will happen later.

Climax

The climax is that point in the play or story where there must be a turning point. Everything up to this time has led to this point, step by step. Everything from the climax on will lead to an ending.

Climax is most important to a play. It often occurs at the end of a scene or an act. Events are then rapidly brought to a close in the next scene or act.

Narrator

When plays are read instead of acted on the stage, one is limited to dialogue. Since no scenery, props, or action are employed, the narrator keeps the listener aware of changes of place or action which are important to understanding.

While discussing these points, use the plays in this book to illustrate and clarify.

Techniques of Evaluation

Constant evaluation of a child's reading performance is encouraged throughout this book. Lists of questions similar to the following are included in the text:

1. Did you speak clearly and distinctly?
2. Did you match your voice to the character you are playing?
3. Did you come in on time with your part?
4. Did your voice change pitch often enough to hold interest?
5. Did you pay attention to commas and periods?

It is hoped that this type of self-evaluation will enable the child to work for improvement in specific areas prior to class performance.

Evaluation of the same type by members of the group is encouraged through using the tape recorder for the first reading. The tape is then played back to the group and the children evaluate each other as well as themselves.

Occasionally the class is asked to rate a performance. This type of rating can be made on mimeographed slips of paper which are given to each child. After listening to the play, each question is rated as "Excellent," "Good," "Fair," "Poor." The slips are collected and handed to the group leader. Later the teacher can work with the group to identify strong and weak areas.

Example of rating sheet:

1. Did the children speak clearly and distinctly?
2. Did the voices fit the characters?
3. Did the children come in on time with their parts?
4. Did the voices change pitch or were they monotonous and sing-song?

Use such evaluation only often enough to keep children alert. Remember, enjoy these plays and help the children to enjoy them also. Over-emphasis and drill on these skills will defeat the purpose of this book. Casual reading with no understanding of how to improve can be equally devastating. Seek some happy medium which keeps interest high and encourages the best possible reading.

POPULAR PLAYS
for
CLASSROOM READING

Ghost in the House

This is a lively comedy about a ghost who moves in with the Meredith family, and solves a few of their problems.

Read the play to yourself and then choose parts.

When you read the play aloud together, remember that this is a humorous play, and you should keep the pace brisk.

There are several ways the ghost might sound. He could be *mysterious, ordinary, frightening*. Discuss with the group the way you think is most amusing.

Talk about what kind of a man you think Mr. Newman is. How should his part be read?

When people first meet the ghost, they are frightened. Practice showing fear with your voice so that even though the ghost cannot be seen, your listeners will understand that he is a scary sight.

Are you ready to read for an audience, or are there places in the play that could be improved? If there are, practice them until they sound right.

Read for the class, and ask them to evaluate your performance. How do they rate you—fair, good, or excellent?

GHOST IN THE HOUSE

by Helen Louise Miller

Characters

(4 boys, 3 girls, and a narrator)
NARRATOR
MR. MEREDITH
MRS. MEREDITH, *his wife*
BOB MEREDITH, *their teen-age son*
MRS. POTTER, *a neighbor*
MARGIE NEWMAN
MR. NEWMAN, *her father*
GHOST

NARRATOR: This play takes place on Halloween, and it even has a genuine ghost who moves right into the Meredith household. As the play begins, the living room is piled with radios, a sewing machine, hair dryers, a vacuum cleaner and boxes and cartons of all shapes and sizes. And at the center is a portable cardboard closet marked "This End Up!" and "Fragile!" Mr. Meredith is talking on the telephone, and seems a little upset—

MR. MEREDITH: But I tell you we *have* been looking for a house for months, and there just isn't one available in this town. . . . I can't help it if the six months are up. We still haven't found a place to go. . . . I know the law says the owner can have occupancy in six months, but what can I do about it? . . . If you'd only change your mind and sell this house to me, I'd be glad to buy it. . . . O. K., O. K. I'll tell you what, Mr. Newman, come over to the house early this evening, and we'll talk it over again. . . . All right. We'll expect you then. . . . (*Laughs*) Yes, I imagine we'll be seeing your daughter before we see you. Too bad she can't influence you to let us stay. . . . O.K., Mr. Newman. Goodbye.

NARRATOR: As Mr. Meredith hangs up, his son Bob comes in, wearing a Halloween mask.

BOB: Hi, Dad. How do you like the mask I bought for the Halloween party tonight? Margie's bringing the rest of my costume over later.

MR. MEREDITH: She'll be coming with her dad, I suppose. He's coming over for a final round about the house. He still insists we have to move when our six months are up.

BOB: I don't see how Mr. Newman could have such a great daughter as Margie, and be such a tough character.

MR. MEREDITH: And even if we do find a house—what a job it will be to move all the stuff your mother has won.

BOB: Yes, if Mom keeps winning contests, we'll have to live in a warehouse or a museum.

MR. MEREDITH (*Impatiently*): We're living in one now. Look at this place. Everything in triplicate—radios, mixers, blenders—just name it. With so much stuff coming in almost every day—your mother's prizes—it's no wonder we can't find closet space for anything! Maybe that new portable closet will help.

BOB: Is that what that thing is?

MR. MEREDITH: Yes, your mother ordered it yesterday. Our clothes closets are so jammed with hair dryers, electric blenders, and transistor radios, there's no room for our clothing.

BOB: Don't tell me she actually bought and paid for this portable closet! If she had waited a while, I'm sure she could have managed to win one.

MR. MEREDITH (*Dryly*): Right now she'd better direct her talents toward winning us a house.

BOB: I'd settle for a trailer. By the way, where *is* my female parent?

MR. MEREDITH: Down at the Britannia Beauty Salon. Remember that slogan she wrote: "Britannia Rules the Waves"? Well, it won first prize, so your mother is now being made beautiful for free.

BOB: I wish she'd hurry home. I'm hungry. What's for dinner?

MR. MEREDITH (*Wryly*): Salmon, I suspect. She just won a whole case.

BOB (*Groaning*): Last week it was baked beans, the prize for her essay on a thousand and one ways to serve beans. Now it's salmon! Brother! Why can't she win some hamburgers and French fries for a change?

MRS. MEREDITH: Did I hear someone mention food? I'll bet you're both starved.

BOB: You said it.

MRS. MEREDITH: Well, just hold on a little longer and I'll give you some nice broiled salmon with baked bean relish.

BOB (*Groaning*): Have a heart, Mother. Do we have to eat everything you win?

MRS. MEREDITH: Nonsense, dear. We're lucky to have all these good, nutritious foods given to us. But we'll skip the salmon tonight, and I'll make some pumpkin soufflé in honor of Halloween. By the way, did I get any mail today?

MR. MEREDITH: Here's a batch of letters, but it doesn't look as if you've won any more contests.

MRS. MEREDITH: I thought there might be some news on my oatmeal jingle. No, not a thing. Oh, well . . . (*Pauses*) Look at this! It's certainly unusual looking. I've never received a black envelope before.

BOB: Don't tell me you've entered a contest for undertakers.

MRS. MEREDITH: Don't be silly. Let me see what it says. (*Pauses*) For heaven's sake! This must be a joke.

MR. MEREDITH: What is it?

MRS. MEREDITH: Here, George, you read it and see what you make of it.

MR. MEREDITH: Hm-m. It's from The Supernatural Society of

America. I never knew there was such a group. Let's see what they want. (*Reading*) "Dear Madam: We are happy to inform you that your essay, 'Why I Do Not Believe in Ghosts,' has been awarded first prize. You will therefore receive one complete ghost, fully equipped and in perfect running order, ready for instant use."

BOB (*Howling with laughter*): Wow! That's a winner, all right —a complete ghost! Just what we needed.

MR. MEREDITH: That's what it says—"One complete ghost in perfect running order." Then it goes on—(*Reading again*) "Should everything not be in perfect condition, please let us know, and our adjusters will call at once. With our heartiest congratulations, Very truly yours. . . ." This is the weirdest thing I've ever heard of.

MRS. MEREDITH (*Uncomfortably*): It's just plain silly!

MR. MEREDITH (*Laughing*): Imagine winning a ghost!

MRS. MEREDITH: And in good working order!

BOB: It might be fun at that.

MRS. MEREDITH: Let's forget this idiotic letter. To the kitchen!

MR. MEREDITH: I second the motion. But wait a minute, Emily. You're not going to leave that portable closet right in the living room, are you?

MRS. MEREDITH: Oh, that! I hadn't noticed it. I'm glad they sent it out so promptly. We'll take it upstairs right after dinner. Wait a minute. I'd better take a look at this. I especially told the man I wanted the kind with the regulation door, not one of those roll-up types. Here, George, help me tear the paper off it.

BOB: Thy've sure gone to a lot of trouble in wrapping this.

MRS. MEREDITH: Oh, good! The right kind of door after all! It's so much easier to open—see?

ALL (*Screaming*): What's that?

NARRATOR: What is it? The ghost, of course, standing motionless in a white suit, his hands and face swathed in bandages like a mummy.

ALL: Close that door! It's the ghost!

MRS. MEREDITH: George, Bob, help me close the door! I can't shut it. The ghost's coming out!

GHOST: Of course I'm coming out. You're not afraid of me, are you, Mrs. Meredith?

MRS. MEREDITH (*Her teeth chattering*): Of course not.

MR. MEREDITH (*Bravely*): Who are you, sir? Is this a trick to frighten my wife half to death?

BOB: To say nothing of scaring the daylights out of Dad and me!

GHOST: I hardly think it necessary to explain my presence here. You must have received word of my arrival. Congratulations, ma'am. Yours was by far the most convincing letter I read. It almost made me stop believing in myself.

MRS. MEREDITH (*Gasping*): You mean I really did win you?

GHOST: You did. And although we disagree on fundamentals, I congratulate you from the bottom of my spirit. Now, where would you like me to put my suitcase?

BOB (*Bewildered*): Your suitcase? Have you come to stay?

GHOST: Naturally. I thought the letter explained all that. (*A bit hurt*) Surely you were expecting me.

MRS. MEREDITH: Well—er—not exactly. The fact is, we . . . well . . . we're a little crowded just now. The guest room is full of prizes. There's so little space, I'm afraid you wouldn't be comfortable.

GHOST: Nonsense, my dear lady. I wouldn't dream of taking your guest room. The attic is the place for me. I take it you *have* an attic?

BOB: Sure, but it's pretty full, too.

GHOST (*Cheerfully*): I'm sure I'll find it quite cozy. If you'll just show me the way, young man, I'll get settled.

BOB: Well—er—if you're sure you want to stay.

GHOST: I'm sure. If you only knew how tired I get of mausoleums and burial crypts, you'd realize how I appreciate a real home with central heating.

Mrs. Meredith: Burial crypts! Oh, George! (*Weakly*) Do something. Don't just stand there!

Mr. Meredith: You will pardon me for being a bit curious, Mr. . . . er . . . Mr. Ghost, but . . .

Ghost: Oh, come now, since we're all members of the same household, why not call me Spec? That's short for Specter. I'll call you George. What do you say?

Mr. Meredith: I don't know what to say. I've never talked to a ghost before.

Bob: Excuse me, sir—I mean, Spec, but were you in some sort of accident?

Ghost: Why do you ask?

Bob: All those bandages you're wearing. . . .

Ghost: Not bandages—clothes. After all, you can't expect me to run around in my ectoplasm. These bandages are really my winding sheet. They put it on me right after my body was pulled out of the Tiber River where I was drowned. Confidentially, my own brother pushed me in, but I managed to drag him down with me, and we perished together.

Mrs. Meredith: George! A murderer!

Ghost: No cause for alarm, ma'am. I'm your guest. And now if you'll show me to my attic cell, I'll hook up my sound effects and go to work.

Mr. Meredith: Sound effects?

Ghost: I take them wherever I go—moans, shrieks, howling dogs, clanking chains, death rattles and assorted screams. I have them all here in my suitcase, carefully recorded.

Mrs. Meredith: Oh, dear! This is too much for me. I feel faint. George, George, make him go away.

Mr. Meredith: Can't you see you're upsetting my wife? Really, Spec, this has gone far enough.

Ghost: Don't worry. She'll get used to me in time, and so will you. I daresay after I've been here a while, we shall all be very good friends. We can help each other.

Mr. Meredith: How? How could a ghost help people?

GHOST: Wait and see, George, just wait and see. And now, if you please, I really must see my quarters. Bob, will you lead the way?

BOB (*Half afraid*): O.K., Spec, but remember, we're pals. No ghostly tricks behind my back.

GHOST (*With a terrible laugh*): My boy, you can trust me like a brother.

BOB (*Frightened*): But you murdered your brother.

GHOST: Don't hold that against me. It was all in the family. Let's go.

BOB: O.K. This way.

MRS. MEREDITH (*After a moment*): George, what are we going to do?

MR. MEREDITH: Why ask me? This is *your* ghost, not mine.

MRS. MEREDITH: But he can't stay here. What will our friends say?

MR. MEREDITH: Let's make him so angry that he'll leave.

MRS. MEREDITH: You can't do that. He might kill us all! Oh —there's someone at the door. Who can that be? We just can't have any company now! George, you'll have to tell them to go away.

MR. MEREDITH: I'll see who it is from the window. (*Pause*) It's Mrs. Potter.

MRS. MEREDITH: Oh, no! She's come to pester me about taking the P.T.A. presidency. Don't let her in!

MRS. POTTER (*Calling*): Yoo-hoo! Emily! Hello, Emily—Mr. Meredith. The outside door was open, so I walked right in.

MRS. MEREDITH: How are you, Mary?

MRS. POTTER: Just fine. . . . Now, Emily . . . Why, what's that closet thing? Another prize? (*Rambling on*) I always said, if there's one smart woman in this town, it's Emily Meredith.

MRS. MEREDITH: You really must excuse me, Mary. This room is a mess. I was late getting home, and . . .

MRS. POTTER: I know just how it is, and I won't keep you a minute. I just dropped in to ask you to reconsider your decision about the P.T.A. You must take the presidency, Emily. We need women like you.

MRS. MEREDITH: But, Mary, I'm too busy. I've told you a thousand times I just can't do it this year.

MRS. POTTER: Nonsense! (*Airily*) We all have time to do the things that really matter, and there's nothing quite so vital as the welfare of our children. Now isn't that true, dear?

MRS. MEREDITH: It's true enough, Mary, but I still can't be president of the P.T.A. My contests take up too much time, and besides that, we have to move, and we can't find a house, and well . . . I'm just too upset to take on anything more.

MRS. POTTER: Emily, we're not going to give up so easily. It won't be any trouble at all. When Sue Ryan was president, she had all the time in the world.

MR. MEREDITH: Then, why don't you get Sue Ryan again?

MRS. POTTER: Oh, we can't have her this year, Mr. Meredith; she's just a nervous wreck.

MRS. MEREDITH: And that's just what I'll be, if you don't stop pestering me, Mary.

GHOST (*Shrieking, from distance*): Eee-e-k!

MRS. POTTER: What in the world was that?

MRS. MEREDITH: George, it's the ghost. He's gone into action.

MRS. POTTER (*Frightened*): Ghost? What ghost? Where? What are you talking about? What was that awful noise?

MRS. MEREDITH (*Casually*): It was just Spec, our ghost.

MRS. POTTER: Your—your *ghost?* Emily Meredith, have you lost your mind?

MR. MEREDITH (*Blandly*): We are both entirely sane, I assure you, Mrs. Potter. But Emily just won a ghost in a contest.

MRS. POTTER (*Excitedly*): Impossible! I don't believe it!

GHOST: Woo-ooo!

MRS. POTTER (*Terrified*): What is that ghastly sound?

MR. MEREDITH: Not ghastly, Mrs. Potter—*ghostly*.

MRS. MEREDITH (*Calmly*): It's our ghost, up in the attic with Bob, getting settled.

MRS. POTTER (*Incredulously*): Settled?

MRS. MEREDITH (*Matter-of-factly*): Yes, he's going to live here. I guess he's coming downstairs now.

MRS. POTTER (*Agitatedly*): Downstairs? Is he coming in here?

MR. MEREDITH (*Mildly*): Yes, but don't be frightened.

MRS. MEREDITH (*Slightly disapproving*): Although he *did* kill his brother.

MRS. POTTER: Let me out of here!

NARRATOR: Bob and the ghost appear in the doorway. The ghost is glowing with an eerie light. He raises his arms toward Mrs. Potter with a threatening gesture, and she screams in terror and runs out of the house.

MR. MEREDITH (*Laughing*): That was terrific, Spec. Just great! We've never been able to get that woman out of the house in less than an hour, and you did it in three seconds.

BOB: And did you hear Spec's sound effects?

MRS. MEREDITH (*Relieved*): I must say I'm grateful to you, Spec. That woman has been bothering me to death.

GHOST: It's nothing, dear lady.

MR. MEREDITH: By the way, Spec, why do you seem to glow all the time?

GHOST: Oh that! I forgot to turn it off. There. You see, since I am now a member of your family, I am visible to you at all times. But I am invisible to strangers, unless I turn on my battery and glow. It's a case of now you see me—now you don't.

MRS. MEREDITH: Then we could have company without frightening them.

GHOST: Of course. I don't want to scare your friends away— just the nuisances.

BOB: I'm glad of that. I'm expecting my girlfriend any minute, and I wouldn't want her scared out of her wits.

GHOST: Don't worry. I'll be on my best behavior.

BOB: Good. I don't want to upset Margie before the Halloween party.

GHOST: Maybe I could go along. I'm sensational at Halloween parties.

BOB (*Uncertainly*): I don't know. I'd have to talk that over with Margie.

MR. MEREDITH: Emily, what about dinner? I'm starved.

MRS. MEREDITH: So am I. What about you, Spec? Are you hungry?

GHOST: I seldom get hungry, ma'am, and when I do, I have peculiar tastes, which I satisfy in my own way.

MRS. MEREDITH: You're certainly a strange one, Spec. Come on, George. I'll need your help with dinner.

BOB: I think there's someone at the door. It must be Margie. Now listen, Spec, turn off your glow and make yourself invisible and don't get out of line. I don't want anything to frighten her.

GHOST: You can count on me, Bob. She can't see me now. I'll just sit in this armchair quiet as a mouse.

BOB: Hi, Margie. You look fantastic. That's a cool Spanish costume.

MARGIE: Do you like it?

BOB: I sure do. What did you get for me to wear?

MARGIE: I had bad luck. That skeleton costume I thought I could borrow turned out to be for someone half your size. So I just brought an old sheet. You can go as a ghost.

GHOST: What a coincidence!

BOB: A ghost! I don't know about that, Margie. I don't know if I want to be a ghost . . . at least not a ghost in a sheet.

MARGIE: Well, why not? Lots of people use a sheet for a ghost costume.

GHOST: She's right, but don't they look awful?

BOB: Yes, they do . . . but . . . but . . . well, the fact is, Margie, a sheet isn't really the right costume for a ghost.

GHOST IN THE HOUSE 13

MARGIE: Since when are you such an authority on what the well-dressed ghost will wear?

BOB: Since tonight . . . since I've seen . . .

MARGIE: Since you've seen what?

BOB: Since I've seen how funny people look in sheets.

MARGIE: But that's the idea. Everybody is supposed to look funny at a masquerade.

BOB: You don't. You don't look a bit funny. You look beautiful.

MARGIE: Thanks. But ghosts aren't beautiful; they're always horrible and ugly.

GHOST: She's awfully insulting, isn't she?

BOB (*Aside, to* GHOST): She doesn't mean it. She just doesn't know any better.

MARGIE (*Angrily*): Bob Meredith, what kind of talk is that? I know as much about ghosts as you do, and I say a sheet is correct.

BOB: It would be O.K. if it were a winding sheet.

MARGIE (*Puzzled*): What's that?

BOB: We could make one out of this sheet, if we cut it into strips.

MARGIE: Well, you can't cut this sheet into strips. My mother would have a fit.

BOB: Then I won't wear it.

GHOST: Good for you, Bob. Stand up for your rights.

BOB: That thing would make a self-respecting ghost turn over in his grave.

MARGIE: Bob, I don't know what's come over you. You were never like this before. Come on, let me try it on you.

BOB: No. If I'm going to be a ghost, I want an authentic costume.

MARGIE (*Irritated*): But this is authentic.

BOB: How do you know? Did you ever see a ghost?

MARGIE: Of course not, and neither did you.

BOB: I did so.

MARGIE: Don't be silly.

BOB: I'm not silly. What would you say if I told you there's a ghost in this room right now?

MARGIE: I'd say you were crazy.

BOB: But what if I can prove it?

MARGIE (*Impatiently*): Oh, Bob, don't be tiresome. It's getting late. I'll sit here in the armchair and wait for you, while you go round up a costume to suit your peculiar ideas of what a ghost should wear.

BOB (*Loudly*): No! Not there! Don't sit there.

MARGIE: For heaven's sake, why not?

BOB: Because it's occupied.

MARGIE: Occupied? Bob Meredith, you *are* crazy.

BOB: No, I'm not. But you just can't sit in that chair . . . not now.

GHOST (*Wearily*): Never mind, I'll get up.

BOB: No, stay where you are. Margie, you say you've never seen a ghost. Would you like to see one?

MARGIE: I'd like to see one, if there really *were* such a thing.

BOB: And you wouldn't be scared, of course.

MARGIE (*Hesitantly*): No—I don't think so . . . not if I had somebody with me.

BOB: Well, here, take my hand. Now, promise not to scream.

GHOST: Should I make myself visible?

BOB: O.K., Spec, light up.

NARRATOR: The ghost begins to glow. Margie stares at him open-mouthed and then screams.

MARGIE: Bob, who or what is that? It looks like a ghost. I'm frightened.

GHOST: It is a ghost. But don't worry.

MARGIE: It even talks.

BOB: Stop calling him "it." His name is Spec, and he lives here.

MARGIE: Then I'm going home.

BOB (*Soothingly*): Now calm down, Margie. Nothing's going to hurt you. Mother won him in a contest. After you get to know him, you'll like him.

GHOST: I'm really not so bad, Margie.

MARGIE (*Calmer*): Are you an honest-to-goodness ghost?

GHOST (*Proudly*): I'm the real, genuine article. I can appear and disappear at will. I haunt houses. I clank chains. Yes, Margie, I am a ghost. But I'm a useful ghost, as you'll find out when you get to know me better.

MARGIE (*Uncertainly*): I'm not sure that I want to know you better.

BOB: Don't be rude, Margie. He's our guest.

MARGIE: I'm sorry, but—well—I just don't know how to behave with a ghost.

NARRATOR: Mr. and Mrs. Meredith enter.

MR. MEREDITH: I see Spec has his light on. So now you've met our house ghost, Margie. What do you think of him?

MARGIE (*Hesitantly*): I just don't know, Mr. Meredith. He makes me rather nervous.

MRS. MEREDITH (*Cheerfully*): That's the way he affects everyone at first, but you'll get used to him. Now why don't you and Bob come into the dining room for a snack before you leave for the party.

MR. MEREDITH: I'm expecting your dad here any minute, Margie.

MARGIE: He had to stop in town to do an errand, but he's coming right along. (*Embarrassed, pauses briefly*) Oh, Mr. Meredith, I'm so sorry Dad has been so stubborn about this house. I've begged, pleaded, and cajoled him, but he won't listen to reason.

GHOST (*Significantly*): People who won't listen to reason sometimes have to learn the hard way.

MR. MEREDITH (*Puzzled*): What do you mean by that, Spec?

GHOST (*Casually*): I simply mean that perhaps Margie's father has never had to reckon with supernatural power, and when he meets it face to face . . .

MARGIE (*Frightened*): You're not going to hurt him?

GHOST: No, just some gentle persuasion. I take it, my dear, that your father is a stubborn old rascal who's determined to turn me out of house and home.

MARGIE: Why, he's no such thing! And how could he turn you out of house and home?

GHOST: Because this is *my* home now, Margie. And I like it here. I have no intention of moving.

MR. MEREDITH (*Eagerly*): You mean you're going to try your —er—persuasive powers on Mr. Newman?

BOB: And I'll bet it will work, too. Come on, Spec, let's see if things are in working order in the attic.

MARGIE (*Fearfully*): What are they going to do? What's happening?

MRS. MEREDITH: I'm not sure, but I think they are planning a surprise for your father.

MARGIE (*Relieved*): I think I catch on. I hope it works. It would be a shame if you had to move to another town now that Bob and I are—well—such good friends.

MR. MEREDITH: That must be your father at the door. I'll let him in.

MRS. MEREDITH: Is your father a nervous man, Margie?

MARGIE: Not very. I don't think he believes in ghosts at all.

MRS. MEREDITH: Then we'll have to convince him. (*Pauses*) Why, hello, Mr. Newman.

MR. NEWMAN: Ah, good evening, Mrs. Meredith. Hello, Margie. I thought you and Bob would have left for the party by now.

MARGIE: I thought so, too, but (*Pretending fear*) some terrible things have been happening here.

MR. NEWMAN: What sort of things? Is anyone sick?

MRS. MEREDITH: Oh, no, it's just that . . .

MR. MEREDITH: The fact is, Newman, that while you haven't changed *your* mind, something has happened to make us change ours. (*Seemingly disturbed*) We're not only willing to move, we want to leave this house as soon as possible.

MR. NEWMAN (*Puzzled*): I don't understand. What's wrong? What's happened to change your mind? You've always liked this house.

MR. MEREDITH: We hate to have to tell you this, but after what has happened here this evening, you'd have to pay most people to get them to stay here overnight.

MR. NEWMAN: I don't understand.

MR. MEREDITH: In plain words—this house is haunted.

MR. NEWMAN (*Bursting into laughter*): For heaven's sake, I thought it was something serious. Haunted, indeed!

MR. MEREDITH: This is no laughing matter. You should take it seriously.

GHOST (*In the distance, shrieking*): Ahh-hh! (*Laughs evilly*)

MR. NEWMAN (*Startled*): What in the world was that?

MARGIE: I'm scared, Daddy. Please take me home.

MR. MEREDITH: That's what I've been trying to tell you, Newman. That's our not-so-friendly ghost.

MR. NEWMAN: You're all crazy!

MR. MEREDITH: Then you still don't—or won't—believe there's a ghost in the house?

MR. NEWMAN: If there is a ghost that haunts this house, where is it?

MR. MEREDITH: In the attic, of course.

MR. NEWMAN: Nonsense! I'm going up there to investigate. On second thought, maybe I'd better wait a while.

MRS. MEREDITH: I think you're wise. I wouldn't intrude on him when he seems so agitated.

NARRATOR: Loud clanking of chains is heard.

MR. NEWMAN (*Less sure of himself*): What was that?

MR. MEREDITH (*Blandly*): It's his signal. He always clanks his chains before entering a room.

MR. NEWMAN (*Uneasily*): You mean he's—he's coming in here?

MARGIE (*Pretending to be afraid*): Oh, yes, Daddy—and it's terrifying! I saw him. Oh—oh—here he comes!

NARRATOR: The ghost is standing in the doorway, glowing with a pale blue light. Mr. Newman draws back in disbelief, then fear, as Bob returns.

MR. NEWMAN (*Almost speechless*): Why, why—it really *is* a ghost!

BOB: Look out, Mr. Newman, he seems to have it in for you.

MR. NEWMAN: What did I ever do to him?

GHOST (*In a hollow tone*): Plenty. You are a threat to my new-found comfort and security. I like it here. I refuse to move.

MR. MEREDITH: You see, it's just as I told you. The house is haunted.

MR. NEWMAN (*Blustering*): I'll—I'll have the law on you.

GHOST: I am beyond the law. As long as there is any unfriendly presence in this house, I will haunt it. If you try to interfere with me, you will know no peace. All night long, you will hear me—(*Laughs maniacally*) in one way or another. And even if you fall asleep, you'll be awakened by icy fingers (*Threatening*) caressing your throat. (*Eerie laugh*) Where-ever you go, whatever you do, I'll be there, watching—wait-ing. . . . (*Eerie laugh.*)

MR. MEREDITH: You see how it is?

MR. NEWMAN: This is outrageous. No one could possibly live here now.

MR. MEREDITH: You're convinced of that, are you?

MR. NEWMAN (*Dejectedly*): It's a total loss. I'll never get a cent out of it.

MR. MEREDITH: Don't worry, Newman, old friend. Perhaps there's still a way out.

MR. NEWMAN: You think someone would buy it?

MR. MEREDITH: Tell you what I'll do. I'll call your office

tomorrow and talk this over. Perhaps if the price is right, we can still reach an understanding.

MR. NEWMAN (*In disbelief*): You mean you'd still buy it . . . after this . . . ?

MR. MEREDITH: I'd have to give it serious thought.

GHOST: Remember, once a house is haunted, it stays haunted.

MR. NEWMAN: That's just what I'm afraid of. The reputation of this place is ruined. George, if you care to call at my office tomorrow, I think I can say that no reasonable offer will be refused.

MR. MEREDITH (*Casually*): I'll think it over.

MR. NEWMAN: Come, Margie, we must go now. I'm not leaving you here another minute!

MARGIE: O.K., Dad. I'll meet you later at the party, Bob. Will you be wearing a sheet?

BOB: I'm not saying. But if a couple of good-looking ghosts show up, I'll be one of them.

MR. NEWMAN: Margie, come along this minute. This is no place for us. Goodbye!

MRS. MEREDITH: Oh, George, you were wonderful.

BOB: It was all Spec's doing. Spec, you're terrific!

GHOST: I think we'll get along fine.

MRS. MEREDITH: I'm sure of it. As soon as we ever finish dinner, I'm taking the electric heater up to the attic so you'll be comfortable.

GHOST: Don't bother, Mrs. Meredith. I'm used to the cold and damp.

BOB: And if you still want to go to that party, Spec, let's get a move on.

GHOST: Thanks a lot, Bob. I'd love to. Together we'll add some real spirit to the party.

MRS. MEREDITH: Have a good time, and be home early.

BOB: We will. 'Bye.

MR. MEREDITH: Well, Emily, I must say your contests really came in handy this time. But don't you think we've had

enough? Someday you might win something really dangerous. Promise me you'll give it up.

MRS. MEREDITH: I've been thinking of quitting, George, but
last week I saw a contest I know I could win.

MR. MEREDITH: What on earth was it?

MRS. MEREDITH: It was an essay contest. . . . One hundred
dollars for the best true story on "A Night in a Haunted
House."

MR. MEREDITH: That should be a cinch . . . and just to make
sure you'll win, what do you say we get Spec to ghost-write
the whole thing?

THE END

Take Me to Your Marshal

Here is an unusual combination of outer space, an ordinary family, and the Wild West.

Read the play silently, then discuss with the group how Zanthus should sound. Remember, he's a man from another planet imitating a cowboy. Have several people read a few lines of his part to see who gives the best reading:

> ZANTHUS: I've been studying your lingo for nigh onto five years, day and night. If you don't mind my saying so— you're mighty strange folks.

When you decide who will make the best spaceman, choose the other parts and read through the play aloud. Did you get across the idea that the Reeds are at first frightened and then relieved about their visitor?

The television performers should be exaggerated. Did they sound that way?

1. Did you come in on time with your part, with no pauses?
2. Did you vary the pitch of your voice to show feeling?
3. How would you rate your reading—fair, good, or excellent?

Arrange to read the play to the class.

TAKE ME TO YOUR MARSHAL

by Claire Boiko

Characters

(7 boys, 3 girls, and a narrator)
NARRATOR
MR. REED
MRS. REED
ROBBIE
JIM
LORI
ZANTHUS
THREE MEN ⎱
ONE WOMAN ⎰ *voices from TV set*

NARRATOR: On a warm summer evening, the Reed family are relaxing in their living room. Robbie, Jim, and Lori are seated cross-legged on the floor in front of the television set, eyes and ears glued to a science fiction program. Mrs. Reed is knitting, and Mr. Reed is reading the newspaper. Let's hear what the TV program is all about . . .

1ST MAN (*From TV set*): So, earthlings. You have invaded the planet Mars. Little did you know the Giant Angleworms from the Vermiform Nebula have already colonized Mars.

2ND MAN (*From TV set*): Yes. Little did we know. But listen, Giant Angleworm—people and worms can coexist.

ROBBIE: Yeah—people and worms get along fine on earth.

1ST MAN: Never! You have too many arms and legs. You are unsightly. Ugh! I will expedite you.

2ND MAN: Very well. Expedite me. But let my trusty technician, the girl scientist and cook, Dr. Cynthia Cyborg, go free.

LORI (*Excited*): Oh, yes, let the girl go free!

WOMAN (*From TV set*): No. No, Smash Borden, Commander of the Mars Exploration Module. I must stay with you. Duty calls. Loud and clear!

2ND MAN: R-r-roger, Dr. Cynthia Cyborg. You are . . . you are all heart. By Jupiter, you're a real *girl!*

WOMAN: Oh, Smash. You never called me "girl" before. Giant Angleworm, we are prepared to meet our doom.

1ST MAN: Splendid. Line up single file. Perhaps you have noticed my highly efficient corkscrew nose? My highly efficient corkscrew nose is actually a lethal weapon. Stand still, earthlings. I am going to *bore* you to death!

3RD MAN (*From TV set*): Well, junior spacemen! Will Captain Smash Borden and his trusty technician, Dr. Cynthia Cyborg, girl scientist and cook, actually be *bored* to death? What a way to go! Tune in next week and find out what ghastly future awaits our dauntless duo in the episode entitled, "The Giant Angleworm Meets the Mighty Mole!"

LORI: Boy! That was scary. Imagine—a giant angleworm. I can't even stand little earthworms.

ROBBIE: Dad, do you think there are such things as giant angleworms on other planets?

MR. REED: Well, Robbie, there certainly could be. Somewhere in the galaxy there are bound to be other forms of life.

MRS. REED: Of course. Look at the range of life here on earth: everything from human beings to giant squid.

JIM: Boy, I hope they stay home. I hope they don't decide to start a real estate development on earth.

LORI: Real estate—that's nothing, Jim. I'd gladly give them a few acres of land. But what if we're the main dish on some outer space menu?

ROBBIE (*In a mechanical voice*): Ah, here is my appetizer.

Knuckles of earth-girl in mud pie sauce. Very tasty, but next time, go easy on the mud.

LORI (*Nervously*): Now stop that, Robbie. It's not funny. All kinds of things could be flying around up there.

JIM (*Soberly*): Yeah. We've been making a lot of noise in space lately. Maybe we've been attracting attention.

MRS. REED: Funny you should say that. I heard that the airport has been reporting strange blips on the radar. They can't account for them.

MR. REED (*Impatiently*): Oh, now, Janet. There are hundreds of reasons for unidentified radar blips, including an unscheduled flight of sea gulls.

NARRATOR: The lights flash on and off. Robbie goes to the window and peers out.

LORI (*Gasping*): What's wrong with the lights?

ROBBIE: The whole sky lighted up.

MR. REED: Heat lightning. That's all.

ROBBIE (*Excited*): Dad—come here!

NARRATOR: Robbie is pointing at something outside. Mr. Reed joins him at the window while the rest of the family crowds in behind them, trying to see.

JIM: Holy smoke! What is that?

MR. REED: Say—it's a fireball. A real fireball zooming around over our house.

MRS. REED: A fireball! Is it dangerous?

MR. REED: Of course not. It's a kind of static lightning. It's quite harmless, but rather rare. I never expected to see it this close.

JIM: Hey—look. What a neat fireball. It has little windows in it and an antenna. Oh boy!

MRS. REED: Harry—should a fireball have little windows and an antenna?

MR. REED: Come on, Jim. You're imagining things. (*Gasping*) Good heavens! Listen, everybody. Don't panic. Do exactly what I tell you to do. Come away from the window slowly

—as if everything were normal. Children—sit down by the television set, just as you were. Janet—you knit or whatever. I'll sit here and read the paper.

NARRATOR: Everyone exchanges puzzled glances, but they do what he says.

MRS. REED (*Whispering*): Harry, for goodness' sake! What did you see?

MR. REED: That fireball has little windows and an antenna. I think it's a flying saucer.

ALL (*Loudly*): Oh!

MR. REED: Sh-h-h. It's important that we don't attract the attention of whoever or whatever is behind those windows.

LORI (*Whispering tearfully*): Oh, Daddy. I don't want to be anybody's blue-plate special.

MR. REED: We have to have a plan now. Listen . . . This is Plan A. Got that? If anything comes through that door, I will simply pick up a poker from the fireplace and hit it on the—on whatever it uses for a head.

JIM: But, Dad, we don't have a fireplace.

MR. REED: Then we'll use Plan B. I'll tackle it as it comes through the door. Robbie, you sit on its feet. Janet, you call the police, and Jim, you stand by your sister.

ROBBIE (*In a small voice*): But, Dad, suppose it doesn't have any feet? Suppose it has slimy tentacles?

MR. REED: In that case, Plan C goes into effect. We try diplomacy. I will greet it in the name of Earth. Robbie, you bow very low. Janet, you call the State Department. And Lori, you break out the ladyfingers and the ginger ale.

LORI: But suppose it'd rather have *real* ladyfingers.

MR. REED: Oh, for heaven's sake. We don't know what kind of creature it is. It might be nothing more than a giant carrot.

MRS. REED (*Wailing*): Oh, no!

MR. REED: Now what!

MRS. REED (*Breaking down*): We had carrots for dinner. Maybe it's offended!

MR. REED (*Exploding*): Oh, for Pete's sake. You can't offend a carrot. Now listen, everybody. Keep cool. Chances are that it's looking for the power lines to refuel. (*Whispering hoarsely*) Pretend that nobody's home. (*There is a moment of total silence.*)

MRS. REED: Harry—I hear footsteps coming toward the house.

MR. REED: Sh-h-h. I'm trying to hear how many feet it has.

ROBBIE: It's on the porch.

JIM: Dad, it's at the front door.

ROBBIE: Which plan, Dad? Which plan?

MR. REED: Get behind the door with me, boys. Janet and Lori, crouch down behind the sofa. When it comes through the door, we'll tackle it.

ROBBIE: What signals, Dad?

MR. REED: Six-twenty-forty-two-hike.

MRS. REED: It's coming in!

NARRATOR: Zanthus cautiously opens the door and comes in. The Reeds stare at him in amazement: he is a perfectly ordinary creature from outer space in a bright green space suit and helmet with two antennae.

MR. REED (*Suddenly*): Six-twenty-forty-two-hike!

NARRATOR: Robbie, Jim and Mr. Reed tackle Zanthus and land in a heap on top of him.

ZANTHUS (*Faintly*): H-e-e-lp!

ROBBIE (*Astonished*): The thing said "help"!

JIM: Hey, let's see what kind of thing the thing is.

MR. REED: Stand back, boys. He may have a weapon that could evaporate you.

ZANTHUS: Don't hit me! Don't hit me!

JIM: Hey, what do you know? It's an English-speaking thing.

ROBBIE: With one head, two arms and two legs. And no tail.

MR. REED: We're not out of danger yet. He may have strange powers beyond those of mortals. Smile, everybody. Show your teeth. We friends. We no hurt spaceman. Understand?

ZANTHUS (*In a pronounced Western accent*): Sure I understand. You're the kind of friends that ambush a feller in the dark and set on him when he's paying a social call. I come down all the way from the back of the moon to ask you a favor, and you push me down and set on me! By doggies, that ain't nice.

ROBBIE: Dad, I think we goofed.

JIM: Hey! It's an English-speaking-cowboy-thing.

MRS. REED: Oh dear. Harry—do you suppose he's an ambassador from another planet? Have we caused an incident?

MR. REED: Probably. It'd be just our luck. I'll do what I can to pacify him. Ah—sir. Sir, we apologize for our rough reception. We've never had a spaceship land in our back yard. We didn't know what to expect.

MRS. REED: Invite him to sit down, Harry. That is, if he sits.

MR. REED: Would you like to sit down? You do sit down, don't you?

ZANTHUS (*Relieved*): Why, sure. That sounds more like it. (*There is an awkward pause.*)

MR. REED: Well!

ZANTHUS: Well! So, this here is the Earth.

MRS. REED (*Brightly*): That's right. That's absolutely right. Did you have a long trip?

ZANTHUS: Mighty long. Yes, ma'am. Well. So this here is the Earth.

MR. REED: Oh, yes. This is definitely the Earth.

MRS. REED: Have you visited us before?

ZANTHUS: No. This is my first trip down to the surface.

MRS. REED: Imagine that, Harry. This is his first trip down to the surface. (*Silence falls again.*)

ROBBIE: Boy-oh-boy. A guy from outer space lands in our back yard. It must be the most historic moment since the discovery of fire, and nobody can think of a thing to say!

MR. REED: We're dumbfounded. Just dumbfounded. Are you a little dumbfounded, too?

ZANTHUS: Yes sirree. Dumbfounded.

JIM: What's your name?

MRS. REED: Sh-h-h, Jim. It might not be polite. Perhaps he'd rather not disclose his name.

ZANTHUS: Shucks, I don't mind. My name is Zanthus, son. Zanthus Amanthus from the planet Radamanthus in the constellation Orion. You can call me Buck.

MR. REED: Well, this is fantastic. I don't know exactly how to proceed. Is there someone you'd like to make contact with? Somebody official? Would you like to meet our President?

ZANTHUS: Shucks, I'm not here on an official mission. Matter of fact, I sneaked off for a visit. My boss doesn't even know I'm here—I hope.

MRS. REED: Your . . . boss. Oh, dear. Are there more of you —just waiting to invade us?

ZANTHUS: No, ma'am. Just me. I'm your friendly Pry in the Sky.

ROBBIE: What's a Pry in the Sky?

ZANTHUS: A monitor. A sky-jockey. A feller who sits up on a rocky pasture up on the moon and watches and listens.

MRS. REED (*Sighing with relief*): Then, you're not going to invade us?

ZANTHUS: Shucks, no. We've got a nice planet of our own. We're keeping an eye out to see that you don't invade us. Matter of fact, this is my last tour of duty. Tonight I go back to Orion for good.

NARRATOR: A rapid beeping sound interrupts him.

MR. REED: What's that?

ZANTHUS: My boss. I knew it was too good to last. He's sent a probe and he wants to know what I'm doing down yonder. He's telling me to get going right away.

NARRATOR: Zanthus takes out a silver whistle and blows some notes that sound like code.

ZANTHUS: There. That ought to hold him for a while.

JIM: Say, Buck. Why do you talk like a cowpoke? Where'd you learn English?

ZANTHUS: From your television. We tap your frequencies. I've been studying your lingo for nigh onto five years, day and night. If you don't mind my saying so—you're mighty strange folks.

MR. REED: Wait a minute. I'm beginning to understand. What particular frequency have you tapped?

ZANTHUS: It's called Channel Seven.

MR. REED: Channel Seven! No wonder he sounds like a cowboy, Jim. Channel Seven runs nothing but Westerns!

ZANTHUS: Say now. I've been forgetting my manners. You folks go right ahead. I know all about your customs. Go right ahead. Break.

LORI (*Bewildered*): Break? Break what?

ZANTHUS: Break for a commercial.

LORI (*Laughing*): We don't break for commercials. We'd never get anything done.

NARRATOR: A louder bleeping sound is heard.

ZANTHUS: There's my boss calling again. Never gives me a minute's peace. I swear! I'm not going back until I've shaken the hand of the mighty man from Dodge.

JIM: Who's the mighty man from Dodge?

ZANTHUS: Why, that's the favor I was going to ask you. There's one feller above all the others who sticks in my mind as I watch the posses come and go on my receiver up there. A feller who walks six and a half feet tall. Quick on the draw. Honest and strong. My hero. Marshal Dillon. Take me to your Marshal!

ROBBIE: Oh, boy, are we in trouble!

JIM: But, Buck. You don't understand . . .

MR. REED (*Interrupting; aside*): Not now, Jim. . . . It's Zanthus's last night on earth. You can't tell him there's no real Marshal Dillon. It's too cruel. Let me handle this. Do what I say.

NARRATOR: Mr. Reed whispers something in Jim's ear. Jim nods and leaves the room.

ZANTHUS: Marshal Matt Dillon. I sure admire that man.

MR. REED: Zanthus—uh—Buck. I'm sorry to have to tell you this. You're about a thousand miles away from Dodge City.

ZANTHUS (*Regretfully*): I am? Why, I thought sure as shooting I was right on target, on the outskirts of Dodge.

MR. REED: We don't want you to get in any trouble with your —uh—boss, Zanthus. I'll tell you what we'll do. When we next see Marshal Dillon, we'll give him your regards. Won't we, everybody?

ALL: Yes, yes.

ZANTHUS: Why, that's mighty fine of you folks. Mighty fine. Just tell Marshal Dillon that somebody up there likes him.

NARRATOR: Jim comes running in carrying a belt with holsters, two six-guns and a Stetson.

JIM: Wait, Buck! We can't let you go back to your planet without official souvenirs of Earth.

NARRATOR: Jim holds out the cowboy gear to Zanthus who takes it, overcome with delight, and puts it on.

ZANTHUS: Why, you even cut two holes in the Stetson for my antenna. Thank you kindly, folks. I sure am sorry I can't return the favor. But I'll tell you this. We've been monitoring you for a quite a spell. Some of the reports haven't been so good. We put you on the intergalactic blacklist for tourists. But you folks have been so fine, that I'm going to put four stars after my report.

MRS. REED: Four stars? What does that mean?

ZANTHUS: It means approved for tourists from outer space. You just wait, ma'am. You're going to be the luckiest lady in your territory. Inside of thirty days, spaceships from just about everywhere are going to be landing in your backyard!

JIM, ROBBIE, *and* LORI: Hooray!

MR. *and* MRS. REED: Oh, no! Not again!

THE END

The Mechanical Maid

A space-age household helper causes confusion and comedy in this play.

Read the entire play silently to yourself. Then discuss with the group how you think Mary should sound. How would her phrasing be different from ordinary conversation? When she breaks down, she would sound still different. How would you show this?

Madame Dupont is French. How should she sound? There are a few foreign phrases in the play. If you need help with them, ask your teacher about the pronunciation and meaning:

"*La bonne nouvelle, comprenez?*"

"*Marie, parlez-vous français?*"

"*Un peu, Madame, mais pas bien.*"

"*Mary, kannst du Deutsch sprechen?*"

"*Ja, ja, Ich kann . . . aber nicht so gut.*"

Choose parts and read the play together. Ask yourself these questions:

1. Did I come in with my part at the right time?
2. Did I sound natural, as if I were having an ordinary conversation?
3. Were there too many pauses?
4. Did I make my part as amusing as I can?

When the group feels it is ready, arrange to read for an audience or record the play on a tape recorder and listen to the tape.

THE MECHANICAL MAID

by Virginia Payne Whitworth

Characters

(1 boy, 6 girls, and a narrator)
NARRATOR
MRS. ABBOTT
MR. KING
MARY
MRS. BROWN
MRS. CLARK
MADAME DUPONT
MRS. ELLIS

NARRATOR: On a bright, sunny morning, Mrs. Abbott and Mr. King of the Modern Mechanical Maid Company are unwrapping a large box that stands in the middle of the Abbott living room. In the adjoining dining area, the table is set for a buffet luncheon.

MRS. ABBOTT: I'm so glad you could deliver this package immediately, Mr. King. My maid walked out on me today, of all days, just when I'm expecting friends for luncheon.

MR. KING: We take pride in being right up to the minute, with up-to-the-minute delivery service, at the Modern Mechanical Maid Company.

MRS. ABBOTT: What a relief it will be to have a mechanical maid! My other maid was always flying into tantrums—and her last one was her best. The kitchen is a mess.

MR. KING: Mary will take care of it for you quickly—and she is guaranteed never to have tantrums. Here she is, fresh from the factory and absolutely sanitary.

NARRATOR: Mr. King opens the front of the box and reveals Mary, who stands stiffly, looking straight ahead.

MRS. ABBOTT: Why, it looks almost human!

MR. KING: It's even better than a human maid.

MRS. ABBOTT: Can it walk?

MR. KING: Of course. There's a switch on her back that makes her walk. I'll show you how she works.

NARRATOR: Mr. King reaches behind Mary and turns a switch. Mary walks stiffly out of the box. Her movements are jerky and her face has no expression. She turns around slowly, showing the control box on her back—knobs, dials, and levers. Then she stops, with her back to Mr. King and Mrs. Abbott. Mr. King shows Mrs. Abbott how to work the controls.

MR. KING: Now you see, Mrs. Abbott, this switch is set to make her come when you call and go when you dismiss her.

MRS. ABBOTT: I see. What do I call her?

MR. KING: Wait till I adjust her talking mechanism. Now ask her her name.

MRS. ABBOTT: You mean ask her just as I would a real—I mean —anyone? All right. What is your name, please?

MARY (*In a mechanical voice*): Ma-ry.

MRS. ABBOTT: Isn't that amazing!

MR. KING: Now, do you see these dials? They're already set for routine duties—front door, back door, telephone, dishes, beds, daily sweeping, dusting, vacuum cleaning, etc. Over here you have special duties—heavy cleaning, formal dinner, luncheon, afternoon tea, late supper, breakfast in bed . . .

MRS. ABBOTT: Breakfast in bed! Oh, lovely! I never could get my other maid to do that right.

MR. KING: You see, Mrs. Abbott, this modern mechanical maid has no will of her own.

MRS. ABBOTT: Of course. I keep forgetting. She looks so real. I almost hate to talk about her or stare at her.

MR. KING: She doesn't mind in the least.

MRS. ABBOTT: All these controls are marked so plainly, I don't see how I *could* make any mistakes. Can she be set for serving a buffet luncheon?

MR. KING: Certainly. I'll adjust her for you. I gather you're expecting your guests soon.

MRS. ABBOTT: Yes, they'll be coming in a few minutes.

MR. KING: Well, there are a few more things I must go over with you, but I have another appointment now. I could call back later.

MRS. ABBOTT: Oh, do. Maybe I'll have some more customers for you, if Mary does a nice job.

MR. KING: I'd appreciate that, Mrs. Abbott. Let's see; I'll set her to call you by name. (*Spelling*) A-B-B-O-T-T. Just call her, Mrs. Abbott.

MRS. ABBOTT: Mary!

MARY (*Mechanically*): Yes, Mrs. Absom.

MR. KING (*Laughing*): Oh, I don't have that quite right. Just a minute. Now, try her again.

MRS. ABBOTT: Mary!

MARY: Yes, Mrs. Abbott.

MRS. ABBOTT: That's fine. Come here, Mary. Turn around. My! Such fun!

MR. KING: Suppose you try her out on something a little harder before I go.

MRS. ABBOTT: Well, let me see. Mary, see who's at the front door.

MARY: Yes, Mrs. Abbott.

NARRATOR: As Mr. King and Mrs. Abbott watch, Mary goes to the front door, opens it, looks out, closes the door and goes back to the middle of the room.

MARY: No one is there, Mrs. Abbott.

MRS. ABBOTT: Amazing! She almost seems to think!

MR. KING: It's the photo-electric eye, you see.

MRS. ABBOTT: Of course. I certainly do thank you for bringing her.

MR. KING: Thank you, Mrs. Abbott. Here is the book of instructions . . . oh, and I must show you about the Main Control Switch. Mary, come here . . . turn around . . . see? Here it is, the Main Control Switch. In case anything should go wrong, be sure to pull this. You'll get a complete shut off and can set your dials all over again before throwing the switch on.

MRS. ABBOTT: I see. That's easy.

MR. KING: And here are some folders to show your friends, with our complete listing of models and prices.

MRS. ABBOTT: Good, good.

MR. KING: I think you'll get along all right if you'll just keep to the simpler things until you get used to her.

MRS. ABBOTT: I will. It's really a very simple luncheon I'm having.

MR. KING: Just go over the items with her and get her to repeat them after you and you should have no trouble. And remember, use the Main Control Switch in case of trouble.

MRS. ABBOTT: I see. What's this little box with the red handle?

MR. KING: I was going to tell you about that. I must run along for my appointment, but I'll be back around two. Just be sure *not* to touch that little red handle. Thank you again, Mrs. Abbott.

NARRATOR: Mr. King leaves. Mrs. Abbott sinks down in a chair and looks at Mary, who is standing stiffly in the middle of the room.

MRS. ABBOTT: A mechanical maid. This is exciting. Now, what shall I have her do? Hm-m. Bring me a glass of water, please, Mary.

MARY: Yes, Mrs. Abbott.

NARRATOR: Mary walks jerkily out of the room to the kitchen. Mrs. Abbott watches nervously. After a moment, Mary returns with a glass of water on a tray.

MRS. ABBOTT: Why, thank you, Mary, you chose just the right glass and tray. What am I saying? She doesn't need to be praised. Come here, Mary. Turn around. (*Reading*) "Care of small children, care of teen-agers, feeding dogs, cats, canaries, pick up papers." That's a good one. Mary, pick up this wrapping paper. Now put it in the box, and carry the box out to the back porch. My, but she's clever. It's amazing what scientists can do these days. (*Pause*) Very good! Now, come with me to the kitchen, and I'll tell you about the luncheon. I will serve the soup at the table from the tureen. I want you to arrange the salad plates and put out the hot rolls.

MARY: Tureen . . . salad plates . . . hot rolls.

NARRATOR: Mrs. Abbott and Mary go off to the kitchen. After a moment, the doorbell rings. Mary enters from the kitchen and opens the front door. Mrs. Brown and Mrs. Clark come in.

MRS. BROWN: We're Mrs. Brown and Mrs. Clark.

MARY: Won't you come in? May I take your things? Step this way, please. Please be seated. I will tell Mrs. Abbott you are here.

NARRATOR: Mary goes to the kitchen while Mrs. Brown and Mrs. Clark sit down.

MRS. BROWN: Strange! Alice didn't tell me she was getting a new maid.

MRS. CLARK: There is something funny about her, don't you think so?

MRS. BROWN: Rather stiff, yes. Needs dancing lessons. I've sent my maid to ballet school. I'm hoping she won't break so many dishes if she learns to move properly.

MRS. CLARK: She has a lovely complexion, hasn't she?

MRS. BROWN: Too good. It looks like enamel.

NARRATOR: Mrs. Abbott comes in from the kitchen.

MRS. ABBOTT: Betty! How are you? And Clare! I'm delighted to see you.

MRS. BROWN: Hello, Alice.

MRS. CLARK: How are you?

MRS. ABBOTT: I'm fine. And did you notice my new maid?

MRS. CLARK: Yes! Tell us about her. Where did you get her?

MRS. ABBOTT: I'll tell you later, when Evelyn Ellis and her friend, Madame Dupont, from Paris, get here.

NARRATOR: The doorbell rings, and Mary comes from the kitchen to open the door. Mrs. Ellis and Madame Dupont enter.

MARY (*Announcing*): Mrs. Ellis and Madame Dupont.

MRS. ABBOTT: How do you do, Madame Dupont? Hello, Evelyn. That will do, Mary. You may get the soup now. Madame Dupont, I should like to present my friends, Mrs. Brown and Mrs. Clark . . . Madame Dupont, of Paris.

MRS. BROWN: *Bonjour*, Madame Dupont.

MADAME DUPONT (*With French accent*): How do you do? You speak French, yes, Mrs. Brown?

MRS. BROWN: Oh, just a very little.

NARRATOR: Mary brings a soup tureen, small trays, and soup plates from the kitchen and puts them on the table. Before returning to the kitchen, she announces—

MARY: Luncheon is served, Mrs. Abbott.

MRS. ABBOTT: Will you come to the table? Please serve yourselves.

NARRATOR: The women take trays and serve themselves soup. Then they sit about on the sofa and chairs and chat as they eat.

MRS. BROWN: I don't see how you can get used to this town after Paris, Evelyn.

MRS. ELLIS: I really enjoy the peace and quiet after that rush trip we made.

MRS. CLARK: We are all so happy, Madame Dupont, that Mrs. Ellis could persuade you to come back with her.

MADAME DUPONT: *Merci beaucoup*. And I am so-o delightful to be here!

MRS. CLARK: Tell us about Paris, Evelyn. Did you buy a lot of clothes?

Mrs. Ellis: I bought a couple of hats. Madame Dupont took me to some darling little shops.

Mrs. Abbott (*Calling*): Mary! You may remove the tureen, Mary. Mary, is anything the matter? Mary! Come here. (*To her friends*) Pardon me a minute, ladies.

Narrator: As Mrs. Abbott starts to go to the kitchen, Mary comes in and stands still. Mrs. Abbott goes to her, examines her controls, and pushes a button. Mary gets the tureen and returns to the kitchen. Mrs. Abbott sits down again.

Mrs. Brown: Doesn't she feel well?

Mrs. Abbott: Oh, yes, it isn't that. It's just—that—well . . .

Mrs. Clark: They all get that way sometimes when there are guests—sort of stage fright.

Mrs. Ellis: Mrs. Abbott has a new maid—*la bonne nouvelle*, *comprenez*, Madame Dupont?

Madame Dupont: *Oui*, Madame, I understand well.

Narrator: Mary returns with a large tray and removes the soup plates from the ladies' trays. Then she hurries out to the kitchen.

Mrs. Abbott: Mary, what are you doing? We haven't finished. Bring those back!

Narrator: Mary hurries in with a broom and dustcloth and starts to sweep and dust rapidly.

Mrs. Abbott: Mary! Stop! Oh, dear, what shall I do? This is terrible. I may as well tell you, girls. She's a mechanical maid, and I just got her, and I haven't learned to handle her yet.

Mrs. Brown: Mechanical maid!

Mrs. Clark: You mean she isn't real?

Mrs. Ellis: What?

Mrs. Abbott: That's right. I must have pressed the wrong buttons or something. Let me look at the instructions. (*Reading*) Washing, ironing, spring housecleaning, luncheons, dinners. How on earth do you get her to *stop* working? Oh, here it is —Main Control Switch.

NARRATOR: Mary is now on her hands and knees, polishing the floor. Mrs. Abbott works the knobs on her controls and Mary stops working. Mrs. Abbott presses some buttons as she reads from the instruction booklet.

MRS. ABBOTT: Buffet luncheon, second course, resume serving. That ought to do it.

MRS. CLARK: Amazing!

MRS. ABBOTT (*Very distinctly*): Mary, take those cleaning things to the kitchen and bring in the next course.

MARY: Yes, Mrs. Abbott. Second course.

NARRATOR: Mary stands up and walks stiffly to the kitchen. As the others talk, she brings in the second course of salad and rolls and serves the women.

MRS. BROWN: Tell us about her, Alice.

MRS. CLARK: Are mechanical maids expensive?

MRS. ELLIS: Let me see that book.

MADAME DUPONT: Ah, your America!

MRS. ABBOTT: Here are several booklets.

MRS. BROWN: If Rosa leaves, I shall certainly get one of these.

MRS. CLARK: How is she at making beds?

MRS. ABBOTT: I don't really know. She arrived only half an hour ago.

MADAME DUPONT: Can she speak French?

MRS. ABBOTT: I hardly think so.

MADAME DUPONT: *Marie, parlez-vous français?*

MARY: *Un peu, Madame, mais pas bien.*

MADAME DUPONT: *Mais, non,* Marie, you speak French very well.

MARY: Oh, *merci,* Madame.

MRS. BROWN: I simply don't believe it.

MRS. ELLIS: It says here, "To keep Mechanical Maid clean, just wipe off once a week with a damp cloth. Use no scouring powder." Might spoil her delicate complexion, I suppose.

MRS. CLARK: And listen to this (*Reading*): "If you're building a new home, or changing your color scheme, return Mechanical Maid to factory. A new paint job will be furnished at a reasonable cost."

MADAME DUPONT: Your country! How I marvel!

MRS. ELLIS: What I don't understand is the French she spoke.

MRS. ABBOTT: Well, you see I ordered Type Z-21. Oh, here. (*Reading*) "Type Z-21, American Experimental Model, with a smattering of several languages." You can get maids with French accents, or who speak Swedish, German, or Japanese.

MRS. ELLIS: Do you mean to say she can actually speak several languages? Mary, *kannst du Deutsch sprechen?*

MARY: *Ja, ja, ich kann . . . aber nicht so gut.*

MRS. BROWN: Oh, I just hate the thought of my dull, sulky, old Rosa. I wonder if Bob would buy me a Mechanical Maid.

MRS. CLARK: They're very reasonable, too, when you consider how much a real one eats.

MRS. ELLIS: And they'll never get tired.

MRS. CLARK: Will she call us by name? Mary?

MARY: Yes, Mrs. Clark.

MRS. ELLIS: Mary!

MARY: Yes, Mrs. Ellis.

MRS. ELLIS: How on earth . . . ?

MRS. ABBOTT: I set her for that before you came.

MRS. CLARK: I want to touch her. Come here, Mary.

MARY: Yes, Mrs. Clark. Yes, Mrs. Clark, (*Louder*) yes, Mrs. Clark, yes, Mrs. Clark—

MRS. ABBOTT: Gracious! Something's gone wrong again!

MRS. CLARK: I'm sorry. I probably touched a sensitive spot.

MRS. ABBOTT (*Frantically*): Where is that Main Switch? Oh, here!

MARY: Yes, Mrs. Cl—

MRS. BROWN: Let me look at those switches, Alice. I'm pretty good at mechanical things. Hmm!

NARRATOR: Mrs. Brown pokes at several buttons, while Mary

stands perfectly still. Suddenly she starts moving with a jerky motion, speaking in a rush as she goes to front door, opens it, closes it, turns and rushes to the kitchen.

MARY: At once, sir, yes, sir, five dollars and fifty cents, sir, collect, the boy is waiting, madam, no answer, sir, call again, certainly madam . . . certainly madam. . . .

NARRATOR: Mary rushes into the kitchen, and a loud crash is heard. Mrs. Abbott runs into the kitchen, her hand to her forehead.

MRS. CLARK: So you're good at mechanical things, Betty?

MRS. BROWN: Well, I can repair iron cords.

MRS. CLARK: Never mind, Betty. I think it was my fault for poking at her.

MRS. ELLIS: Maybe she's ticklish.

MADAME DUPONT: She is very funny, *mais non?*

MRS. BROWN: Well, Alice—much damage done?

MRS. ABBOTT: Would you believe it? All that noise, and only two old mason jars broken. I have her straightened out now, I hope, so let's go on with our lunch. I put her near an open window to cool down.

MADAME DUPONT: This *salade*, Madame Abbott, it is so *delicieuse!*

MRS. ABBOTT: Thank you, Madame. I'm sorry everything's so hectic.

MRS. BROWN: Don't apologize, Alice. We're having a grand time. I'm almost too excited to eat. I don't care if they do act up occasionally. I want to order one.

MRS. CLARK: It says here in the booklet that they can sew, mend, take care of small children. I wonder if my husband would let me order one.

MRS. ABBOTT (*Worried; to herself*): The salesman said not to open the little box with the red handle. Betty, did you touch a little box with a red handle on Mary's back?

MRS. BROWN: I don't think so. Why?

MRS. ABBOTT: What *was* it Mr. King said about that little red box?

MRS. ELLIS: Betty, lend me your pencil. I want to fill out this order blank.

MRS. BROWN: I wish I could have six!

MRS. ELLIS: I'm ordering the same kind as yours, Alice—Type Z-21.

NARRATOR: As the women write out their order blanks, a loud humming noise comes from the kitchen.

MRS. BROWN: What's that strange noise, Alice?

MRS. ABBOTT: I can't imagine.

MRS. CLARK: Sounds like a jet engine. Careful, Alice. It's getting louder.

MRS. BROWN: Heavens! Something went past the window.

MRS. ELLIS: Look! Up in the sky!

MADAME DUPONT: Oo, la la!

MRS. ABBOTT: Mary is *gone!*

MRS. BROWN: What?

MRS. CLARK: Gone!

MRS. ELLIS: How did it happen?

MRS. ABBOTT: She disappeared through the door. Whoosh! Just like that.

MRS. ELLIS: Alice! It says here in the booklet that Type Z-21 is—is an experiment! An outer space experiment!

MRS. BROWN: Outer space?

MRS. CLARK: That maid?

MRS. ABBOTT: The little red handle! That was it!

MRS. ELLIS: That's what put her in orbit.

MRS. BROWN: Was it my fault? Do you think I set her off?

MADAME DUPONT (*Puzzled*): She flies away, the maid?

MRS. ABBOTT: My lovely new maid!

MRS. CLARK: She's just a speck in the sky now.

MRS. BROWN: I'm awfully sorry, Alice.

MRS. ABBOTT: It's not your fault, Betty. If only I hadn't tried so many new things all at once.

THE MECHANICAL MAID 43

Mrs. Ellis: Don't worry, Alice. It says here: "If by mistake you touch the red handle marked *Orbit*, Type Z-21 is set to return to factory, after circling the earth three times. This should take about fifty-eight minutes."

Mrs. Abbott: Oh, I'm afraid our lunch has been a failure, and I wanted it to be so nice.

Mrs. Clark: Not a bit, Alice.

Mrs. Brown: We'll just go back to the good old days when the guests got busy and helped with the dishes.

Madame Dupont: *Oui! C'est bon!*

Mrs. Ellis: Yes, let's get the table cleared and the dishes washed before she gets back.

Mrs. Brown: Fifty-eight minutes. That's not long.

Mrs. Clark: Then we can call up the factory and have Mary tell us all about what it's like in outer space!

THE END

Fish in the Forest

This is an old Russian folk tale. It tells about a clever peasant and his not-too-clever wife, and how they discover a fortune.

This is not a difficult play. Read it through to yourself to be sure you understand what is happening.

Olga cannot keep a secret—how would you read her scenes with Anna and Sonia? The Count and Countess would probably speak somewhat differently from the others in the play. How do you think they should sound?

Choose parts and read the first scene of the play aloud. How did it sound? Do the two people playing Ivan and Olga need to improve? If so, they should practice their scene together again. Now read the second, third and fourth scenes. Check to be sure you know all the words. If you think you still need practice, read the play through again.

Read the play for the class, and have a discussion about how Ivan was able to fool the Count.

FISH IN THE FOREST

adapted by Hazel W. Corson

Characters

(4 boys, 5 girls, and a narrator)

NARRATOR
IVAN, *a poor peasant*
OLGA, *his wife*
ANNA ⎫
SONIA ⎬ *friends of Olga*
COUNT
COUNTESS
SOFIA, *her maid*
COURT OFFICIAL
OFFICER POPOFF

SCENE 1

NARRATOR: This folk tale takes place long ago in Russia. In the first scene, Ivan and his wife, Olga, who are poor peasants, are in the forest gathering mushrooms.

OLGA: We were lucky to find so many mushrooms, Ivan. Now we can have good mushroom soup to go with our black bread.

IVAN: This was a good idea of yours, Olga.

OLGA: Do you think there may be fish in that little pond over there?

IVAN: I'm sure there are some. I'll set some fishing lines, and I'll also set a snare by this old stump. If I can catch a rabbit, we will have some meat.

OLGA: Do you think you should do that, Ivan?

IVAN: Why not? Surely we need meat, and we have no money to buy any.

OLGA: You know how angry the Count gets if he hears that someone has been hunting in the forest.

IVAN: The Count is always angry. Besides, what the Count doesn't know won't hurt him. Just once, don't tell anyone, that's all. What is this? Something is hidden in this hollow stump. Why, it's an old leather bag.

OLGA: It must have been in the stump for many years. See how old and moldy the leather is! What is in it?

NARRATOR: Ivan shakes the bag, and hears a clinking sound. He puts his hand into the bag and draws out some coins, then lets them drop, one by one, back into the bag.

IVAN: Gold! We are rich! What a wonderful thing! We are rich! We are rich!

OLGA: Now I can have a new skirt, and a new shawl, and some new shoes, maybe even a ring to wear on my finger, like the Count's wife. I cannot wait to tell Anna!

IVAN (*Angrily*): Not so fast, wife! Not so fast! We must not speak of this to anyone!

OLGA: Why not? Surely our friends would rejoice in our good fortune.

IVAN: Indeed, they would. And they would talk about it to everyone.

OLGA: And what of that?

IVAN (*In exasperation*): Why, sooner or later, the Count would hear of it.

OLGA: Ha! I will tell him myself. And at the same time I will tell him that we do not need to slave for him any longer.

IVAN: Oh, Olga! It is not as simple as all that. The Count will say that the forest is his, and that anything found in the forest is his. He will have his soldiers take the money from us. No, we must not speak of this to anyone.

OLGA: Can't I just whisper it to Anna, and Sonia, and maybe Sofia?

IVAN (*Sternly*): No, Olga! You must not whisper it to anyone! I forbid it!

OLGA: But all our friends are as poor as we are. What can I tell them when they ask how I can have a new skirt and new shoes, and a new shawl, and new dishes and new . . .

IVAN (*Interrupting*): Enough, Olga! We cannot have new things. We must hide the treasure. We must live as we have been living. Otherwise, the Count will suspect something.

OLGA: If we can't spend any of the treasure, what good is it? Why not give it to the Count? He might give us a reward, and we could spend that.

IVAN: The Count is a rich man. He does not need the money, and he would never use it to help anyone. If we hide the treasure and say nothing about it, we can use it, little by little, to help the poor.

OLGA: So we can help the poor! And who is any poorer than we, I'd like to know?

IVAN: We can use a little sometimes. But we must not buy a great many things that will make us seem richer than our friends. Now, help me plan where to hide the treasure.

OLGA: Why not hide it in our house, under the hearth? Surely it will be safe there.

IVAN: That *is* a good plan. We will bury it tonight, when no one is about. Remember, I forbid you to speak of this!

OLGA: All right! All right! But I see no harm in whispering it to Anna.

IVAN (*Frustratedly*): Olga! Must I beat you?

OLGA: Oh, all right! All right!

* * * * *

SCENE 2

NARRATOR: Ivan and Olga go off to their home to hide the gold. In spite of what Ivan has said, Olga cannot keep their secret. So, a few days later, when she meets her friend Anna—

ANNA: Hello, Olga!

OLGA: Hello, Anna!

ANNA: Where have you been? I have not seen you all this week.

OLGA: Oh, Ivan has been keeping me busy helping him. But I know it is not so much help he wants.

ANNA: Ivan has always been a good husband. Does he now make you work hard?

OLGA: He doesn't make me work hard. He just doesn't want me out of his sight, because he thinks I can't keep a secret.

ANNA (*Eagerly*): Oh! So you and Ivan have a secret?

OLGA: Whatever made you think that?

ANNA: You must know something Ivan doesn't want you to tell. Surely you can whisper it to your old friend Anna!

OLGA: He thinks if I say anything about what we found, the Count will hear of it. So I will not breathe a word of it.

ANNA: Oh, come, Olga! I am your good friend! You can tell me your secret.

OLGA: I mustn't. Ivan will beat me.

ANNA: All right, Olga, whatever you say. I must be going now. See you later.

OLGA: Goodbye, Anna.

NARRATOR: As soon as Anna leaves, Sonia strolls by.

SONIA: Good morning, Olga.

OLGA: Good morning, Sonia. Isn't that a new skirt?

SONIA: Yes. Stefan brought it to me from the fair. Do you like it?

OLGA: It is beautiful. I might have many new things if Ivan were not so afraid of the Count.

SONIA: What has the Count to do with a new skirt?

OLGA: Oh, Ivan is so foolish. He says it might make the Count think we had found something valuable, and he would dig under the hearth and take it away from us.

SONIA (*Eagerly*): So you found something valuable? What is it? Where did you find it?

OLGA: How do you find out these things? I will not say another word.

NARRATOR: Olga puts her hand over her mouth and runs off. Sofia comes along, and Sonia runs up to her to tell the news.

SONIA: Have you heard the news, Sofia? Ivan and Olga Petrovich have found a fabulous treasure, and are as rich as czars!

SOFIA (*Excitedly*): Really? That's marvelous news. (*Hesitating*) But, it would be most unfortunate for Ivan if the Count should hear of this.

SONIA: Ah, yes, but I know you will not tell.

SOFIA: Nothing could drag it from me. But I must hurry. The Countess gets very angry if I am not there the minute she wants me. Goodbye, Sonia.

SONIA: Goodbye, Sofia.

NARRATOR: Sonia leaves as the Countess enters. She is carrying a mirror and comb, which she gives to Sofia.

COUNTESS: Here you are at last, Sofia. Fix my hair.

SOFIA: All the servants are buzzing this morning, Your Ladyship.

COUNTESS: The servants are always buzzing. What is it this time?

SOFIA: It seems that someone in the village has found a fabulous treasure . . . gold, silver, jewels . . . who knows what? Enough for a czar's ransom.

COUNTESS: Really? And who might that be?

SOFIA: Oh, that I couldn't say, Your Ladyship. It is a great secret.

COUNTESS: I am sure it is. Lay out my riding clothes, Sofia. I will take a ride this morning.

NARRATOR: Sofia leaves to lay out the Countess's clothes. After a moment, the Count joins the Countess.

COUNTESS: Good morning, my dear husband. The news from the village is that someone has found a fabulous treasure.

COUNT: That is most interesting! And who is the lucky person?

COUNTESS: No one knows, of course.

COUNT: Hm-m-m. Why don't you ride into the village, and do a little talking among the women?

COUNTESS: That is what I plan to do. I think I'll start with Olga Petrovich. She never can keep a secret. She has given me much information from time to time.

COUNT: Well, you have a way of finding out things from the women that I can't get from the men, even with torture. Just bring me the name of that scoundrel. I'll make such an example of him that no one else will dare to hide anything.

* * * * *

SCENE 3

NARRATOR: While the Countess goes off to find out what the gossip is in the village, and the Count returns to his palace to think over what he has heard, Ivan has gone to the forest. He looks all around to be sure that no one is watching. Then he goes up to the rock near the spot where he found the money. He sets down the basket he is carrying and starts to dig with the spade he has with him.

IVAN: I'll have to hurry. I don't have much time before Olga arrives. First, I'll bury the treasure under this big rock. Then I'll put these fresh fish along the path. If only these cakes will just stay tied to the tree! Now, where did I set that snare? Ah, here it is, with a fat rabbit in it! Suppose I fasten it to a fish hook, and throw it into the pond like this? Well, I'm finished. I am afraid that Olga's talking has made enough trouble in the past. Maybe no one will pay much attention to her stories after this. She should be here by now. Ah, there she is.

OLGA: Hello, Ivan. Why did you want me to meet you in the forest? Do you think we'll find more treasure?

IVAN: Stop talking about the treasure, Olga. It will only get us into trouble. There was a heavy rain last night. We might find anything. Just keep your eyes open.

OLGA: Oh, look, Ivan! A fine fat fish! Imagine finding it in the forest like this!

IVAN: Have you never heard that one often finds fish in the forest after a heavy rain?

OLGA (*Excitedly*): No, I never have! But it must be so. Here is another, and another. Into my basket you go, my pretty fish. Why haven't we done this before, Ivan?

IVAN: Well . . . one doesn't always find them. One has to come at just the right time, or the forest animals will have eaten them up.

OLGA: Oh, Ivan! Look! There are cakes on this little tree! Fresh cakes! Now who put them there, do you suppose?

IVAN: It rained quite hard last night. Perhaps there were cakes on the ground as well as in the tree. Animals probably ate them up.

OLGA (*Incredulously*): But I never knew it could rain cakes! How wonderful!

IVAN: It doesn't happen everywhere, so it isn't a thing one talks about. Otherwise all the world would rush to the spot and no one would have anything.

OLGA: How fortunate we are!

IVAN: Let's see if I caught anything on the fishing lines I set in the pond.

OLGA: How strange! A rabbit in the pond!

IVAN (*Matter-of-factly*): I do not think it strange. Have you not heard that rabbits, as well as fish, may be found in water?

OLGA: No, indeed! I knew it not!

IVAN: Well, you have seen it with your own eyes. And as for us, we have food fit for the Count himself.

OLGA: Yes, we have. Let's go home and cook it.

* * * * *

SCENE 4

NARRATOR: Meanwhile, the Count has learned more of the rumors about a great treasure that Ivan has found. So, a few days later, the Count calls everyone in the village together at his palace. Everyone is there—Anna, Sonia, Sofia, their neighbors, and, of course, the Court Official, servants, and pages.

COURT OFFICIAL (*Loudly*): His Lordship has something to say to you.

COUNT: I have called you all here today because there is something I wish you to see and hear. Some of my people are not here because they could not be spared from their work, but every family is represented.

COURT OFFICIAL (*Loudly*): Soldiers of the guard with Ivan Petrovich and his wife, Olga.

NARRATOR: Two guards bring Ivan and Olga into the room. They kneel before the Count.

COUNT (*Sternly*): Do you have anything to tell me, Ivan?

IVAN: What should I tell you, sir?

COUNT: Did you not find a great treasure in my forest? Do you not have it buried under your hearth?

IVAN: A great treasure under my hearth? Your Lordship knows that I am a poor man. Surely you jest, sir.

COUNT (*Furiously*): I never jest! It is only fair to tell you that I know all about it. News of this reached the Countess. She visited Olga. (*Loudly*) Countess, tell this liar what you discovered by this visit.

COUNTESS: Olga hinted that she and Ivan found treasure in the forest, and that it was buried under their hearth.

OLGA (*Indignantly*): But, Your Ladyship! This was a secret between women. I did not think that you would tell the Count.

COUNT: Silence, Olga! This secret between women is now a question for men to settle.

COURT OFFICIAL: You know that what is found in the Count's forest belongs to him. You should have come to him at once with the treasure. Doubtless he would have given you a reward.

COUNT: True! However, I may not punish you too severely if you tell me about the treasure at once.

IVAN: But, sir, there is no treasure under my hearth.

COUNT (*Sternly*): Do not lie to me, Ivan, or it will go hard with you. Do not forget that I can put you to the torture.

IVAN: But Your Lordship can send soldiers to my house to dig under the hearth.

COUNT: I have already done that, Ivan. They should be here soon with the treasure. Now do you wish to change your story?

IVAN: Would that I could, my lord!

COURT OFFICIAL (*Loudly*): Officer Popoff of the palace guard, to report to the Count!

COUNT: Good! Let him come forward.

OFFICER POPOFF: I took four soldiers to the house of Ivan Petrovich, Your Lordship. I had them dig under the hearth, and under the whole house. There was no treasure, sir.

COUNT (*In amazement*): No treasure?

COUNTESS: No treasure?

IVAN (*Pleadingly*): I beg of you, Your Lordship, do not be hard on poor Olga. I see I can no longer hide the truth. Some days Olga is quite all right. Other days she imagines things and does not know what she is saying. She does not mean to lie. She just imagines things at times.

OLGA (*Indignantly*): I do not imagine things! It is the truth! You did find treasure in the forest, and you did bury it under the hearth!

IVAN (*Gently*): Olga, when did I find treasure in the forest?

OLGA: Now let me see. Why, it was a few days before we went into the forest and found the fish.

COUNT (*Surprised*): You found fish in the forest?

OLGA: Yes, Your Lordship. And a fine lot of plump fresh fish we found, too. We gathered a basketful of them along the path. Then Ivan fished in the pond and caught a fat rabbit. I shall never forget that day! Perhaps you will remember that day, Your Ladyship. It rained cakes the night before.

COUNTESS (*Dumbfounded*): It . . . rained . . . cakes?

COUNT: So this is where you get your information, wife! I fear you are not a good judge of character.

COUNTESS: I am amazed!

COUNT: Guards, show these two out. They are wasting my time.

OLGA: Are you going to make Ivan give up the treasure, Your Lordship? We might as well give it up. Ivan won't give me any of it to spend.

COUNT: No, Olga. Ivan may keep his treasure, along with any fish he may find in my forest.

THE END

A Howling Success

This play is about a Broadway actor who plays a very un-usual role. Read the play through to yourself, and then discuss with the group the following questions:

What kind of a man is Lyle Bannister? Is he a conceited star or a down-to-earth person? How should his part be read?

What is Sheila's life's ambition? How does she behave in the play? How would you show this in reading her part?

Bonny isn't impressed with all the goings-on; how should she sound?

Choose your parts and read the play out loud. Did it sound right to you? Are there places that need more practice before you are ready to read for an audience? Did you come in at the right time and use the right tone of voice?

Read the play into a tape recorder and play it back. How did you sound? Do you still need improvement? If so, practice un-til you sound smooth and natural.

A HOWLING SUCCESS

by *Juliet Garver*

Characters

(5 boys, 4 girls, and a narrator)
NARRATOR
MR. ALLEN
MRS. ALLEN
SHEILA ⎤
BONNY ⎬ *their children*
ROGER ⎦
LYLE BANNISTER, *Mrs. Allen's cousin, an actor*
MARTHA MILLER, *President of the Ladies' Literary League*
JOHN RANDOLPH, *President of the Men's Club*
AL CASEY, *a reporter*

NARRATOR: This play is a comedy, and it takes place in the living room of the Allen family. As it begins, Mr. Allen is reading a newspaper, Mrs. Allen is dusting the furniture, and Sheila, a teen-ager, is leafing through a movie magazine. Bonny, her younger sister, is sitting on the floor, sandpapering a wooden box.

MRS. ALLEN: I wish we had some new drapes or slipcovers—something to dress this room up.

MR. ALLEN: We don't have to put on a front for your Cousin Lyle.

SHEILA: I wish our house looked like this one in *Movie Moments*. I wonder what Cousin Lyle is going to think of us in our—uh—provincial surroundings.

MR. ALLEN: Provincial, huh? Well, I don't care what Cousin

Lyle thinks of us. He still owes me ten dollars from the last time I saw him—and that was a mere ten years ago.

SHEILA (*Ignoring her father*): To think we have a real actor in our family! A Broadway star on his way to Hollywood.

BONNY: Me, I'd rather have a nice, dead Egyptian mummy.

SHEILA (*Shocked*): What?

BONNY: I saw a mummy in the museum last week. Gee, it was neat.

SHEILA: How horrible!

MR. ALLEN (*Amused*): I think Bonny's right. A guy like that would probably be much better company than Cousin Lyle.

MRS. ALLEN (*Protesting*): Now, George . . .

SHEILA: Maybe he'll do a scene for us from his Broadway play.

MRS. ALLEN: Maybe I could get Lyle to do a scene for the Ladies' Literary League meeting on Thursday! I'll call Martha Miller and tell her.

NARRATOR: Mrs. Allen goes to the phone and dials.

MRS. ALLEN (*Excitedly*): Martha? Lorraine Allen. I have the most exciting news. My cousin, Lyle Bannister, is a Broadway actor and he's coming here this afternoon. I think we could persuade him to come to our Thursday meeting and do a scene from his Broadway play *The Last Snow*. . . . Oh, I'm sure you can count on it. . . . I'll call you when he gets here. 'Bye. (*Happily*) There. It's all settled.

BONNY: I still wish he were a mummy . . . a nice, rotted one.

NARRATOR: The telephone rings, and Sheila answers it.

SHEILA: Hello? Oh, yes, Mr. Randolph, he's here. It's for you, Dad.

MR. ALLEN: Hello, John, how are things going? . . . Oh? Everything happens to us. We'll just have to get another speaker, that's all. . . . Mm . . . whom can we get at the last minute?

MRS. ALLEN: Cousin Lyle! I'll bet he'd be glad to be the guest speaker at the Men's Club.

MR. ALLEN: Say, John, wait a minute. My wife's cousin, a

Broadway actor, is coming here this afternoon. . . . He could talk to us about acting—be a nice change from all those business tycoons we've had lately. . . . Don't worry, I'll ask him as soon as he gets here. . . . 'Bye.

BONNY: Looks like Cousin Lyle's going to be mighty busy once he gets here.

MRS. ALLEN: Which reminds me . . . you and Sheila had better go upstairs right now and get busy. Clean up your room, and then get dressed.

SHEILA: All right, Mom. I want to look glamorous when Cousin Lyle arrives. After all, maybe he'd know of a spot in Hollywood for little old me.

BONNY: Ha!

SHEILA: Never you mind. (*Dramatically*) Someday . . . someday, my picture will be on all the billboards. My name will be in lights . . . I'll be famous.

BONNY: What a ham!

MRS. ALLEN: Girls, please. Sheila, go upstairs.

SHEILA: All right . . . but someday, you'll see. I'll be famous, and then I won't even speak to Bonny.

MRS. ALLEN: Bonny, you go up, too. Take all that mess with you—the sandpaper, too.

BONNY: If you insist. But you don't know how you're damaging my personality. Someday when I'm lying on a psychiatrist's couch . . . well, I'll really have stories to tell that psychiatrist. I'll probably make medical history.

NARRATOR: Bonny follows Sheila out of the room. Roger, a teen-ager, comes in wearing old jeans and a shirt streaked with grease.

ROGER: Greetings, everyone!

MRS. ALLEN: Roger, what have you been doing?

ROGER: Helping Sandy fix up his car.

MRS. ALLEN: You'd better get cleaned up before Cousin Lyle gets here.

ROGER: O.K. O.K. For you, Mom, I'll wash my hands . . . on both sides.

MRS. ALLEN: You'll do more than that. You'll take a good, hot bath.

ROGER: A bath! Mom, do I have to?

MRS. ALLEN (*Firmly*): Absolutely.

ROGER: Gee, I might drown on an empty stomach.

MRS. ALLEN (*Insistently*): You'd better hurry. Cousin Lyle will be here any minute.

ROGER: I was much happier under Sandy's car.

MRS. ALLEN: I'm going to put on my new black dress. I don't want Cousin Lyle to think marriage has changed me into a drab, old housewife.

MR. ALLEN: Not you, my dear—never.

NARRATOR: Mrs. Allen and Roger leave to change their clothes as Bonny comes dashing in, all cleaned up. Just as she speaks to her father, the doorbell rings.

BONNY: I haven't been this clean since my sixth birthday party. I'll get the door, Dad.

MR. ALLEN: Maybe that's our bright light from Broadway now.

BONNY: Cousin Lyle?

LYLE: In person. Lyle Bannister—of Broadway and Hollywood. Hello, George.

MR. ALLEN: Hello, Lyle. The family is still upstairs, getting ready. It isn't every day that we have a Broadway actor come to visit us. This is Bonny, our youngest daughter.

LYLE: Bonny, I'm delighted to meet you.

BONNY (*Pleased*): Well, gee—I—maybe you're just as nice to have around as a nice, dead mummy.

LYLE (*Puzzled*): What?

MR. ALLEN: Just a family joke. Come in, sit down, Lyle. Everyone will be down in a few minutes, I'm sure.

NARRATOR: Sheila makes a grand entrance, comically overdressed in an evening gown, false eyelashes, bracelets, necklaces—and a long scarf.

BONNY: So that's what took you so long. What a waste of time.

MR. ALLEN: Sheila, for goodness' sakes, what are you dressed up for? A masquerade?

SHEILA (*Ignoring all comments*): What's wrong with this uncultured family? Isn't anyone going to introduce me?

MR. ALLEN: I'm almost ashamed to admit it, but this is my daughter, Sheila.

SHEILA (*Dramatically*): Cousin Lyle, I believe?

LYLE: My pleasure, young lady. A pleasure to make your acquaintance. I can see you're interested in the theater.

SHEILA (*Thrilled*): Oh, I knew you'd understand. I just knew it. Acting is very close to my heart—very close. I know a lot of girls want to be actresses. New York is probably full of them.

LYLE: Well, there are quite a few.

SHEILA: But with me, it's different . . . it goes deep. I feel it way down deep inside of me.

BONNY: You probably just ate too much for lunch.

SHEILA: How can you say such a thing? You see, Cousin Lyle, nobody in this family understands me . . . this feeling I have, this flame inside of me.

BONNY (*Disgusted*): Ugh! And I have to share a room with her. Honestly, sometimes sisters are more than sisters can bear.

NARRATOR: Mrs. Allen and Roger come in.

MRS. ALLEN: I though I heard the doorbell before. Lyle, how nice of you to come and visit us.

LYLE: Lorraine! I would have known you anywhere—even in the middle of Times Square.

MRS. ALLEN (*Flattered*): Would you?

LYLE: You haven't changed a bit. Time has only made you lovelier.

MRS. ALLEN: Well, thank you, Cousin Lyle. I'm not used to such compliments.

MR. ALLEN (*Slightly peeved*): I haven't taken up acting yet.

MRS. ALLEN: This is my son, Roger.

LYLE: How are you, Roger?

ROGER: Right now, I'm slightly starved. I haven't had anything to eat for hours.

MRS. ALLEN: I'll serve some snacks here in the living room.

LYLE: I hope you're not going to any extra trouble on my account.

MRS. ALLEN: I want everything to be especially nice for your visit, Cousin Lyle. Roger, the tray is all fixed. Please get it out of the refrigerator, and don't eat anything while you're in the kitchen.

ROGER (*Complaining, good-naturedly*): What a dog's life I lead! I'll be back in a flash. My stomach is so empty I could put all of New York in it.

LYLE: Speaking of dogs, that reminds me of my play.

SHEILA: How can there be a dog in *The Last Snow*? Or do you mean someone leads a dog's life in it—a terrible, unhappy, miserable life?

LYLE: No. There really is a dog in *The Last Snow*.

SHEILA (*Impatiently*): All right, there's a dog in your play, but what part do you play, Cousin Lyle?

LYLE (*Proudly*): I play the part of the dog.

SHEILA: But I thought you had the lead.

LYLE: I do. The biggest part in the play is that of an imaginary dog. That's me. I play behind the scenes.

MRS. ALLEN (*Trying to help*): I'll bet he influences everyone's life in the play.

LYLE: You're right. Without me, there'd be no play.

SHEILA: But, Cousin Lyle, what exactly do you do?

LYLE: I bark. (*Starts to bark*) Woof—woof—woof.

MR. ALLEN: For this you get paid?

LYLE (*Proudly*): Four hundred and fifty dollars a week.

MR. ALLEN: I'm in the wrong business.

SHEILA: You mean all you do on the stage is bark?

LYLE: It's not as simple as all that, Sheila. Not everyone can bark as convincingly as I do. It took me years to learn, and now I'm going to do it in the movies. Of course, the movies pay a lot more.

SHEILA (*Disappointed*): I can't believe it.

LYLE: Yes, there I was, starving in New York, eating in drug-stores when I could afford it—and then I learned to bark. What a great day that was for me.

MRS. ALLEN: And I wanted you to entertain the Ladies' Literary League. We do very literary, highbrow things. Last year, we did some scenes from Shakespeare.

MR. ALLEN: And I arranged for you to speak at our Men's Club.

SHEILA: I'll never live this down. I've told everybody all about you. And yesterday, the principal came into our room, and I told *him*. He wants you to come to school one day and make a speech.

NARRATOR: The doorbell rings. Bonny opens the door and Al Casey comes in.

AL CASEY: Hello, I'm Al Casey from the *Daily Journal*.

SHEILA (*Horrified*): A reporter!

LYLE: Tell the young man to come in, Bonny. I always like to stay on good terms with the press.

SHEILA: Oh, Cousin Lyle, you shouldn't tell your public everything. Be sort of mysterious. Keep your secrets hidden.

LYLE (*Laughing*): I stay hidden long enough, backstage.

AL: Mr. Bannister?

LYLE (*Pleasantly*): Yes, yes, I'm Lyle Bannister.

AL: I hope you don't mind if I ask you a few questions.

LYLE: No, no, not at all. Lyle Bannister is always glad to co-operate with the press.

AL: Thank you, Mr. Bannister. Of course we have a lot of clippings on you in our morgue.

BONNY: Morgue? Isn't that for dead people?

MR. ALLEN: Not in a newspaper office, Bonny. It's just a fancy word for file cabinets.

BONNY (*Disappointed*): Oh.

AL: And I'm a regular subscriber to the New York *Times* so I know what's going on in the theater world, even though we're miles from Times Square.

SHEILA: Then you know all about the play Cousin Lyle's in . . . *The Last Snow?*

AL: Yes, indeed, read all the reviews. Quite an unusual play.

LYLE: And an unusual part in it for me, if I may say so.

AL: Yes, sir, it certainly is. Now, Mr. Bannister, please, just a few questions. How long are you planning to stay here in town?

LYLE: Oh, just a short while. I have to be in Hollywood by the end of next week. We're going to make *The Last Snow* into a movie.

AL: You'll be here long enough to fulfill some speaking engagements?

LYLE: Speaking engagements? What speaking engagements?

AL: A Mrs. Miller called the paper a while ago and told our Society Editor that you were going to speak at the next Literary League meeting.

LYLE: Well, I . . .

MRS. ALLEN: I didn't think you'd mind, Cousin Lyle, but, of course, if you'd rather not—

LYLE: Why, I'd be delighted.

AL: What do you think of our little town, Mr. Bannister?

LYLE: Great—a great little town.

AL: One more thing. What advice would you give to young people who want to become actors and actresses?

LYLE: My advice to everyone is—if you have a dream, don't give it up.

AL: Thank you, Mr. Bannister. We have all the other information we need.

BONNY: In the coffins?

AL (*Puzzled*): Coffins?

MR. ALLEN: I think she means the morgue.

AL: Oh, yes, young lady . . . in our morgue we do have some dead people but also some pretty live ones. Well, thanks a lot, Mr. Bannister. Goodbye, everyone. I'll let myself out.

LYLE: Well, I'd better go upstairs and unpack. Have to shake the wrinkles out of my two-hundred-dollar suits.

MRS. ALLEN: Bonny, go upstairs and show Cousin Lyle where he can put his things.

BONNY: All right. Come on, Cousin Lyle. This way.

SHEILA (*After a pause*): I'll die. I'll positively die when everybody finds out that all Cousin Lyle does on the Broadway stage is *bark*!

MR. ALLEN: I can see the headlines now—BARKING DOG DOESN'T BITE . . . DOG WEARS TWO-HUNDRED-DOLLAR SUITS . . . LYLE BANNISTER PUTS ON THE DOG.

MRS. ALLEN: Oh, stop teasing Sheila. It's—it's kind of a shock to all of us, but (*Giggling*) it is funny.

MR. ALLEN (*Laughing*): It is. And now, Sheila, you can go upstairs and take off that Mata Hari disguise.

SHEILA: Oh, this family! It's so . . . so humiliating. I'll bet my friends will bark at me when I walk down the street.

MRS. ALLEN: I wonder what happened to Roger. I forgot about him in all the excitement, but I sent him to the kitchen quite a while ago.

SHEILA: Roger probably got his head stuck in the refrigerator.

MRS. ALLEN: I'm going to see what he's up to.

NARRATOR: Mrs. Allen goes off to the kitchen as the telephone rings again. Sheila speaks over her shoulder to her father as she answers.

SHEILA: I'll bet the news is all over town about Cousin Lyle. . . . Hello? . . . Who? . . . Yes, just a moment. (*In a whisper*) Dad, it's the Crunchy Munchy Dog Biscuit Company. They want to talk to Cousin Lyle.

MR. ALLEN: Now I've heard everything!

SHEILA (*Calling*): Cousin Lyle—telephone.

NARRATOR: Lyle, Bonny and Roger come in.

SHEILA: Telephone for you, Cousin Lyle.

LYLE: Thanks, Sheila. . . . Hello, Lyle Bannister speaking . . . Yes? . . . Well, I might consider it. . . . Yes, you can send someone over and we'll talk about it . . . Thank you. Goodbye.

BONNY: Does somebody want to take a picture of you eating dog biscuits?

LYLE: Not exactly.

ROGER: I get hungrier than most people but even *I* would never stoop to that.

LYLE: The Crunchy Munchy Dog Biscuit Company wants to use me as a . . . well, a clever tie-in for their advertising— magazines, television commercials and so forth. They'll pay me five thousand dollars.

MR. ALLEN: Five thousand dollars!

LYLE: That's what the man said. Well, excuse me. I'm going out to the kitchen to find a cup of coffee.

MR. ALLEN: I'll never understand it. A man doesn't need talent or anything—just has to bark like a dog and five thousand dollars falls into his lap.

NARRATOR: Mr. Allen stares after Lyle in amazement. The doorbell rings and Roger opens the door. Mrs. Miller, the President of the Ladies' Literary League, rushes in, just as Mrs. Allen comes from the kitchen.

MRS. ALLEN: What happened, Martha?

MRS. MILLER: I've never been so humiliated in all my life.

MRS. ALLEN: It can't be that bad.

MRS. MILLER: I'll have to resign. I can't be president of the Ladies' Literary League after this. Imagine, having a man bark like a dog, and he gets paid for it. I just heard all about it. My cousin, (*Angrily*) who works for the paper, called me and told me about your Cousin Lyle and his *unusual* talent. You didn't tell me that your cousin barked.

66 *A HOWLING SUCCESS*

MRS. ALLEN: I didn't know.

MRS. MILLER: I have an uncle who whistles like a bird but I never tried to pass him off as a famous Broadway celebrity. I wouldn't have the nerve!

NARRATOR: Mrs. Miller storms off. The Allens look at each other in dismay.

MR. ALLEN: Don't look at me, Lorraine. He's *your* cousin.

MRS. ALLEN: Oh, George, what are we going to do? I'll bet the story about Cousin Lyle will be on the front page of the paper tonight.

MR. ALLEN: Just like your Cousin Lyle to put on the dog.

MRS. ALLEN: Don't mention the word "dog" to me.

BONNY: Cousin Lyle became famous barking. How many people can say that?

SHEILA (*Unhappily*): I'm sure he's the only one.

ROGER: And he was just offered five thousand dollars for doing an ad.

MRS. ALLEN: He was?

MR. ALLEN: Yes. I guess it pays to bark. Maybe it's the up-and-coming thing. Maybe we can learn to do it to music.

MRS. ALLEN: George!

NARRATOR: The doorbell rings once again, and Roger goes to answer the door.

ROGER: This is probably someone from the American Kennel Club—maybe they want to make Cousin Lyle an honorary dog.

NARRATOR: Roger opens the door to Mr. Randolph, who goes to Mr. Allen and shakes his hand.

MR. RANDOLPH: George, I wanted to come over and tell you myself. We had a special meeting of the Board of the Men's Club, and we voted to pay your cousin two hundred dollars to speak at our next meeting.

MR. ALLEN: What?

MR. RANDOLPH: Everybody was for it.

MR. ALLEN: We never pay our speakers anything like that.

MR. RANDOLPH: I know, but we've never had a famous actor before. A real celebrity here in Westlake.

MR. ALLEN: John, you're an old friend of mine. I've got to tell you the truth. Cousin Lyle, well—uh, he—

SHEILA: He has a peculiar talent.

MR. ALLEN: Uh, yes, that's it—peculiar.

MR. RANDOLPH: Oh, you mean the barking?

MR. ALLEN: You know?

MR. RANDOLPH: Sure. My wife reads everything she can about New York theater. She gets all the magazines on the stands. I read about it a long time ago . . . must take a lot of talent. Say, anybody can play the part of a man, but a dog!

MR. ALLEN (*Weakly*): I guess so.

MR. RANDOLPH: Could I—I mean—I'd like to meet this great theater personality.

MR. ALLEN: He's out in the kitchen. But first, Roger . . . quick, get me the telephone book.

ROGER: Huh? What for?

MR. ALLEN: I want to look up dog kennels.

SHEILA: Dog kennels?

MR. ALLEN (*Shouting*): Yes, dog kennels!

BONNY: Cousin Lyle's fame has gone to Dad's head.

ROGER: But what for?

MR. ALLEN: I'm going out to every dog kennel in town and learn how to bark.

SHEILA (*Amazed*): What?

MR. ALLEN: Look at the money in it. It's better than buying an oil well or digging for gold. I don't see why Cousin Lyle should have a corner on the market. There are lots of actors in Hollywood who can sing. Why should there be only one who can bark? I'll bet with a little practice I can do it. (*Starts to bark*) Woof—woof—woof—woof—(*Everyone laughs heartily, as he continues to bark.*)

THE END

Doctor Know All

This play is an old folk tale about a man who pretends to be a wise man, and manages to catch some thieves in spite of himself.

Read the play silently and then discuss it as a group. What do the names of the characters show about them? Would they sound like people in a play set in the present day? What sort of a person is Mary?

Remember that the characters should be exaggerated in this play. Their speeches are not always like ordinary conversation. Remember to come in promptly with your speeches and speak clearly.

Choose your parts and read the first scene. Can you suggest any improvements? If so, work on the parts that need it before going on to the second and third scenes. Do the same for them.

Ask yourself these questions:

1. Do I understand all the words?
2. Did I make my part funny while still speaking so that others can understand me?
3. Did I pay attention to punctuation and my tone of voice?

When the group thinks it is ready, you can arrange to read for your class, or into a tape recorder.

DOCTOR KNOW ALL

adapted by Helen L. Howard

Characters

(8 boys, 4 girls, and a narrator)
NARRATOR
CRABB, *the farmer*
MARY, *his wife*
MR. PROSPER, *a rich man*
CROOK ⎤
CRAFTY ⎬ *his servants*
CUNNING ⎦
DR. LAZARUS
MRS. AIKINGBAK ⎤
MR. PAYNE ⎥
MRS. HERTZ ⎬ *patients*
IAN HERTZ ⎥
MISS QUALM ⎦

SCENE 1

NARRATOR: This play begins in Dr. Lazarus's office. The doctor is sitting at his desk, talking to one of his patients, Mrs. Aikingbak. Another patient, Mr. Payne, is sitting on a bench, holding a pair of crutches and waiting his turn. As Dr. Lazarus talks with Mrs. Aikingbak, the farmer Crabb comes into the office and stands at one side.

MRS. AIKINGBAK: Oh, Dr. Lazarus, I don't know how I could have stood the pain another day. You are so wonderful! How much do I owe you?

DR. LAZARUS: That will be one piece of silver, Mrs. Aikingbak.

MRS. AIKINGBAK: I'm so happy to give it to you.

DR. LAZARUS: I'm so glad I could help you, Mrs. Aikingbak.

MRS. AIKINGBAK: Goodbye, Dr. Lazarus.

DR. LAZARUS: Thank you, Mrs. Aikingbak. Goodbye.

NARRATOR: As Mrs. Aikingbak leaves, Mrs. Hertz and her son, Ian, come in and wait their turn.

DR. LAZARUS: Now, Mr. Payne, what can I do for you today?

MR. PAYNE: Good day, Dr. Lazarus. I've come to pay you for setting my broken leg and putting it in the cast. How much do I owe you?

DR. LAZARUS: Well, now, Mr. Payne, just let me look in my book, here. That will be five pieces of silver.

MR. PAYNE: I'm glad to pay you, Doctor. It was a bad break.

DR. LAZARUS: Thank you, Mr. Payne. Good day to you.

NARRATOR: Mr. Payne leaves the office, passing Miss Qualm, who rushes in.

MISS QUALM: Oh, Dr. Lazarus, I've just stopped in to pay you for taking care of that tiny freckle on the end of my nose. (*Affectedly*) Everyone says I'm much more attractive than I was before.

DR. LAZARUS: And so you are, Miss Qualm. I'm glad others think so, too. If you will just sit down and wait until I talk with Mrs. Hertz and Ian, I'll discuss the matter with you.

MISS QUALM (*Indignantly*): Well, I never! The idea—asking me to wait!

DR. LAZARUS: I'm sorry, Miss Qualm, but I always take my patients in turn. Now, Mrs. Hertz, what can I do for you?

MRS. HERTZ: I just came to pay you for making Ian feel good again.

IAN: I didn't like having the fever, but now I can go out and play ball again, and fly my kite. Thank you, Dr. Lazarus.

DR. LAZARUS: You are certainly welcome, Ian, and I'm glad you're feeling well.

MRS. HERTZ: How much do I owe you, Doctor?

DR. LAZARUS: That will be one silver piece.

MRS. HERTZ: Here it is, Doctor.

DR. LAZARUS: Thank you, Mrs. Hertz. Goodbye.

MRS. HERTZ: Goodbye, Doctor.

DR. LAZARUS: Now, Miss Qualm, you are next.

MISS QUALM: Well, I should think so! I'm practically the only one here. How much do I owe you?

DR. LAZARUS: Ten silver pieces, Miss Qualm.

MISS QUALM: Here you are!

DR. LAZARUS: Oh, Miss Qualm, I did hope that after I removed the freckle from your nose you'd feel like smiling a little.

MISS QUALM (*Shyly*): To tell the truth, I do feel like it, but it has been so long since I smiled. . . .

DR. LAZARUS: I'm sure you can, if you try.

MISS QUALM: Why, I can smile! I do feel so much better. I'm sorry I was so rude. I'll catch up with Mrs. Hertz and Ian and take them home in my carriage. Goodbye, Doctor.

DR. LAZARUS: Now, Farmer Crabb, what can I do for you?

CRABB: If you please, sir, I've brought the load of wood you ordered.

DR. LAZARUS: Oh, yes. How much do I owe you?

CRABB: Five copper pieces.

DR. LAZARUS: Here you are.

CRABB: Thank you, sir.

DR. LAZARUS: What's the matter, Crabb? Didn't I give you enough money?

CRABB: Yes, sir.

DR. LAZARUS: Then why are you waiting?

CRABB: I was thinking, Doctor. Here I spent a whole day cutting the wood and bringing it to you in my cart. I get only five copper pieces. You sit here and take in silver pieces all afternoon. I'd like to be a doctor.

DR. LAZARUS: Well, since it's so easy, why don't you get a black coat and a sign that says you are Doctor Know All. Hang the sign in front of your door and wait in your black coat for customers.

CRABB: What a good idea! That's just what I'll do! Thank you, good Doctor.

DR. LAZARUS (*Laughing*): I wish you luck, Doctor Know All!

* * * * *

SCENE 2

NARRATOR: Crabb rushes home, full of plans to become the great Doctor Know All. His only problem is his scatter-brained wife, Mary.

MARY: Now, tell me once more what I'm to do if somebody docks at the noor? I mean knocks at the door? Oh, now I remember! I'm to say, "The great Doctor Know Nothing will—"

CRABB: Oh, no! No! No! The great Doctor Know *All*.

MARY: Oh, yes! I'll remember. The great Doctor Know Nothing will see you—

CRABB: No, Mary, no! That's all wrong. The great Doctor Know *ALL*. And you do not bow and kiss the hand! You curtsy, like this, and say, "The great Doctor Know All will see you at once!" Oh, Mary, you are so awkward! What am I to do with you? There's someone at the door now! Look— a fine carriage has stopped outside, and a man in rich clothes is knocking at our door. Go quickly and open the door, Mary.

MARY: To be sure I will.

CRABB: No, no! That way is the kitchen! Do you think my patients will come through the kitchen? The front door! Put down the broom! What are you taking it for?

MARY: To sweep off the boots of the fine gentleman, so he won't get my floor dirty!

CRABB: Don't be silly! A fine gentleman won't have dirty boots. Leave the broom and go and answer the door before he goes away.

NARRATOR: Crabb goes to the table and sits, pulling his black robe around him and trying to look dignified. Mary leaves the broom on the floor and answers the door to admit Mr. Prosper.

MARY: Good day, sir.

MR. PROSPER: I've come to see the doctor.

MARY: Doctor? No doctor here except my husband, and he is Doctor Know Nothing.

MR. PROSPER: But the sign outside your house says "Doctor Know All."

MARY (*Laughing*): Oh, yes! That's right! I can never remember whether it is all or nothing! Come in. It's my husband you want to see.

NARRATOR: Mr. Prosper follows Mary into the room. Crabb gets up, but as he starts toward Mr. Prosper, he stumbles over the broom and falls to the floor. Mary takes the broom and begins sweeping furiously. Crabb staggers to his feet and turns to Prosper.

CRABB: Ah, good day, sir. What can you do for me? I mean, what can I do for you?

MR. PROSPER: Are you the great Doctor Know All?

CRABB: I am. (*Aside*) Mary, stop sweeping!

MARY (*Loudly*): What do you want?

CRABB: Nothing! Nothing!

MR. PROSPER: Well, Doctor Know All, I came to you to help me find a bag of gold that has been stolen.

CRABB: A bag of gold!

MR. PROSPER: Yes. My bag of gold has disappeared. I suspect my three servants, Crafty, Cunning, and Crook, but I don't know how to find out who stole it or where it is hidden.

CRABB: Yes. And what do you want me to do? Give you a powder for your nerves?

MR. PROSPER: Oh no! I want you to find my gold.

CRABB (*Astonished*): Me? Me find your gold?

MR. PROSPER: Why, surely. If you are the great Doctor Know

All, you must know everything. You must know, then, where my bag of gold is hidden. I shall give you half of the gold when you find it for me. I'll take you to my house at once and you may stay there until you find the gold.

CRABB: You want me to go with you!

MARY (*Whispering*): Take me, too.

CRABB (*Whispering*): No!

MARY (*Louder*): Yes!

CRABB: Oh, very well. Mr. Prosper, may my wife go, too? I always take her with me.

MR. PROSPER: Why, yes, I suppose so. Come, are you ready?

CRABB: As soon as I get my hat and cane. We're going out the front door, Mary, not the kitchen!.

MARY: All right. Oh, my broom! I nearly forgot my broom!

* * * * *

SCENE 3

NARRATOR: And so this odd little group makes its way to Mr. Prosper's house—Mr. Prosper himself in his fine clothes, Crabb in his black cloak, high hat and cane, and last of all, Mary, wearing her bonnet and carrying her broom. When they reach Mr. Prosper's fine house, he ushers them into the dining room, seats them at the brocade-covered table, and lights the candelabra. Mary holds tight to her broom.

MR. PROSPER: I have told my servants that you are the great Doctor Know All and that they are to do whatever you ask them to do. It is necessary for me to be away for a while but my servants will give you your dinner here. Good day.

MARY: My! My! What a hice nouse he has! I mean, what a nice house. Just look at this cloth. It must have cost a mot of loney —I mean a lot of money.

CRABB: Now I must explain to you about the way food is served in rich men's houses. Come and sit down before someone comes in. Now in rich men's houses they do not put all of the food on the table at once. They serve the food in courses.

MARY: Courses? What's that? Are they golden dishes?

CRABB: No, no! Here comes someone. I haven't time to explain. I'll tell you as each course comes in.

NARRATOR: A servant named Crafty comes in with a tray.

CRABB: Now, this is the first!

CRAFTY (*Aside*): Ah, he knows that I am the first thief! He is indeed the great Doctor Know All! I must run and warn the others!

MARY: He dropped the tray on the floor. What a funny place to put the food! So that is the first course. Do we sit on the floor for it?

CRABB: No, no! The food on the tray was the first course. Now comes the second course. But hush! Someone else is coming!

NARRATOR: A second servant called Cunning comes in with a tray of food.

CRABB: This is the second.

CUNNING (*Aside*): Ah, woe is me. He knows everything! He is the great Doctor Know All. He knows that I am the second thief! I must run away!

MARY: How strange, to bring in food and run out again with it before we can eat. I think I like our way better, even if it isn't so stylish! At least I get something to eat.

CRABB: Hush, here comes another course.

NARRATOR: The third servant, Crook, comes in carrying a covered dish.

CRABB: And this is the third!

CROOK (*Aside*): Crafty and Cunning are right! He does know everything. He knows that I am the third thief! Sir, my master told us that you are the great Doctor Know All. Now, if you know everything, tell me, what is in this covered dish I am carrying?

CRABB (*Aside*): What am I to do? I don't know what is in the dish. I'm ruined! They'll know that I am not the great Doctor Know All! Oh, what shall I do! (*Aloud*) Oh, wretched Crabb that I am!

CROOK: Crab! You're right! The covered dish does contain a crab! Oh, sir. Spare us! You know that Crafty, Cunning and I stole the money! You know also that we hid it in the well!

CRABB: I'll not tell your master on you if you will go and get the bag of gold and bring it to me. At once!

CROOK: Oh, thank you, great Doctor Know All! We will get the bag of gold at once!

CRABB: Promise never to steal again!

CROOK: We promise!

NARRATOR: Crook runs out. Mary looks at Crabb, puzzled.

MARY: But how did you know what was in the dish? And how did you know that the servants stole the money? And how did you know where the money was hidden?

CRABB (*Pleased*): Why, because I am the great Doctor Know All!

THE END

The Ten-Penny Tragedy

This is a comedy about how gossip and some misunderstood words start a rumor in a high school. It is not a difficult play, but it should move along briskly.

After you read the play to yourself, discuss with the group how you can make sure a listener would understand the way the rumor about Andrea spreads.

The characters in this play are all about the same age. How can you make each one sound like an individual? Of course, you should try to make the conversation sound natural, because the play is taking place in an ordinary school. Mr. Faddle is the only character who might be exaggerated.

1. Choose parts and read a few pages. Did you sound lively and natural? If not, practice until you read smoothly, with no pauses. Use the right tone of voice.

2. Practice reading the whole play out loud together. Go over it until everyone comes in on time and reads without hesitation.

3. Have your chairman plan a time to read the play for an audience.

THE TEN-PENNY TRAGEDY

by Josef A. Elfenbein

Characters

(4 boys, 4 girls, and a narrator)
NARRATOR
ANDREA NEVINS ⎫
MARJ HIGGINS ⎪
MARILYN ⎪
DELIA ⎬ *high school students*
GERALD ⎪
PHIL ⎪
ALEX ⎭
MR. FADDLE, *the principal*

NARRATOR: This play shows what happens when gossip and misunderstandings turn a high school upside down. Andrea Nevins is sitting at the Information Desk outside the principal's office, selling tickets to the Spring Carnival. She is talking on the telephone with her open notebook, textbooks, and tickets in front of her. While she is talking, Gerald comes up to the desk and waits until she has finished.

ANDREA: Yes, Miss Furbush. Tickets for the Carnival are available today. . . . They're ten cents each. . . . No, *ten* cents. A dime. That's right. . . . Yes, I can bring one up to you. Are you in the English office? . . . No, no trouble at all. I'll be glad to. Marjorie Higgins takes over this desk when the bell rings. I'll bring one ticket with me when I come. . . . At the end of the period. . . . Yes, and thank you. Goodbye.

GERALD: Here's your ten cents, Andrea. I just got my allowance for the week, so I guess I can afford a ticket.

ANDREA: Here's your ticket, Gerald. Now, where will I put your dime? I don't have a cash box yet, and I don't have pockets in this dress. I'll lose the dime.

GERALD: Tie it in your handkerchief. You won't lose that.

ANDREA: I shouldn't. It's my mother's best handkerchief. Dad gave it to her for her birthday last month. She lent it to me, and I promised I'd take care of it.

GERALD: I won't hurt the handkerchief. Here, give it to me. This way you'll hang on to the money.

ANDREA: Hurry, Gerald. The period is almost over and I have to get a ticket up to Miss Furbush. Marj should be along any minute.

GERALD: Here, all fixed.

NARRATOR: Gerald ties the dime in a corner of the handkerchief and hands it back to Andrea, who slips it in her notebook and puts it on the desk as the bell rings.

ANDREA: Thanks. We're going to be late for class.

GERALD: Here comes Marj down the hall now.

ANDREA: She'll have some good excuse for being late, I know.

MARJ (*In a great hurry*): Sorry I'm late, Andy, but Mr. Burton was hung up on a dangling participle, and we were kept dangling with him. You can take off now. Don't forget your books.

ANDREA: I'll just take my poetry book. I'll get the others later.

GERALD: Sell lots of tickets, Marj. The basketball team needs new uniforms.

MARJ: I'll do my best.

NARRATOR: Gerald and Andrea leave for class. The telephone rings and Marj answers it.

MARJ: Hello, Spring Carnival tickets. Ten cents each. A dime apiece. Marjorie Higgins speaking. . . . Oh, yes, Miss Furbush, she just this minute left. She'll get it right up there, I'm sure. . . . Yes, ma'am, all classes after 2 p.m. on Friday are cancelled. . . . Yes, I'm sorry, too. I'll miss algebra. . . . It *is* too bad. But the team needs new uniforms. . . . Well, the moths chewed up the old ones this summer. . . . No, there wasn't enough left to sew together. They even ate the numbers off the backs. . . . Oh, they *will* take better care of them next summer. Lots of moth balls. . . . All right, Miss Furbush, if I see her. . . . Goodbye.

NARRATOR: The bell rings for the start of the next period. Andrea and Gerald come in, looking worried.

MARJ: Andrea! Gerald! What are you doing here? Are you cutting English?

ANDREA: No, I'm looking for a handkerchief I lost. It has a dime in it.

GERALD: It was her mother's and Andy lost it somewhere.

MARJ (*Repeating*): A diamond? Lost?

ANDREA: How can I face my mother tonight?

MARJ: It was your mother's?

GERALD: Her father gave it to her mother.

MARJ: Gosh, I didn't see it.

GERALD: Let's go back and look in the hall, Andrea.

MARJ: I certainly hope you find it.

ANDREA: I'm worried sick!

NARRATOR: Andrea and Gerald leave, searching the hallway. Marj watches them, stunned. Alex comes up to the desk and raps for attention.

ALEX: Cash customer! Cash customer! A ticket to the Carnival.

MARJ (*Slightly dazed*): What did you say?

ALEX: I want a ticket to the— Say, what's the matter with *you?*

MARJ: Poor Andy.

ALEX: What's the matter with "poor Andy"?

MARJ: It's terrible, Alex. Awful! Even worse than that.

ALEX: What's so terrible?

MARJ: Andrea . . . Andrea lost her mother's diamond somewhere in school.

ALEX: What?

THE TEN-PENNY TRAGEDY 81

MARJ: It was the one Mr. Nevins gave to Mrs. Nevins.

ALEX: Their engagement ring! I'll bet it was their engagement ring!

MARJ (*Sadly*): You're probably right. She just has to find it.

ALEX: I know what! I'll tell the team about it. They'll help find it. Here's my ten cents.

MARJ: Thanks. Here's the ticket.

ALEX: Imagine Andrea losing her mother's engagement ring. Wow!

NARRATOR: Alex leaves, passing Marilyn on the way.

MARILYN: Hi, Marj. How are tickets going?

MARJ: Oh, Marilyn, who can think about tickets, when there is tragedy brewing right here in this very school!

MARILYN: Tragedy?

MARJ: Andrea lost her mother's huge engagement ring.

MARILYN: So that's it. I knew something terrible had happened.

MARJ: What do you know about it?

MARILYN: I saw Andrea in the hall and she was crying something awful!

MARJ: She says she can't bear to face her parents.

MARILYN: Afraid of her father?

MARJ: Most likely.

MARILYN: He's a big man. He'll probably beat her when he hears about it.

MARJ: Oh, no!

MARILYN: Beat her within an inch of her life.

MARJ: Poor, poor, *poor* Andy.

MARILYN (*Confidentially*): If I were her, I'd run away!

MARJ: I would, too. Imagine a father beating a girl her age.

MARILYN: I'd better go after her. If she's going to run away, I'll let her spend the night in *my* house.

MARJ: You're a really true friend, Marilyn.

MARILYN: I'll go right away and find her.

NARRATOR: Marilyn hurries off to find Andrea. The phone rings and Marj goes to the desk to answer it.

MARJ: Hello, Spring Carnival tickets. . . . Yes, Miss Furbush. I know Andrea was supposed to take you a ticket but something *terrible* has happened. . . . She lost her mother's diamond engagement ring. . . . Yes, and her father is going to beat her for it. . . .

NARRATOR: Marj speaks in a low voice as Andrea and Gerald return. Marj has her back to them and does not notice them.

ANDREA: We've been over every inch of the floor from here to 109. I don't know what to do. (*She sniffs.*)

GERALD: There's no point crying over a handkerchief and a dime, Andrea. Here, this is my week's allowance. I'll lend it to you. Run downtown and buy another handkerchief just like the one you lost. Maybe the store has another one just like it.

ANDREA: But what about my English class?

GERALD: Explain it to the teacher later.

ANDREA: All right. I'll run as fast as I can so I won't miss the next class.

GERALD: It's the only thing to do. Go ahead.

NARRATOR: Marj hangs up and gasps as she turns to see Andrea and Gerald.

MARJ: Andy! Gerald! Haven't you found it yet?

ANDREA: No.

MARJ: Well, what are you going to do?

ANDREA: No time to talk now. I have to run.

MARJ (*Misinterpreting her*): You have to *run?*

ANDREA: Yes, Marj, I have to go right now. Goodbye.

MARJ (*Calling after her*): Andrea! Andrea, come back! Don't run off like that.

GERALD: It's the only thing she can do under the circumstances. It's the only way.

MARJ: Oh, poor Andy! What'll she do for money?

GERALD: I lent her my week's allowance. That'll help. Well, I'd better get back to English. See you later.

NARRATOR: As he leaves, Gerald bumps into Phil.

PHIL: Watch where you're goin', fella! Hm! Where's he going in such a rush? He'll kill himself on the stairs. The jerk doesn't even watch where he's going.

MARJ: He's not a jerk. He's a gentleman. A knight in shining armor.

PHIL: Gerald, a knight in shining armor? What brought all this on?

MARJ: Well, Andy lost her mother's huge diamond engagement ring. Then she was afraid that her father would beat her within an inch of her life, so she's running away. Gerald gave her his week's allowance so she could escape.

PHIL: Whew! No kiddin'? That's a shame. Andy's mother would be sick if she knew all this.

MARJ: She'll probably faint dead away when she does hear.

PHIL: Any woman would.

MARJ: Imagine, a furious father, a fainting mother—no wonder she's running away from home.

NARRATOR: Now Delia comes in, upset by the rumors she has heard.

DELIA: Is it true what I heard about Andrea, Marj?

MARJ (*Seriously*): Yes, Delia, it is.

DELIA: I saw her running out of the building—hair flying, tears running down her cheeks, and her face as white as chalk.

PHIL: Sounds sick to me.

MARJ: She said she was sick about it.

DELIA: She must be sick. She was wild-eyed!

PHIL: Do you think she really is sick?

DELIA: Phil, I said she was chalk-white and wild-eyed.

PHIL: She must be sick as a dog.

DELIA: What do you expect? All this trouble. Nervous tension. Besides, measles are going around.

PHIL: If she has the measles, she should have a doctor.

MARJ: Instead she's all alone, running through the streets.

PHIL: I wonder where she caught the measles.

DELIA: From her little brother, of course. All the kids have them now.

MARJ: I could weep for Andy.

DELIA: What about her mother? Think of it! A cruel husband who beats his daughter. A son down with the measles. A treasured diamond engagement ring lost. And a loving daughter sick and running away from home.

PHIL: It's enough to make a person collapse from the strain, or something.

DELIA: That's no joke. She might very well have a nervous collapse over this situation.

MARJ: My heart is racing right now and I'm not even related.

PHIL: My health teacher says that nerves can be very serious.

DELIA: Don't say another word, Phil. It's all too tragic.

MARJ: Something ought to be done.

DELIA: Maybe we ought to tell Mr. Faddle about it. After all, he's the principal of this school—where the diamond was lost.

MARJ: You're right. Phil, go tell Mr. Faddle all about it before Mrs. Nevins gets any worse.

PHIL: I don't know if I should, but I will. Be right back.

DELIA: Exactly what did Andrea say when she left?

MARJ: She stood right . . . here, like this. Her hand clutching her throat. She smiled sadly, but sweetly, and whispered in husky tones, "I have to run."

DELIA: "Have to run"? I see, she felt the pressure on her. She knew the beating her cruel father would give her . . . knew about her sick brother . . . and her mother with her bad nerves.

MARJ (*Dreamily*): Gerald was magnificent through it all.

DELIA: What did he do?

MARJ: He stood strong and generous. He gave her his week's allowance. He knew her problem; he understood.

DELIA: Did he say anything?

MARJ: As Andrea fled through the hall, he called me back, saying wisely, "It's the *only* thing she can do under the circumstances. It's the *only* way!"

DELIA (*Thoroughly engrossed and moved*): Beautiful, Marjorie. Beautiful and sad.

MARJ: It was like a great movie. A movie right here in the main hall. And I . . . I was a part of it all.

DELIA: I only wish I had been part of it myself.

NARRATOR: Mr. Faddle, the principal, rushes from his office.

MR. FADDLE: This is incredible!

PHIL: They felt you ought to know, Mr. Faddle.

MR. FADDLE: And they were absolutely right. Now, then, Marjorie, call Andrea's father at this number. It's his business phone.

DELIA: I'm glad you're doing something about this, Mr. Faddle.

MR. FADDLE: It's my duty. Just part of my job. Just part of the job of a school principal. All in a day's work, you know. Give me the phone, Marjorie. Hello, Mr. Nevins? This is Herman Faddle, principal at the high school. . . . Yes. . . . I have some distressing news to discuss with you that needs immediate attention. . . . I know you have a business to operate, but this is more important. . . . Well, I hate to discuss it over the telephone. It's about your wife's collapse, and your daughter's losing Mrs. Nevins's engagement ring, and running away from home, and you threatening to beat her. . . . No . . . I am not crazy.

DELIA: If you ask me, he's the one who's crazy.

PHIL: Sh-h! I can't hear.

MR. FADDLE: I do not choose to argue over the phone. I shall expect you in my office at once, if not sooner. Goodbye.

PHIL: What did he say?

MR. FADDLE: He denied the whole thing.

DELIA: Pretense. That's what it is. Plain out-and-out pretense.

MR. FADDLE: Used very strong language.

MARJ: Trying to cover up for himself.

MR. FADDLE: Are you *sure* you have the facts straight?

DELIA: Mr. Faddle, there are three of us here who are witnesses.

PHIL: The entire school knows about it by now.

MR. FADDLE: Oh, my!

MARJ: I hope the newspapers don't hear about it.

MR. FADDLE: We must keep it out of the papers. Bad publicity for the school.

DELIA: It's almost a *scandal!*

MR. FADDLE (*Shocked*): A scandal?

DELIA (*Dramatically*): I can see the headlines now. "High school girl runs away from home to escape beating by brutal father."

MR. FADDLE: Heavens!

DELIA: "Mother collapses."

MR. FADDLE: Oh!

DELIA: "Priceless diamond ring lost near principal's office."

MR. FADDLE: Please, Delia, please. That's enough.

MARJ: But, it *could* happen, Mr. Faddle. It could happen.

MR. FADDLE: Not if we keep it to ourselves.

PHIL: Keep it to ourselves? With the whole basketball team scouring the building for the missing ring?

DELIA: Besides, Miss Furbush knows all about it.

MR. FADDLE (*Overcome*): Not Miss Furbush. . . . Excuse me. I'm going to lie down in my office. I don't feel well.

NARRATOR: Mr. Faddle returns to his office, his hand to his head. Alex comes down the hall and up to the desk.

ALEX: Any news about the great diamond loss?

DELIA: It's no joke, Alex. Andrea has run away because of it.

ALEX: Andrea ran away?

MARJ: We have to bring her back. We have to locate her.

ALEX: There's only *one* way to locate a missing person.

PHIL: What's that?

ALEX: Call the police.

DELIA: The police?

ALEX: The only way.

MARJ: Alex is absolutely right. I'll call the police right away.

PHIL: Now, wait a minute, Marjorie. We ought to check with Mr. Faddle before we call the police.

MARJ: He's lying down, resting. Operator, give me the police. Hurry, this is an emergency. A life is at stake.

DELIA: Make it sound really urgent so the police will get right over.

PHIL (*Sadly, but thoughtfully*): Somehow, I'm beginning to regret this whole mess.

MARJ: Hello? Police department? . . . This is Marjorie Higgins at the high school. . . . Yes. . . . One of our students, a Miss Andrea Nevins, has run away from home. She lost her mother's valuable diamond ring and her father has threatened to beat her within an inch of her life. . . . Yes, and her mother has collapsed and her brother is down with the measles. . . . Sure I know what I'm talking about. It's serious. . . . Our principal had a terrible argument with Mr. Nevins right on this phone. Yes, and *he* nearly collapsed. . . . Mr. Faddle nearly collapsed. He's lying down right now. . . . We'll give you the details when you arrive. Better bring some of your men. . . . We're right in the main hall. . . . Yes. Goodbye.

DELIA: Now we'll get some *real* action!

PHIL: I wonder how Mrs. Nevins is.

DELIA: In a state of complete shock, I'd guess.

MARJ: Should I call and check?

ALEX: Might as well. You've called everybody else.

PHIL: I think I ought to go home.

DELIA: Stay right where you are. We'll need you when the police arrive.

PHIL: I was afraid of that!

ALEX: Who are you calling?

MARJ: Andy's mother.

ALEX: Oh.

MARJ: There's no answer.

DELIA: Call her doctor and see what he says. Their doctor is Dr. Fine, I think.

PHIL: I think you ought to hang up.

MARJ: Hello, Dr. Fine? . . . This is Marj Higgins. I called to ask about Mrs. Nevins. . . . She collapsed from strain and nerves. . . . Nobody called you? . . . Didn't you even know about it? . . . Yes, this afternoon. I just tried to get her on the phone but there was no answer. . . . No, nobody's home with her. . . . Yes, you certainly ought to get right over there. . . . Billy is sick, too . . . and Mrs. Nevins may be unconscious. Perhaps you ought to get the ambulance from the hospital . . .

NARRATOR: Marilyn comes to the desk in a hurry.

MARILYN: Marj, get off the phone. Miss Furbush has been trying to call down here for the last ten minutes. She's furious.

MARJ (*Ignoring her, still talking on phone*): If Mrs. Nevins needs any help, tell her to call on me. . . . Thank you. Goodbye.

DELIA: For one measly ticket, Miss Furbush can wait. This is tragedy here. Pure Greek tragedy.

MARILYN: Miss Furbush will make a tragedy of you, if you don't send up a ticket. There's the phone again.

MARJ (*Answering phone*): Hello, Spring Tragedy . . . I mean, Spring Carnival . . . Miss Furbush? That ticket is on its way up any minute now. . . . No, Andrea isn't back yet. . . . No, I don't know why she was wearing her mother's ring. . . . Yes, it was foolish. . . . No, Mr. Faddle is still resting. . . . Yes, we'll let you know what happens. Goodbye.

PHIL: I never realized before how important a ticket to the Carnival could be.

MARILYN: Miss Furbush is very interested in student affairs.

NARRATOR: The telephone rings again, and Alex puts his hand on the receiver.

ALEX: I have it. You rest, Marj. Hello, Spring Carnival tickets. . . . What? (*Puts hand over receiver; to others*) The editor of the newspaper.

PHIL (*Mournfully*): Uh-oh.

ALEX: About what? . . . The girl who ran away after her father beat her?

DELIA: Oh, no—Mr. Nevins found her and already beat her . . .

ALEX: Yes, the police know that. Yes. . . . Yes. . . . Well, if you want to speak to the principal, you'd better come down here. . . .

PHIL: This gets worse . . . and worse.

ALEX: He's collapsed in his office . . . collapsed. . . . We're in the main hall. All right. We'll be here. . . . 'Bye.

MARILYN: I'm sure Mr. Faddle will be glad to talk to the newspaper.

PHIL: Yes, delirious with joy. Here's Gerald.

GERALD: Andrea back yet?

MARJ: Back *here?* After her father found her and beat her?

GERALD: Found her? Beat her?

MARILYN: That's what the newspaper editor said.

GERALD: What's going on here?

DELIA: Sh! Look down the hall. There!

MARJ: It's Andy!

PHIL: She doesn't look beaten to me.

MARILYN: She isn't even crying.

ALEX: Looks rather happy for someone in trouble.

ANDREA (*Cheerfully*): Hi!

MARJ (*Shocked*): Hi?

DELIA (*Soothingly*): Now, don't get hysterical, dear. Bear up.

ANDREA: Bear up? About what?

ALEX: Your brother's measles.

ANDREA: My brother is in school, and he doesn't have the measles.

MARILYN (*Weakly*): But your mother collapsed.

ANDREA: What? My mother is perfectly well. I just met her downtown in the department store.

DELIA (*Even more weakly*): Didn't your father just beat you within an inch of your life?

ANDREA: My father doesn't beat me. And I haven't seen him since breakfast.

PHIL: You *did* lose something, didn't you?

ANDREA: Yes, but when I was downtown I suddenly remembered where I'd put it. Where's my notebook?

MARJ: Right here.

ANDREA: Just when the bell rang I put it in my notebook. And the notebook was open right here to my French lesson . . . and here it is.

MARJ: The diamond ring in the handkerchief!

GERALD: Diamond ring?

ANDREA: It's not a diamond . . . it's a *dime*.

DELIA (*Faintly*): A dime . . .

ANDREA: Wrapped in my mother's best handkerchief.

GERALD: The one her father gave her mother.

PHIL: Which you couldn't bear to lose?

DELIA: Which if you lost, you couldn't face your mother without?

ANDREA: Yes, this is it. Everything is all right now.

MARJ: And you didn't run away from home at all?

ANDREA: No! What's wrong with all of you?

NARRATOR: Mr. Faddle rushes from his office.

MR. FADDLE (*Sympathetically*): Andrea, poor child. Let me help you. Let me offer my sympathy.

ANDREA: Mr. Faddle, do you feel well?

MR. FADDLE: It's all right, child. We know all. We will help you in your great distress. Trust us. We are your dear friends.

GERALD: Something mighty strange is going on here.

ANDREA: Mr. Faddle, I don't know what's been going on. But, I didn't run away. I didn't lose a diamond ring. My brother doesn't have the measles. My mother did not collapse and my father didn't beat me.

MR. FADDLE: What?

ANDREA: All I lost was this dime and this handkerchief.

MR. FADDLE (*Weakly*): Somebody help me to a chair. But they said . . . I called your father . . . Miss Furbush. . . . Get me a glass of water. My nerves are gone. . . . I . . . I . . .

PHIL: Golly, look at the commotion outside.

MR. FADDLE: What commotion?

PHIL: There's an ambulance, the editor of the newspaper with a photographer, Mr. Nevins, Dr. Fine and a whole car full of police. And they're all rushing up the front steps of the school!

MR. FADDLE: No, no, no! (*He is almost sobbing.*)

PHIL: I think we'd better go now.

ALEX: Yeah. Our work is done.

MR. FADDLE: Don't leave me. Don't leave me. You got me into this. Stay and share the blame. Oh, my nerves. My poor taut nerves.

NARRATOR: Mr. Faddle sinks into a chair. The students all tip-toe out except Delia and Marj.

DELIA (*Softly*): He doesn't look well.

MARJ: He kept complaining of his nerves.

DELIA: Probably won't last another week.

MARJ: We can expect a new principal on Monday.

DELIA: He was such a *nice* man.

NARRATOR: As Marj and Delia shake their heads, the telephone rings and Marj answers.

MARJ: Hello, Spring Carnival tickets. . . . Miss Furbush? . . . I'm bringing your ticket up myself. . . . What? . . . You decided not to go? We're awfully sorry. . . . Oh, by the way, Miss Furbush, is it true Mr. Faddle is leaving school because of a nervous breakdown? . . . I mean, who will be our new principal? . . . You didn't know about it? . . . Well, it's like this . . .

THE END

Another Way to Weigh an Elephant

This play is based on a Chinese story. In it, a child shows the Empress of China how to solve a problem.

The language in this play is not quite the same as ordinary English. The sentences are short, and certain words are omitted to make you think you are hearing a foreign language. Read the play through to yourself. Then practice reading these lines aloud, two or three times, to learn the new speech patterns:

DANG: Problem has no solution.
DONG: Imperial Highness is not kind-hearted and generous.
DANG: Mighty Majesty is heartless and cruel.

Now choose parts for the play and read the play together. Discuss how the problem of the elephant's weight was solved. Do you understand how it was done? What sort of a person do you think the Empress is—haughty, kindly, proud, friendly?

Are there any places that you should practice? If so, work on them until the play moves smoothly.

Arrange to read the play into a tape recorder or for the class soon.

ANOTHER WAY TO WEIGH AN ELEPHANT

by Lenore Blumenfeld

Characters

(4 boys, 3 girls, and a narrator)
NARRATOR
EMPRESS, *a haughty lady*
Ho-Jo, *the Empress's parasol-bearer*
DING ⎫
DONG ⎬ *villagers*
DANG ⎭
MOTHER
CHILD

NARRATOR: It is long ago, in ancient China. In the beautiful Imperial Garden of the Empress, we see a lily pond surrounded by an edging of pebbles. What else do we see? A great, big, wiggling, dancing elephant, whose name is Plum Blossom. Plum Blossom is the Empress of China's favorite pet. And now comes the Empress herself, followed by her parasol-bearer, Ho-Jo, who is dragging along an enormous bag of peanuts.

EMPRESS: Ah, Plum Blossom, my pet. Leave the peanuts and be gone, Ho-Jo. And see that I am not disturbed. And prepare the imperial riverboat for my afternoon cruise. (*Changing tone*) Here, my pretty. Peanut time.

NARRATOR: Ho-Jo bows to the Empress and backs away. The Empress begins to feed Plum Blossom peanuts, which the elephant takes with her trunk. The villagers, Ding, Dang, and Dong, come in, followed by a mother and her child. The mother carries embroidery and the child, a toy boat. The Empress is so busy feeding Plum Blossom that she does not notice them.

CHILD (*Whispering*): I'm hungry, Mother.

MOTHER: Hush, child.

EMPRESS: Mind your manners, Plum Blossom, you playful imp.

DING: Your Imperial Highness—

EMPRESS: Who dares to interrupt the Empress?

CHILD: Mother, may I take a peanut?

MOTHER: Sh-h-h.

DANG: O powerful ruler, mistress of multitudes—

DONG: And possessor of uncounted riches—

EMPRESS: Ah, yes—well, get on with it. What do you want? My elephant is hungry.

CHILD: I'm hungry too.

MOTHER: Go play quietly with your boat at the pond before you get us all beheaded.

DING: Imperial Empress, the child speaks for all of us.

DANG: Everyone in our village is hungry.

EMPRESS: Lazy peasants! Go harvest your grain and you'll have plenty to eat.

DONG: But, Empress—

EMPRESS: Imagine, my pretty Plum Blossom! They leave fields of ripe grain to come sniveling for free handouts. Here, sweetie, have another peanut.

DING: Last night, Your Worship—

DANG: While the entire village slept—

DONG: An army of grasshoppers came and ate every morsel of grain!

EMPRESS: Preposterous! Too late in the season for grasshoppers. Idlers! Go harvest your crops. Go! Leave!

NARRATOR: Ding, Dang, and Dong turn to leave, their heads hanging in despair. Suddenly the Empress clutches her neck and shrieks.

EMPRESS: Oh-h-h! Something is creeping up my imperial neck.

DING: It is just a grasshopper, Imperial Highness.

EMPRESS: Well, get it off!

NARRATOR: Dong flicks the grasshopper away, and the three turn again to leave.

EMPRESS: Halt!

DONG: Imperial Highness?

EMPRESS: Did grasshoppers really eat all your grain?

DONG: Every morsel.

EMPRESS: In that case—

DANG: Yes, Imperial Magnificence?

EMPRESS: I, your mighty Empress, ruler of multitudes, possessor of uncounted riches—

CHILD: I'm hungry.

MOTHER: Hush.

EMPRESS: Hmph. As I was saying—I, your kind-hearted and generous Empress, will purchase food from a nearby kingdom—

DING, DANG, *and* DONG (*Together*): Long live our kind-hearted and generous Empress!

EMPRESS: Enough food to equal the weight of—of—the imperial elephant!

DING: A feast!

DANG: A banquet!

DONG: Bring on the egg rolls! (*They cheer.*)

EMPRESS: However (*Sudden silence*)—I do not approve of giving something for nothing.

DING: Imperial Highness, we have no money.

DONG: But we're willing to work for our food.

DANG: We'll dig ditches—

DONG: We'll pave roads—

DING: We'll build stone walls—

EMPRESS: Silence! Don't you know what happens to people who do hard work on an empty stomach?

DANG (*Sadly*): They make mistakes.

DONG: They weaken.

DING: And sometimes they faint.

EMPRESS: Do you think I want my kingdom cluttered up with unconscious citizens?

DING, DANG, *and* DONG: No.

EMPRESS: Exactly. So, I won't make you work to earn your food—

DING, DANG, *and* DONG: Ah!

EMPRESS: But I *will* make you think!

DING, DANG, *and* DONG: Oh!

EMPRESS: I have often wondered how smart my subjects are.

DONG: We villagers are well-educated, Imperial Highness.

DANG: We know how to read and write.

DING: And we know how to add and subtract.

DONG: Give us any problem and we'll solve it.

EMPRESS: Very well. If you want Plum Blossom's weight in food, you must tell me how much she weighs.

DANG: Simple.

DONG: Elementary.

DING: Get a scale.

EMPRESS: Halt! No scale in the kingdom is big enough for Plum Blossom to stand on. That is the problem. You must think of another way to weigh an elephant. Have a peanut, sweetie.

DING: Impossible.

DANG: Problem has no solution.

DONG: Imperial Highness is not kind-hearted and generous.

DANG: Mighty Majesty is heartless and cruel.

DING: We may as well return to our empty fields.

CHILD: I know another way to weigh an elephant.

MOTHER: Hush!

DONG: Let the child speak.

DANG: Let us open our ears to the wisdom of youth.

DING: What do we have to lose?

MOTHER: Gracious and illustrious Majesty, this small person—

EMPRESS: Get on with it. You're delaying Plum Blossom's dinner.

CHILD: Pretend this water lily from the imperial pond is the imperial elephant. (DING, DANG, *and* DONG *laugh.*)

EMPRESS: Silence! There is indeed a resemblance between that lily blossom and my Plum Blossom. Both are beautiful and fragrant. Proceed, small person.

CHILD: Put the elephant on the imperial riverboat. Mark how high the water rises on the side of the boat. Lead the elephant to dry land.

NARRATOR: The child demonstrates by putting the lily on toy boat, lifting the boat out of the pond and marking the water line with chalk. The child removes the lily from the boat and lowers it to the ground beside the pond, singing a slow marching chant.

CHILD (*Chanting*):
Left, right, left, right,
Da dum, da dum, da dum, da dum.

ALL (*Chanting*):
Left, right, left, right,
Da dum, da dum, da dum, da dum.

CHILD: Silence! (*All are silent.*) Now load the boat with enough stones to make the water reach the same mark. Then weigh each stone, add the weight of all the stones, and you have the weight of the elephant!

EMPRESS: Brilliant! Ho-Jo! Send messengers to purchase food from the neighboring kingdom. Clear the deck of the imperial riverboat to make room for Plum Blossom. And find stones for weighing. And you, wise child—what special reward can I bestow upon you?

CHILD: Please, Imperial Empress, may I have a peanut?

EMPRESS: Let us all have a peanut!

THE END

The Impossible Room

In this play, an amateur detective solves a baffling mystery without leaving his living room. There is plenty of opportunity for drama, however, as Professor Wilbur uncovers a plot to steal some jewels.

Read the play through to yourself. Then discuss it with the group. Did you understand how the Professor discovered who the criminal was? What clues does he have to work with?

After you have chosen parts, read the play aloud together. If there are any words that cause you trouble, get help with them. When you have read the play once, see if the group has any suggestions for improvement.

This play is mostly conversation, so keep the pace lively.

When the group is ready, have the chairman arrange a time with the teacher to read for the class.

THE IMPOSSIBLE ROOM

by John Murray

Characters

(4 boys, 4 girls, and a narrator)
NARRATOR
JEFF TURNER, *a reporter*
HELEN PORTER, *his friend*
ANNIE, *a maid*
DR. AMOS WILBUR, *an amateur criminologist*
PROFESSOR ADAMS, *his friendly rival*
VINCENT DUDLEY, *a mystery writer*
MRS. DUDLEY, *his wife*
PAM DUDLEY, *his daughter*

NARRATOR: In this play, an amateur detective solves a baffling mystery. Jeff Turner, a reporter, and his friend Helen are visiting the home of Dr. Amos Wilbur, so Jeff can interview him for his paper. Annie, the maid, shows them into the drawing room.

ANNIE: If you'll wait here, Dr. Wilbur will see you in a few minutes.

HELEN (*Excitedly*): Oh, Jeff, I still can't believe I'm going to sit in on a personal interview with *the* Dr. Wilbur!

JEFF: If you don't be quiet, Helen, there won't be any interview. The doctor is very shy. He has a nice place, though. Does anyone live here with Dr. Wilbur?

ANNIE: No, sir. Ah—the doctor's coming now. I have to get back to the kitchen.

NARRATOR: As Annie hurries out to the kitchen, Dr. Wilbur

and his friend, Professor Adams, come in. They are having a friendly argument, and do not notice Helen and Jeff.

ADAMS: And I say, Wilbur, that you pay entirely too much attention to trivialities. You miss important clues by sorting out the little things.

WILBUR: I have my way, Professor Adams. The little things always tell me about the *big* things.

ADAMS: I can't agree! Your method is old-fashioned. Your style is outdated.

NARRATOR: Dr. Wilbur suddenly notices Jeff and Helen, and goes to greet them.

WILBUR: If my methods and style are at fault, Adams, at least let me salvage something of my manners. We have guests and we continue to prattle like two magpies!

JEFF: Dr. Wilbur! This is a pleasure. I'm Jeff Turner of the *Weekly Dispatch*.

WILBUR: Ah, yes. You're the young man who wishes to interview me for his paper?

JEFF: That's right. Everyone has heard about your work in solving crimes. Our readers want some inside information about your methods.

WILBUR: My methods again! My good colleague, Professor Adams, would have something to say about my methods.

ADAMS: No offense intended, Doctor. I merely said that one can't dwell on the little things anymore. The scientific methods of crime detection have eliminated all that. The day of Sherlock Holmes and the sit-by-the-fire deduction has come to an end.

WILBUR (*Sadly*): You may be right. But we have neglected this young lady. . . .

JEFF: This is Miss Helen Porter, a friend of mine on the paper. She wanted to come to the interview.

HELEN (*Quickly*): I've always wanted to meet you, Dr. Wilbur.

WILBUR: I hope you're not disappointed, young lady. I have just been called a defeated, old-fashioned has-been.

ADAMS: Now, Dr. Wilbur.

WILBUR (*Laughing*): Oh, Adams, you're forgiven. But despite your modern methods, I will still ride along with the little things—the things that everyone overlooks.

ADAMS: What good are those—little things?

WILBUR: Maybe they are a waste of time, but everything must be examined in crime deduction—even the simple things in our lives.

ADAMS: I wish I could agree that simple things solve real-life cases—take those jewel robberies, for example.

HELEN (*Eagerly*): Do you mean those two cases down on Leicester Street last month? Are you working on those, Dr. Wilbur?

WILBUR: No, the police are handling those cases, or *trying* to handle them, at any rate. I work only on cases where I'm privately consulted, you see.

HELEN (*Sadly*): Oh!

WILBUR: You sound disappointed, Miss Porter.

HELEN: Well, I would like to have seen you at work.

NARRATOR: Suddenly Vincent Dudley and his wife and their daughter Pam burst into the room.

PAM: Your maid said you were busy, Dr. Wilbur, but I had to see you. Oh, please help me!

WILBUR: Help you, young lady? But, of course! You're the girl I've often seen in the garden across the street.

DUDLEY: Yes, we've been neighbors for years.

WILBUR: And you're Vincent Dudley! Really, your mystery stories have often kept me up past my bedtime!

HELEN: Mr. Dudley! I read all your books.

JEFF: I'm guilty, too!

DUDLEY: I wrote enough of them, but I'm stumped now. (*Soberly*) That's why I—we need your help, Dr. Wilbur.

WILBUR: I'm honored to be called upon for help, but fiction is really out of my line.

DUDLEY: But this is not a fictional mystery, Doctor. I'm afraid that a real-life mystery has been planted—right on our doorstep!

MRS. DUDLEY (*Haughtily*): You can see, Vincent, that Dr. Wilbur is entertaining friends tonight. We can't very well occupy his time with such nonsense!

PAM: It isn't nonsense, Mother! Oh, please, Dr. Wilbur—won't you help us?

WILBUR: I'm sure your trouble is not that serious.

MRS. DUDLEY: It's a tempest in a teapot! You're making a terrible fool of yourself, Pam. I'm sure that Larry will turn up in a little while and have a good laugh at our expense.

WILBUR: Larry?

DUDLEY: Larry Parker is my daughter's fiancé.

WILBUR: Oh, I see.

PAM: And he's disappeared. He disappeared—into *thin air*. Look—here—this is his photograph. I—I want you to find him for me!

NARRATOR: Dr. Wilbur examines the photograph Pam has handed him, then puts it down on a table.

WILBUR: He certainly seems to be a handsome young man!

MRS. DUDLEY: There, Pam! I told you that Dr. Wilbur wouldn't listen to you.

WILBUR: I'll be glad to listen, but if her young man has chosen to disappear, I'm afraid there's little I can do.

PAM: Oh, but it isn't what you think, Dr. Wilbur. Larry hasn't left me—

DUDLEY: Please let me explain. Pam means that Larry has not gone away because of some foolish lover's quarrel. He has disappeared—practically before our eyes!

HELEN (*Excitedly*): Disappeared?

DUDLEY: Yes. Larry Parker has vanished!

PAM (*Tearfully*): He disappeared in the *Impossible Room*.

ADAMS: The Impossible Room?

WILBUR: You have aroused our curiosity but—*thin air*—*the Impossible Room*—I think we'll need a little explanation.

DUDLEY: I'll try to tell you about the trouble as briefly as possible.

WILBUR: Please do so.

DUDLEY: Mr. Parker—Larry—arrived at our house this afternoon at four.

MRS. DUDLEY: He was to spend the weekend with us.

PAM: You see, we were planning to announce our engagement formally tomorrow night.

DUDLEY: It was going to be a double occasion for us. The engagement—and the publication of my new mystery next week. Naturally, the talk turned to mysteries.

PAM: Larry is quite an enthusiast.

DUDLEY: Larry wanted an outline of the plot, and since my new book deals with the problem of a locked room, Larry was quite fascinated.

ADAMS: A locked room?

DUDLEY: Yes, the problem in the book dealt with a man who escaped from a locked room. Larry said that he could solve my problem of the locked room and could do me one better —by escaping from a locked room, himself!

WILBUR: The whole suggestion of the locked room business was his own idea?

DUDLEY: Yes. I wanted to forget the subject, but Larry was quite insistent. He demanded that I take his challenge.

WILBUR: And what was the challenge?

DUDLEY: Larry Parker insisted that he could escape from a locked room without the aid of keys, sliding panels or an outside confederate!

PAM: Yes. He said that he could escape from the Impossible Room!

WILBUR: You mentioned that room a little while ago, miss, and

I am fascinated—and a little perplexed. What is the Impossible Room?

DUDLEY: The Impossible Room is a pet name for an old room on the second floor of our house. It is off the same hallway as our bedrooms, but it has one outstanding peculiarity.

PAM: There's only one entrance to the room—namely, the door leading into the hall. The door has a snap lock which opens only from the outside!

MRS. DUDLEY: The lock will not work from inside. Why, I was locked in that dreadful room for two hours one day before the maid heard me pounding on the wall!

WILBUR: A peculiar room, indeed. Now, why can't it be opened from the inside?

DUDLEY: The Impossible Room is not really a room at all, but a sort of closet-pantry found in these old-fashioned houses. The house belonged to my grandfather and he used the room as a storage place for old papers, books, and that kind of thing.

WILBUR: Oh, I see. And I suppose the window in the room is too small to offer escape?

DUDLEY (*Soberly*): There is no window in the Impossible Room.

WILBUR: No window?

PAM: The only entrance is the door.

DUDLEY: The room is built with solid walls and lighted with a solitary, dim lamp in the center of the ceiling. After we moved to the house, we threw away all the old papers and other things that Grandfather had gathered.

MRS. DUDLEY: The room is completely empty, Dr. Wilbur.

WILBUR: And Mr. Parker boasted that he could escape from that room?

DUDLEY: He not only boasted, Dr. Wilbur. He *did* escape!

WILBUR (*Musing*): This whole thing started simply enough —but I'm afraid there's something sinister about it.

PAM (*Quickly*): Oh, Doctor, do you think Larry's in danger?

WILBUR: Who can tell? Please go on with your story.

DUDLEY: Finally I consented to Larry's plan. It was agreed that he would be locked in the Impossible Room and remain there for a half-hour. Then, at the end of the time, he would present himself downstairs.

ADAMS: As simple as that?

DUDLEY: Yes. Of course, he didn't tell us his plan of escape but, knowing the Impossible Room, I was quite interested to see him try it.

WILBUR: And who locked Parker in the Impossible Room?

PAM (*Sheepishly*): I—I did. (*More quickly*) Oh, I know what you're thinking. You probably feel that the door wasn't securely locked and that Larry freed himself and is hiding someplace laughing at us.

WILBUR: Well, that's a possibility.

PAM: But it's not true! I know the door was locked. I know it! I tried it after Larry went into the room and the door wouldn't budge!

WILBUR: I believe you, Miss Pam. But I must have more details. Please tell me everything, no matter how unimportant it may seem. I want exact details from the time Parker went up to that room until you made certain the door was locked.

PAM: Now, let me see. When Father gave his permission that Larry could be locked in the Impossible Room, I was terribly excited. Larry and I went up to the second floor to the room, Larry leading the way.

WILBUR: You say "you and Larry." Didn't you go along, too, Dudley?

DUDLEY: No, I'm afraid I didn't. My agent telephoned and I had quite a lengthy conversation about my new book.

WILBUR: And you, Mrs. Dudley?

MRS. DUDLEY: Heavens, no! I don't indulge in mysteries. Besides, I'd just returned from upstairs. I brought my jewels up to the bedroom, as I remember—

WILBUR: Your jewels?

MRS. DUDLEY: Why, yes. I usually keep them in the bank vault, but I took them out earlier in the afternoon for the engagement party.

WILBUR: And you left the jewels in your bedroom?

MRS. DUDLEY: Yes, of course.

WILBUR: I see. Thank you, Mrs. Dudley. Please continue, Miss Dudley.

PAM: Well, when we got upstairs, Larry went right to the door of the Impossible Room. He quickly turned the knob and walked in. He laughed and said something about Houdini and closed the door after him.

WILBUR: You didn't go into the room?

PAM: No, Larry had already closed the door. But he went into the room. I saw him with my own eyes!

WILBUR (*Thoughtfully*): Yes, of course.

PAM: I made certain that the outside spring lock was securely fastened and then—and then—(*Begins to sob*)

WILBUR: Please, Miss Dudley.

PAM: But this is the part that I can't understand. You see, I didn't want Larry to escape without our knowledge and I thought it would teach him a good lesson about bragging, so I—I—

WILBUR: Yes?

PAM: I ran some tape around the door jamb so that he couldn't possibly escape through the door. You see, if the tape were broken, I would know that he had a secret way of opening the door from the inside. Oh, I knew the tape wouldn't hold the door, but it would snap instantly if the door were tampered with.

WILBUR: I see. And what did you do then?

PAM: I called something to Larry to make doubly sure he was in the room, and he answered from behind the locked door.

WILBUR: Did you wait outside the door long?

PAM: No. I went downstairs right away.

WILBUR: And nothing else happened?

PAM: No, nothing.

WILBUR (*Impatiently*): There must be something else. There has to be!

PAM: I—I don't know what you mean.

WILBUR: In order to help you, I must know more about the little things.

PAM: More little things?

WILBUR: Yes, every detail that happened from the time you locked the Impossible Room until you joined your mother and father downstairs.

PAM (*Insistently*): There's nothing to tell. I made certain that the door was locked—that Larry couldn't get out. And I went downstairs! That's all, Dr. Wilbur.

WILBUR: You met no one in the hall or on the stairs?

PAM: No one. (*Loudly*) No one could have helped Larry escape. The door was securely locked and taped. I thought it was impossible for Larry to get out of that room. Why, I even stepped back to admire the good work I had done on the door and then—(*Breaks off*) But, of course you wouldn't be interested in that.

WILBUR (*Quickly*): What is it?

PAM: It's nothing, really. As I said, I stepped back and, as the hall was quite dark, I bumped into Mr. Abercrombie.

WILBUR (*Bewildered*): Who?

MRS. DUDLEY: Pam! I don't think the doctor will be interested in Mr. Abercrombie.

WILBUR: I am interested in every aspect of this case, madam. Now, who is Mr. Abercrombie?

PAM: Mr. Abercrombie is a pet name for an old suit of armor that stands in the hall.

WILBUR: A suit of armor?

PAM: Yes. It belonged to Grandfather and we kept it—well, for sentimental reasons.

WILBUR (*Impatiently*): Where does that suit of armor stand?

PAM: It stands directly across the hall from the Impossible Room—it's in line with the door.

WILBUR: And you stepped backwards and crashed into it?

PAM: Yes, yes—but I don't see what that means.

WILBUR: It makes the case a little more difficult, that's all. If you had mistaken the door of the Impossible Room and had locked Mr. Parker in another room, the suit of armor wouldn't have stood behind you.

PAM (*Suddenly*): No—that's true! Oh, that makes everything worse. And Mr. Abercrombie was behind me—directly opposite the door of the Impossible Room!

WILBUR: Before I can say anything about this business, I must know a little more about the upstairs hallway.

PAM: It's an ordinary hall. There are four doors opening onto the hallway.

WILBUR: Who occupies those rooms?

PAM: I have the first room—my bedroom. Then, there's the Impossible Room. Beyond that, there is the door to my mother's room, and the fourth room is Father's bedroom and study.

WILBUR: Are the doors all the same?

PAM: Yes, they're all uniform in size and color. But, of course, only the door to the Impossible Room cannot be opened from the inside. The others can.

WILBUR: I see. In other words, if a door to the other bedrooms is locked from the outside, that door can be easily opened by turning the knob from the inside?

PAM: Yes, that's the only difference between the doors.

WILBUR (*Musing*): Then that would explain—(*Suddenly*) But never mind. What happened after you joined your parents downstairs?

DUDLEY: Why, we just waited for Larry to turn up. It was a rough half-hour, too.

MRS. DUDLEY: It was almost an hour, Vincent. Don't you remember that you were a little alarmed at six when Larry hadn't appeared?

DUDLEY: At six, I decided that the nonsense had gone far enough. We went upstairs to the Impossible Room.

PAM (*Quickly*): The door was still locked and the tape was in place. Even Mr. Abercrombie was standing watching us.

WILBUR: I think that Mr. Abercrombie could tell us many interesting things. And then?

PAM: I called to Larry and got no answer.

DUDLEY: We quickly pulled the tape off the door and I turned the knob, releasing the outside spring latch.

MRS. DUDLEY: We went into that room—into the dark—and I snapped on the light.

PAM: And Larry was gone! The room was empty!

DUDLEY: It was terrifying! A man had disappeared through a two-foot-thick wall!

PAM: He couldn't have been hiding in that room because there was no place to hide!

WILBUR: What did you do?

DUDLEY: We went downstairs to wait for Larry. Naturally, I felt that he must have discovered some way to escape and he was going to wait until we were really in a frenzy before appearing.

PAM: That was almost two hours ago—but Larry is still missing. Oh, Dr. Wilbur! What are we going to do?

ADAMS (*Defiantly*): Yes, Doctor, what are you going to do?

WILBUR: There is little we can do. I'm afraid the damage has already been done. And yet—there may still be time.

NARRATOR: Dr. Wilbur picks up the photograph of Larry, then he rushes to the telephone, dials, speaks quickly and hangs up.

MRS. DUDLEY (*Quickly*): Doctor! You haven't called the police!

WILBUR: Yes, madam, I have.

MRS. DUDLEY: This is ridiculous! (*Haughtily*) I only consented to come here thinking that you might spare us the embarrassment of the police.

WILBUR (*Strongly*): This is more than an embarrassing situation. Don't you realize that a man has disappeared?

MRS. DUDLEY (*Taken aback*): Yes, but—I—

WILBUR: And the reason for his disappearance will cause you more disturbance than the police!

MRS. DUDLEY: What are you trying to say?

WILBUR: There is a deep-rooted motive behind this. A fiendish scheme!

DUDLEY: Doctor!

WILBUR: Oh, you can put your mind at ease, all of you! I didn't ask the police to go to your house.

DUDLEY: You didn't?

WILBUR: Of course not. I asked them to go to the International Airport and block all exits!

MRS. DUDLEY: What do you mean?

WILBUR: The police have a fairly accurate description of your Mr. Parker. They've had trouble with him before.

PAM: Larry—a criminal? I don't believe it! It's not true, Dr. Wilbur!

WILBUR (*Softly*): Yes, Miss Dudley, it's true enough. It *has* to be that way. It's the only solution to the whole thing. You knew him only a short time, but you told me you were announcing your engagement tomorrow night.

PAM: Yes, I met him six weeks ago. But I won't believe anything bad about him.

WILBUR: Was today the first time he came to your house?

PAM: No, he was there several times.

WILBUR: The visits were—I believe the popular phrase is—to "case" the place.

DUDLEY: What's all this, Dr. Wilbur?

WILBUR: Larry Parker—alias Louis Parkman—is known by the police as one of the cleverest jewel thieves in this part of the country!

DUDLEY: No!

MRS. DUDLEY: A jewel thief?

WILBUR: I'm sorry to say it's true. Oh, yes, he was at your house before. And he must have thought it ingenious when he remembered the Impossible Room.

DUDLEY: This is all too confusing.

WILBUR: On the contrary, Mr. Dudley, it's amazingly simple. Consider—if one's house guest were to arrive and then leave unexpectedly, one might think it rather strange and immediately check for one's personal belongings.

DUDLEY: I might.

WILBUR: However, if there were a strange cloak of mystery about the guest's disappearance, one would be involved with the problem at hand. In other words, Larry Parker wanted to give you something to occupy your minds while he ransacked your house and made off with your jewels!

MRS. DUDLEY (*Shocked*): My jewels!

WILBUR: Yes, madam. Parker probably deduced that you would have your jewels at home to wear to the engagement party tomorrow night and again to the literary functions with your husband next week.

MRS. DUDLEY: Why, yes, it's true—just as I told you! I took my jewels out of the bank vault this afternoon!

WILBUR: A jewel thief uses a great deal of psychology. And, most often, he's correct! If he wanted your jewels, he had to take them today. He had no time to lose. And, in the clever hands of a man like Larry Parker, it was child's play!

ADAMS (*Scoffing*): I wouldn't call disappearing from a locked room exactly child's play.

WILBUR: We'll discuss that later, Adams, but first I think Mr. Dudley should go back to his house and examine Mrs. Dudley's jewel box.

DUDLEY (*Nervously*): Yes, yes, of course.

MRS. DUDLEY: The little carved box, you know, in the second drawer of my dresser.

NARRATOR: Mr. Dudley leaves hurriedly to check on his wife's jewels.

HELEN: I can't believe it—it's fantastic.

WILBUR: People aren't always what they seem. Upon close examination, they often turn out to be disagreeable.

ADAMS: I still don't see how you plan to get around that Impossible Room business. Granted that Parker might have stolen the Crown Jewels of England at some time or another, how did he manage to get out of that locked room?

PAM (*Defiantly*): Yes, Dr. Wilbur, you haven't answered that.

WILBUR: We must look for a logical answer. You saw him go into the room. You locked the door. You taped the door. The man disappeared. That is a chain of events—and somewhere there is a weak link which will solve the entire problem.

PAM: But everything you mentioned is true.

WILBUR: No, Pam, one of the statements must be incorrect. Let us examine them again. First of all, Mr. Parker is missing. We have your father's and mother's verification of that.

PAM: That's right.

WILBUR: Then, we'll let that stand for the moment. Secondly, you taped the door.

PAM: Yes! Mother and Father will swear to that, too. They saw the tape when we went upstairs to the Impossible Room.

WILBUR: Very good. Let's look at the next statement. You locked the door.

PAM: I did! After Larry stepped into the room, I turned the handle and locked the door. The door wouldn't budge!

WILBUR: Well, that brings us to the first statement. We have reason to believe that the last three impressions are correct so the fault must lie in the first statement. And that statement was—"I saw him go into the Impossible Room!"

PAM: He did! He even talked to me from behind the locked door.

WILBUR: Oh, we believe that he entered a room, well enough—but *what* room? That's the question.

PAM: I don't follow you.

WILBUR (*Slowly*): It was a very easy matter for Parker to escape from the locked room. You see, Pam, Larry never went into the Impossible Room!

JEFF: Oh, that's foolish. We have Miss Dudley's evidence.

WILBUR (*Insistently*): She saw Parker go into a room. Well, was he not planning to go into the Impossible Room? Therefore, the mere fact that he entered a room, any room, would instantly establish the place as the Impossible Room!

PAM: I—I couldn't have been mistaken.

WILBUR: You were mistaken, Pam. Parker wanted you to be mistaken. Wasn't it his idea in the first place to pursue the question of the locked room?

MRS. DUDLEY: That's right. He brought the subject up.

WILBUR: You see, the stage was all arranged. He knew that the four doors were identical in size and color. He knew that if he played his cards cleverly, he could lead you to any door of his choice and, in the confusion, make you believe that you were standing in front of the Impossible Room.

PAM: I—I can't believe that I could have made such a mistake.

WILBUR: It was late afternoon. Dusk! The most deceiving time of all. Yes, it could very easily have happened. Oh, it wasn't your fault. The power of suggestion is an amazing thing. It often makes us see things that don't exist at all. And Parker was clever, remember that.

ADAMS: But how can you be so sure that this is true? It's a flimsy explanation, if you ask me.

WILBUR: It's the only possible solution. I first suspected it when Pam mentioned the similarity of doors. And I knew I was right when she mentioned Mr. Abercrombie.

PAM: Mr. Abercrombie! But that makes you wrong! When I stepped back, I bumped into the suit of armor—and Mr. Abercrombie stands facing the Impossible Room!

WILBUR: I'm afraid he didn't this afternoon. Mr. Abercrombie was an unwitting member of the plot. Parker knew that you would be more convinced that he was in the Impossible Room if you were to see some undeniable landmark that you would associate with the room. Therefore, if the suit of armor were moved in front of another door—

JEFF (*Quickly*): Why, she would think that that was the door of the Impossible Room!

MRS. DUDLEY: Oh, that wretched young man—to deceive Pam that way!

HELEN: You mean the suit of armor was moved?

WILBUR: Yes. It was moved in front of Mrs. Dudley's room— the third door. This is what happened: Parker went ahead of you and entered your mother's room. Remember, he quickly closed the door before you had any chance to enter. In the dark hallway and with the added impression of the suit of armor in front of the door, you released the spring lock on the outside and thought he was imprisoned.

PAM: But all the bedroom doors can be opened from the inside.

WILBUR: Precisely! When Mr. Parker knew you were safely downstairs, he ransacked your mother's jewel box, opened the door from the inside, stepped into the hallway, and moved the suit of armor back to its original position in front of the Impossible Room.

PAM (*Insistently*): But that's not right. Remember, I taped the door. If I made a mistake, the tape would be on Mother's door and not on the Impossible Room as we found it!

JEFF: That's right, Dr. Wilbur.

WILBUR: Would it not be easy for Parker to rip the tape off the third door and use the same tape to seal the door of the Impossible Room?

ADAMS: You mean Parker taped the door?

WILBUR: Of course! I told you a great deal of planning went into this deed. When the second door was taped, and the suit of armor was moved back to its original position, he merely stole out of the house and headed for the International Airport. Mrs. Dudley's jewels were safely in his pocket.

NARRATOR: Mr. Dudley returns, greatly excited.

DUDLEY: You were right, Dr. Wilbur! I found the jewel box. Empty!

MRS. DUDLEY: Empty! I had a diamond necklace that was a family heirloom. And my rings!

PAM: Then it's true. Everything's true about Larry.

WILBUR: It's very hard for you, Pam, but it's really better this way. I know you'll find happiness again.

ADAMS: There are some people who value only the material things in life. Larry is one of those people.

NARRATOR: The telephone rings, and Dr. Wilbur answers it.

WILBUR: Hello? . . . Yes, this is Dr. Wilbur. . . . You did? Good! Yes! Yes! I understand. Ah, that's very good! . . . Yes—goodbye! Ladies and gentlemen, I believe we've just seen the last act of the Impossible Room.

PAM: They—they found Larry?

WILBUR: Yes—at the airport.

MRS. DUDLEY: And my jewels?

WILBUR: He had them in a briefcase.

DUDLEY: I don't know how I can thank you, Dr. Wilbur, for putting our minds at ease.

WILBUR (*Sadly*): Yes, but I brought a little unhappiness, too.

PAM: It's all right, Dr. Wilbur. I'll get over it, I suppose.

DUDLEY: Now that you've met your neighbors, Dr. Wilbur, we hope you won't be a stranger.

MRS. DUDLEY: No, indeed!

WILBUR: And I think Mr. Turner and Miss Porter have more than enough material for their interview.

JEFF: I'll say we do. And I'll be sure not to leave out "the little things"!

THE END

Shirley Holmes and the FBI

In this lively mystery, a group of girls and boys, a dish of fudge and hidden money play important parts.

First read the play through silently. Did you understand the "clue" the boys find?

After you have chosen your parts, read the play aloud once. Go back and practice the places the group thinks were not well done. The scene where the boys and girls capture the robbers is important, so make certain it is as exciting as it can be.

1. Did you pronounce all the words correctly?
2. Did you change your voice to show feeling?
3. Did you pay attention to the punctuation?
4. Did everyone come in at the right time?

When you feel everything is going smoothly, read the play into a tape recorder or read for a live audience.

SHIRLEY HOLMES AND THE FBI

by Helen Louise Miller

Characters

(10 boys, 5 girls, and a narrator)

NARRATOR
SHIRLEY HOLMES
DONNA
KATE
JEN
CANDY
JERRY MASON
BRUCE
LARRY
ALF
ADAM
BABY FACE BOYD
CURLY SMITH
OFFICER HIGGINS
OFFICER RYAN
ANNOUNCER'S VOICE

NARRATOR: This play takes place in an abandoned garage-workshop. Baby Face Boyd and Curly Smith, both wearing eye masks, enter the dark garage and stumble over a box. They turn on their flashlights and play them around the walls. There is nothing much in the garage except stepladders and lumber, some sports equipment in one corner and a hot plate and radio on a table. Baby Face looks around hopelessly.

BABY FACE: It must be here someplace, Curly.

CURLY (*Sarcastically*): Oh, sure! All we have to do is find it.

BABY FACE: That shouldn't be too hard with Gentleman Joe's directions.

CURLY: Oh, come off it, Baby Face! I'll bet the cops have gone over every inch of this place.

BABY FACE: You're forgetting that Gentleman Joe was a pretty smooth operator. He made sure there were no clues to connect this hideaway with the big Fairview holdup. Remember, he was five miles outside of town when they caught him. Now let's get moving before they send out a general alarm on our escape.

CURLY: It's so dark in here. There must be a light switch somewhere.

BABY FACE: What do you expect in a garage with no windows? Besides, there wouldn't be any lights here.

CURLY: Who says there's no juice in this place? Here's a light switch.

NARRATOR: Curly flips the switch and the lights go on. They turn off their flashlights and start to examine a paper Curly takes from his pocket.

BABY FACE: Let's have a look at Gentleman Joe's instructions.

CURLY: Here they are, but they're Greek to me. Why couldn't he have told you straight out where he hid the money?

BABY FACE: He never expected us to escape and go looking for it. Besides, Gentleman Joe liked to think he was smarter than the rest of us. He never figured I could dope out his secret code. (*Reading*) Um-m-m—"Four CS . . . One CM . . . One LB."

CURLY: What does CS stand for?

BABY FACE: Take a look at these walls, Curly. What do you see?

CURLY: Cinder blocks. Now I get it. C stands for *cinder* or maybe *cement*. But what about S?

BABY FACE: *S* is for *slabs* or *stones*. If we're right, "Four CS" means *four cement slabs*. Start counting, Curly.

CURLY: But where do we start? From the right? From the left? From the bottom? Or from the top?

BABY FACE: We'll try them all. (*Reading*) "Four CS"—*four cement slabs*. "One CM" . . . Aha! *One cement moves!* In other words, we count four of these cement blocks, and the next one moves. That must be where he hid the money!

CURLY: What about the next letters—LB? What does LB mean?

BABY FACE: *Lift block*, stupid! Now start counting. I'll take this side. You take the other.

CURLEY: But what if somebody comes? We're not armed.

BABY FACE: And we're going to stay that way so nobody gets hurt. Besides, who would come poking around an abandoned garage on a vacant lot?

SHIRLEY (*As if outside garage*): Hurry and open the door! What's the matter? Won't the key work?

CANDY: Hold your horses!

BABY FACE: Hey, someone's coming. We've got to get out of here.

CURLY: Too late. Duck!

NARRATOR: As they crouch down, Shirley, Candy, Donna, and Kate come into the garage, carrying mops, pails, and boxes. Jen follows with a folder of papers. Candy is the first to see Baby Face and Curly. She drops her pail and shouts—

CANDY: Help! Robbers!

SHIRLEY: Oh, for goodness' sake! Be quiet, Candy! They aren't robbers. (*Crossly*) I must say you two boys have a lot of nerve. Maybe you can fool Candy and the others with those masks, but not me. I'd know you anywhere.

CURLY: Let's beat it! The kid is wise to us.

SHIRLEY: You bet I'm wise to you, so don't bother to put on any cheap gangster act! I never thought Jerry Mason would stoop to sending his big brother and his buddy to spy on us!

BABY FACE: Now wait a minute, little girl!

SHIRLEY: What do you say, girls? Now that we have these two big, brawny high school boys in our midst, let's put them to work.

BABY FACE (*Outraged*): High school boys!

JEN: A good idea, Shirley. They can help us clean up this place.

CANDY: They really had me fooled for a minute.

DONNA: I was scared, too, Candy. What's the big idea of the masks?

SHIRLEY: Part of the big plan to scare us off! Jerry and his Super-Sleuths are determined to have this old garage for their meeting place, but the FBI got here first.

CURLY (*Alarmed*): The FBI?

KATE: Female Bureau of Investigators!

SHIRLEY: As if they didn't know! Well, don't just stand there! Stack those boxes along the wall, and hurry up!

CURLY: Boy, this is a switch!

JEN: I honestly don't see how you recognized them, Shirley.

SHIRLEY: Elementary, my dear Watson! Elementary!

JEN: Oh, don't be so smart! And stop calling me *Watson!* Just because your name is Shirley Holmes, you don't have to talk like *Sherlock* Holmes! My name is Jen!

SHIRLEY: But your last name *is* Watson, and you *are* my first assistant detective, and . . .

CURLY: Detective! What is she talking about?

BABY FACE: Easy, boy! It's just some game they're playing.

DONNA: Is that so?

CANDY: I'll have you know we're real, honest-to-goodness investigators with half a dozen mysteries to our credit!

DONNA: And our business is growing. That's why we need this garage for our headquarters.

SHIRLEY: And we're going to have it, too! In spite of Jerry Mason and his Super-Sleuths!

CURLY: There are too many detectives around here, games or no games. Let's split.

BABY FACE: Pardon our hasty departure, ladies, but for once my partner is right! We have urgent business elsewhere.

NARRATOR: Baby Face and Curly run out the door while the girls watch them go.

DONNA: Well, they're gone. Now, what was that all about?

CANDY: Something tells me, Donna, that we're just as well off without that pair.

JEN: You're right, Candy. Even Shirley can't explain how she recognized them.

SHIRLEY: I have my methods, but if we stand here talking all day, we'll never get this place straightened up.

DONNA: Listen! Someone's knocking! Do you think they've come back?

SHIRLEY: Open the door and see.

NARRATOR: Donna opens the door, and Jerry Mason, Alf, Larry, Bruce, and Adam troop in. Jerry carries a white flag on a stick.

DONNA: Jerry Mason, you and your pals get out of here and stay out.

JERRY: Have a heart, Donna. Look! We come under a flag of truce. The Super-Sleuths reporting for duty. Now, what can we do to help?

DONNA: Help?

JERRY: Sure, that's why we came. We thought we could lend a hand.

SHIRLEY: A likely story!

JEN: After that mean trick you just played on us?

ALF: Trick? What trick?

SHIRLEY: Sending Jerry's big brother and his buddy to scare us away from here.

JERRY: What is all this? My brother is away on a basketball trip and so are most of his buddies!

DONNA (*Sarcastically*): Then I guess we only imagined we saw two big boys in here with masks tied over their faces!

BRUCE: Hey, Jerry, they must mean those two guys who almost knocked me over just now, when we were parking our bikes in the alley.

JERRY: But they were no friends of ours!

ADAM: We never saw them before.

SHIRLEY: But I could have sworn I recognized them. I could see their high school letters on their shirts, showing through their sweaters—SPHS!

CANDY: Maybe they weren't high school boys. Maybe they were robbers after all.

JERRY: Did they take anything?

ALF: Is anything missing?

DONNA: Let's take a look.

SHIRLEY: There is so much junk in here, we would hardly know if anything is missing or not.

ALF: This box is full of pots and pans and groceries.

JEN: That's mine. I was going to make some fudge.

BRUCE: Fudge!

LARRY: I'm all for it!

ADAM: Me, too. Let's stick around!

ALF: I'll put the box up on the bench for you.

NARRATOR: Jerry picks up Jen's folder of papers and the robbers' instruction sheet from the workbench. Jerry glances at the paper left by the robbers, then looks at it more closely, surprised.

JERRY: Wait a minute. What's this? Take a look, Alf.

ALF: Um-m. Looks like some sort of code.

JERRY: Right! (*Reading*) "Four CS, One CM, One LB, One CC, Two SQCB."

JEN (*Impatiently*): Secret code, poppycock! That's my fudge recipe! Give it to me.

JERRY: Fudge recipe!

JEN: It's a new one Mother found in a magazine. She typed it for me this morning. I guess it fell out of my folder.

ALF: You could have fooled me. I thought it was a cryptogram.

JEN: That's how much you boys know about cooking! CS is cups of sugar, CM is a cup of milk and LB is a lump of butter.

KATE: I guess CC is a cup of cocoa.

DONNA: Two SQCB. That must be two squares of chocolate, but what's the *B?*

CANDY: *B* for *Bitter*. Even I know you always use bitter chocolate for fudge.

BRUCE: All this is making me hungry. Why don't you go ahead and make the fudge while we pitch in on the clean-up job?

JEN: O.K. I only hope this hot plate is in working order. It seems all right.

CANDY: Let me help you, Jen.

SHIRLEY: I still don't understand this great burst of generosity on the part of you boys.

KATE: Neither do I, not when you were so determined to have this place for your Super-Sleuths meetings!

BRUCE: There's an old saying: "When you can't lick 'em, join 'em!"

SHIRLEY: Nothing doing! The FBI is strictly female, and it's going to stay that way!

JERRY: Oh, come now, Shirley, you know the best detectives in the business are men!

DONNA: Is that so? How about the Mystery of the Missing Notebook, and the Case of the Kidnapped Kitten? We solved those without any help from you!

ALF: Never mind all those arguments now. Let's get to work. If this old radio is working, we can have some music while we work. I'll turn it on.

ANNOUNCER'S VOICE: We interrupt this program to bring you a special news bulletin.

ALF: This old radio works pretty well.

VOICE (*Continuing*): Fairview Police have just been alerted to be on the lookout for Baby Face Boyd and Curly Smith who escaped from the State Prison Hospital Squad early this morning. Prison officials have reason to believe the two men may be heading for Fairview in an attempt to recover the money from the big payroll holdup last spring. The missing prisoners are described as short, slight, and extremely youthful in appearance—easily mistaken for teen-agers. A reward of five thousand dollars is offered for their capture or information leading to their arrest.

CANDY: Shirley, those two weren't high school boys—they were the robbers! I know they were.

JERRY: Some detectives!

ALF: You had those two guys right here, and you let them get away!

SHIRLEY: How could I have been so stupid! Those letters I saw on their shirts—SPHS—I thought they stood for South Penn High School, not State Prison Hospital Squad!

DONNA: But what were those two crooks doing in this garage?

ADAM: Looking for the stolen money. What else?

JERRY: Then it must still be here. Come on. Let's turn this place inside out!

ALF: Hey, Larry, give me a hand with these stepladders and this lumber.

NARRATOR: Alf and Larry move the ladders and lumber aside and reveal an old cupboard. The others gather around, even Jen, who has the pan of fudge she has been stirring.

SHIRLEY (*Astonished*): I never knew that old cupboard was there!

JEN: And I never saw fudge that looked like this. Something's wrong with it.

JERRY: Never mind the fudge now—not at a time like this.

JEN: But look at it—I can hardly stir it. I don't understand what happened to it.

CANDY: You must have made a mistake in the recipe.

JEN: I put in everything the recipe called for.

SHIRLEY: The recipe. Where is it, Jen?

JEN: Right there next to the hot plate. What are you all excited about?

NARRATOR: Shirley picks up the recipe and looks at it. Then she turns to the others excitedly.

SHIRLEY: Jen, you've solved the mystery!

JEN: I've *what?*

SHIRLEY: Your fudge has solved the mystery. Jerry was right. This *is* a secret code. Oh, why didn't I notice this before?

LARRY: Notice what?

SHIRLEY: The proportions are all wrong. No wonder the fudge is too thick! Just one cup of milk would never dissolve four cups of sugar! And why would you use cocoa and bitter chocolate in the same recipe?

JEN: Then it's not the right recipe.

CANDY (*Excitedly*): That's not a recipe at all. Look, Jen. I just found this in your folder. It's labeled "Recipe for Chocolate Fudge."

JEN: Don't tell me I tried to make fudge from a secret code!

BRUCE: If we can crack that code, we'll find the money!

DONNA: If this paper is really the clue to the hidden money, those men will come back.

KATE: I'm scared! Let's get out of here!

JERRY: You're right, Kate. This is a man's job. You girls go home, and let the Super-Sleuths take over.

SHIRLEY: Not on your life! Kate, you run to the nearest phone and call the police. Donna, you go down to the corner and try to find Officer Higgins. I'll lock the door after you.

JERRY: If we can only figure out this crazy code. (*Reading*) "Four CS"—those letters must stand for something right here in this garage.

BRUCE: C! C! What begins with the letter C? Ceiling . . . cement . . . counter . . .

SHIRLEY: Cupboard! *Cupboard* starts with a C! Quick, let's look!

ALF: But it says "Four CS." There's only one cupboard.

SHIRLEY: But maybe it has four shelves.

JERRY: That's it! "Four CS"! Fourth cupboard shelf!

LARRY: Let me look!

JEN: Do you see anything, Larry?

LARRY: A lot of cobwebs. Wait a minute. There's something

shoved back here. It's some sort of bag. Here, Bruce, don't drop it. It's heavy.

BRUCE: It's made of some heavy material.

ADAM: Probably canvas.

SHIRLEY: Of course! It all fits. CM—*canvas mailbag.*

BRUCE: Wow! Look! It's stuffed full of money!

ALL (*Ad lib*): We've found it! The holdup money! It's here! (*Etc.*)

LARRY: Here's a big flat book of some kind.

JEN: It's a ledger book. That must be what LB stands for. Look! More money hidden between the pages!

BRUCE: Anything else up there, Larry?

LARRY: I think so. Yes, here's a can.

CANDY: It's a coffee can. There's the CC we thought was a cup of cocoa! Here's more money!

LARRY: I guess that's all. No, wait a minute. Here are two boxes.

ALF: Cigar boxes.

JEN: Two squares of chocolate—bitter, turns out to be two square cigar boxes.

ADAM: Sh-h! Someone's at the door.

CANDY: Maybe the girls are back with the police.

SHIRLEY: No. They would have given us the signal.

CURLY (*Calling*): Open up in there.

JERRY: You girls take cover.

BABY FACE (*Calling, angrily*): Open up, I say, and be quick about it!

CANDY: They may break down the door.

SHIRLEY: Then let's get ready for them! I'll take the canoe paddle. Jen, you take the baseball bat. Candy, you get that tennis racket.

CURLY (*Calling*): This is a countdown! Ten seconds, and we're coming in!

BRUCE: They mean business!

JERRY: Quick. Set up those ladders at either side of the door. I think we're about to make the catch of the season.

ALF: What are you going to do?

JERRY: You and Adam get up on the ladders, stretch this volleyball net across the doorway and drop it over their heads as they come through the door.

NARRATOR: Alf and Adam set up the ladders on either side of the door. They take the net from Jerry and mount the ladders, stretching the net across the doorway. Bruce and Larry each grab a mop, as the girls line up at either side with their "weapons."

SHIRLEY: We're ready for them, Jerry.

JERRY: All set? (*Pause*) Here we go!

NARRATOR: Jerry opens the door, and Baby Face and Curly plunge through. Alf and Adam drop the volleyball net over them. Both robbers become entangled in it. The others rush at them, bringing them to the floor. Jerry sits astride Curly, and Bruce sits on Baby Face.

BABY FACE *and* CURLY: Help! Help!

NARRATOR: Kate and Donna, followed by Officers Higgins and Ryan, rush in.

DONNA: I hope we're in time.

RYAN: What's going on here, anyway?

DONNA: There they are—the men I told you about! They're the prisoners you're looking for!

HIGGINS: They answer the description all right.

JERRY: And you'll find the missing money right there, too.

BABY FACE: They found the money! They broke Gentleman Joe's code!

CURLY: How did you kids ever figure out that "Four CS" meant *four cement slabs?*

SHIRLEY: It didn't. It stood for *fourth cupboard shelf*, and that's where we found all the money.

BABY FACE: It beats me. The cupboard wasn't even here when we were looking.

RYAN: I wish you kids would fill us in on this code business. I've got to put it all in my report.

DONNA: Well, we surprised these two holdup men here in the garage, but mistook them for high school boys playing a joke.

SHIRLEY: They ran off when they heard the sirens and left a piece of paper here with what turned out to be a code that led us to the money.

ALF: I turned on the radio and we heard the special news bulletin about the escape of these two characters.

JERRY: And Shirley broke the code and led us to the loot . . . with the help of her Female Bureau of Investigators.

SHIRLEY: But it was you and your Super-Sleuths who figured out how to trap Baby Face and Curly in the volleyball net.

HIGGINS: I must say *that* was a new idea to me.

JERRY: Not very new, Officer! Have you ever seen pictures of Roman gladiators trapping their enemies in nets?

HIGGINS: Now that you mention it, I did see something like that in a movie last week. But just the same, you can take credit for making it work on a modern problem . . . and these two certainly are "modern problems"!

RYAN: And this is the money from the payroll robbery, all right. You kids deserve a lot of credit.

HIGGINS: Come on, Ryan. We have to get this pair down to headquarters. And we'll want some of you kids to come down later and tell the whole story to the Chief.

RYAN: And there's the matter of the reward, you know.

ALL: Reward! We forgot all about it!

HIGGINS: Sure thing—five thousand dollars—and you boys and girls have certainly earned it.

RYAN: Let's go, Higgins. Come on, you two. March!

BABY FACE: Trapped by a bunch of kids!

CURLY: And they made everything sound so easy!

HIGGINS: We'll take these two and the money, and I'll send a squad car for you kids in about twenty minutes.

NARRATOR: Higgins and Ryan help Curly and Baby Face to their feet, and march them out the door.

ALF: If we get all that reward money, the Super-Sleuths can build a super-duper clubhouse.

KATE: And what about the FBI?

SHIRLEY: I've been thinking about the FBI, Kate. Maybe we should make a few changes! It's pretty nice to have some husky boys around when you need them.

JERRY: And I've been thinking, too, Shirley. I doubt if the Super-Sleuths could solve a mystery with a pan of fudge!

JEN: Are you talking about a merger?

SHIRLEY: That's what I have in mind.

CANDY: But we'd have to change our name! We couldn't call ourselves the Female Bureau of Investigators if we took in boys!

SHIRLEY: I think I've had about enough of mysteries and investigating. If we get the reward, there's something else we could do.

ALL: What?

SHIRLEY: Well, there are lots of boys and girls in Fairview who have no meeting place for their clubs and societies.

JERRY: I get the idea! Maybe if we talked to the Town Council or the Recreation Department, we could build a clubhouse for the whole town.

SHIRLEY: Jerry, you're a mind reader. How about it, girls?

JEN: I like the idea, Shirley. But I hate to give up our name.

JERRY: It could still be the FBI, you know . . .

SHIRLEY: Only the letters would stand for Fairview Bureau of Improvements.

JEN: Fairview Bureau of Improvements!

LARRY: That sounds great!

JERRY: Let's put it to a vote!

SHIRLEY: All in favor, say "Aye."

ALL: Aye!

THE END

Miss Louisa and the Outlaws

This is an unusual Western play about a schoolteacher who helps capture some dangerous outlaws. It is both a comedy and a drama.

When you read through the play silently, notice the places that are funny and those that are serious. Would you read the parts differently?

In this play, the outlaws and the sheriff and his deputy might have a Western drawl. Miss Louisa speaks very precisely and correctly. Have three of the group read the following lines so that you can see the difference.

BENNY (*In confusion*): Say, what is this? Dan and me got guns. We don't have to take orders from you.

MISS LOUISA: It's Dan and *I have* guns, sir. And as long as you and Benjamin take refuge here, I shall insist that you obey the laws and rules of our schoolhouse. Kindly wipe your feet, gentlemen!

DAN (*Grudgingly*): All right, all right. We'll wipe our feet.

MISS LOUISA: Mind your manners, sir. When I speak to you, you are to answer, "Yes, Miss Louisa."

BENNY *and* DAN (*Meekly*): Yes, Miss Louisa.

Choose your parts, and then read them to yourselves very softly. When you are ready, read the play aloud together. Be sure to read briskly, with no pauses. If you have trouble with any of the words, get help from the group or your teacher.

Read for the class. Ask them if you read well or not, and why.

MISS LOUISA AND THE OUTLAWS

by Frances B. Watts

Characters

(6 boys, 4 girls, and a narrator)
NARRATOR
MISS LOUISA, *the schoolteacher*
THEODORE ⎤
WILLIAM ⎟
ANNABELLE ⎬ *pupils*
CLARA ⎟
REGINA ⎦
BENNY ⎤
DEAD-EYE DAN ⎬ *outlaws*
SHERIFF
ED, *his deputy*

NARRATOR: On an October day, many years ago around the turn of the century, a history lesson is beginning in a little one-room schoolhouse in the West. The teacher is Miss Louisa, and her students, Theodore, William, Annabelle, Clara, and Regina, are sitting at attention with their hands folded.

MISS LOUISA: For our history lesson this afternoon you all were to learn the first three stanzas of "Paul Revere's Ride." Theodore, would you come to the front of the room and recite, please?

THEODORE: Uh—uh—Listen, my-uh-children, and you shall hear. Uh—uh—

MISS LOUISA (*Sternly*): I see that you haven't studied your lesson, Theodore. You will stay after school and learn the lines before you leave this afternoon. Do you understand?

THEODORE (*Mumbling*): Yes.

MISS LOUISA: Remember your manners! Yes *what*, Theodore?

THEODORE (*Speaking with respect*): Yes, *Miss Louisa.*

MISS LOUISA: William, let's see how well you have learned the stanzas.

WILLIAM: Uh—uh. Listen, my children, and you shall hear. Uh—uh. Of the midnight ride of Paul Revere. Uh—uh—

MISS LOUISA: Another shirker! William, you will join Theodore after school. Do you understand?

WILLIAM (*Mumbling*): Yes.

MISS LOUISA: Yes, *what*, William?

WILLIAM (*With respect*): Yes, *Miss Louisa.*

MISS LOUISA (*Sighing*): Boys and girls, I realize that this poem may seem a bit dull and uninteresting. But I'm asking you to memorize it in hopes that you will recognize the courage and strength some of our forefathers possessed when they founded our great country. Do you have any idea what courage is?

CLASS (*After a moment's hesitation*): No, Miss Louisa.

MISS LOUISA: Well, courage is behaving bravely when you are most afraid. All of us, at some time, have been afraid. Those who discipline themselves and control fear in times of stress are exhibiting courage. Is that clear?

CLASS: Yes, Miss Louisa.

WILLIAM (*In a whispered aside*): Ha, I'll bet Miss Louisa has never been afraid in her life! All she ever does is scare *us* to death!

THEODORE (*Aside*): You said it. What does she know about fear? All she has in her veins is ice water!

MISS LOUISA: Annabelle, do you think that you can recite the lines for us?

ANNABELLE: Yes, Miss Louisa. (*Reciting*)

"Listen, my children, and you shall hear
Of the midnight ride of Paul Revere."

NARRATOR: As Annabelle recites the poem, Benny and Dead-Eye Dan, two outlaws, enter the schoolroom with drawn guns.

BENNY: Stay where you are!

THEODORE (*Fearfully*): Outlaws! It's Benny the Kid, and Dead-Eye Dan! The ones who robbed Dodge City Bank last week!

WILLIAM: It is! It is! Their pictures are up in the Post Office. Wanted, dead or alive! A hundred dollars' reward!

NARRATOR: The children scream with terror, and run to the back of the room. Miss Louisa raps on her desk with a ruler for attention.

MISS LOUISA (*Sternly*): Back to your seats, everyone! How often have I told you never to leave your seats without permission! Sit down at once!

DAN: Nobody's going to get hurt, kiddies, as long as you set there quiet.

MISS LOUISA (*With great dignity*): Watch your grammar in front of my pupils, sir. The proper expression is—*sit there quietly*—not *set there quiet*.

DAN (*Baffled*): Huh? Oh. As long as you *sit there quietly*.

BENNY: Just in case somebody tipped off the Sheriff that we're in town, my pal Dan and me are going to hide out here till the two-thirty freight train comes through. Then we'll make our getaway. So don't anybody get any bright ideas like yelling out the window or running for help, see?

DAN: Let's take a load off our feet. We can sit at those two empty desks. May as well be comfortable till train time.

MISS LOUISA (*Firmly*): Just a moment, Daniel! I believe that is your name. You and Benjamin will kindly wipe your feet on the mat in the doorway before you sit down.

BENNY (*In confusion*): Say, what is this? Dan and me got guns. We don't have to take orders from you.

MISS LOUISA: It's Dan and *I have* guns, sir. And as long as you and Benjamin take refuge here, I shall insist that you obey the laws and rules of our schoolhouse. Kindly wipe your feet, gentlemen!

DAN (*Grudgingly*): All right. All right. We'll wipe our feet.

MISS LOUISA: Mind your manners, sir. When I speak to you, you are to answer, "Yes, Miss Louisa." Do you understand?

BENNY *and* DAN (*Meekly*): Yes, Miss Louisa.

MISS LOUISA: All right, you may sit down now.

BENNY (*Aside, puzzled*): I don't know why we let this schoolteacher lead us around by the nose, Dan. By all rights we ought to tie her up in the closet.

MISS LOUISA (*Brisk and efficient*): Well, boys and girls, we shall continue our history lesson tomorrow. It is now time for music. Let's have a song. A jolly one. How about "Old MacDonald Had a Farm"?

REGINA: We can't sing, Miss Louisa. We—we're too scared!

MISS LOUISA: Afraid, Regina? Of what is there to be afraid? As far as we are concerned, we simply have two extra pupils in our room. We will follow our usual schedule.

NARRATOR: Miss Louisa takes her pitch pipe from her pocket and sounds the key. The children begin to sing. Miss Louisa suddenly raps on her desk with the ruler, interrupting the song, and speaks sternly to the outlaws.

MISS LOUISA: Benjamin and Daniel, why aren't you singing?

DAN (*Bewildered*): Huh? Why should we sing?

CLARA (*Earnestly*): Because, when we have music in this school, everybody sings.

ANNABELLE: And that means *everybody*. It's a school rule.

MISS LOUISA: Clara and Annabelle, this is not your affair. (*Firmly*) When we start to sing again, you will sing. Do you understand?

BENNY (*Mumbling*): Yes.

MISS LOUISA: Yes *what*, Benjamin?

BENNY: Yes, Miss Louisa.

NARRATOR: Miss Louisa blows on her pitch pipe again and waves her arms as she leads the song. The children's spirits rise as they sing. The faces of the outlaws are very serious as they sing along with the children. When the song ends, Miss Louisa goes to the window and gazes out with a worried frown. Benny and Dan jump up and draw their guns.

BENNY: Stay away from that window, ma'am. We're not giving you the chance to signal for help.

DAN: You may be a schoolmarm, but you can't outsmart us. Nobody has ever outsmarted Benny the Kid and Dead-Eye Dan.

MISS LOUISA (*Speaking matter-of-factly*): It looks a bit like rain. William, will you and Theodore please go out and bring in the flag?

BENNY: Do you think we're stupid? Why, the minute those kids leave this room they'll run for the Sheriff.

WILLIAM (*Nervously*): Don't insist that we go, Miss Louisa! It really doesn't look like rain.

MISS LOUISA: There are cumulus clouds forming in the west. It is October; showers begin suddenly in fall. It is a rule of our school that we never allow the American flag to become wet. One of you may accompany the boys, if you wish. But our flag must not be rained upon! Do you hear?

BENNY: Oh, all right then.

MISS LOUISA (*Sternly*): What did you say?

BENNY (*Meekly*): Yes, Miss Louisa.

NARRATOR: Benny heads toward the door, motioning to William and Theodore to go ahead of him. They go out the door while Dan keeps his gun drawn. After a moment, Benny, William, and Theodore return. They wipe their feet carefully, and William hands the flag to Miss Louisa, who folds it and lays it on her desk.

MISS LOUISA: Now, boys and girls, we will have a spelling bee. Regina and Clara may be captains. You may start choosing teams, girls.

REGINA: I choose Theodore for my team.

CLARA: I choose William.

REGINA: I choose Daniel.

CLARA: I choose Benjamin.

BENNY: Say, what is this? What's going on?

DAN (*With enthusiasm*): A spelling bee, pal. Ain't you never been in a spelling bee before?

MISS LOUISA: *Haven't you ever*, Daniel. Watch that grammar!

DAN: Haven't you ever been in a spelling bee before?

BENNY: No, and I'm not going to now. Besides, it'll be train time soon. We have to stay on the alert.

MISS LOUISA (*Pauses, then sympathetically*): Very well, Benjamin. I will excuse you from participating in the spelling bee. Naturally, it would be most embarrassing for you to be spelled down by a group of young children.

BENNY (*Blustering*): Who's scared of being spelled down? Look, maybe I haven't had much schooling, but I'm not so dumb that a bunch of little kids can lick me at spelling.

MISS LOUISA: I admire your spirit, Benjamin. You won't mind joining Clara's team then.

BENNY (*Sighing*): Oh, all right.

MISS LOUISA (*Severely*): What's that, Benjamin?

BENNY: Yes, Miss Louisa.

MISS LOUISA: Clara, please spell "doctor."

CLARA: D-o-c-t-o-r.

MISS LOUISA: Correct. Now, Regina, spell "lawyer."

REGINA: L-a-w-y-e-r.

MISS LOUISA: Good. Now, Benjamin, I would like you to spell the word, "thief."

BENNY: Uh—uh. Lemme see. T—h. T-h-e-i-f.

MISS LOUISA: That is wrong, Benjamin. The correct spelling is t-h-i-e-f. You may take your seat.

WILLIAM (*Aside*): Gee whiz! He *is* a thief, and he can't even spell it!

BENNY (*Sulkily*): Aw, so what if I'm not a good speller. I still make a good living.

DAN (*Suddenly*): What's that sound? Yeow! There goes the two-thirty freight train!

BENNY (*Angrily*): I told you it was time to get out of here! But you had to let that crazy schoolteacher talk us into a spelling bee!

NARRATOR: Suddenly, the Sheriff and Ed, his deputy, enter, their guns drawn. They catch the outlaws off guard.

SHERIFF: Hands up.

ED: You're covered.

NARRATOR: Benny and Dan raise their hands, as Ed takes their guns. The children cheer as the Sheriff steers the men toward the door.

THEODORE: Sheriff, how did you know the outlaws were here?

SHERIFF: I didn't know, son. But I gathered that something was wrong when I happened to look out of my office window and saw that the school flagpole was bare.

ED: Why, you know as well as I do that, unless it's raining, Miss Louisa never lowers the flag until sundown. It's a rule of the school. Remember, Miss Louisa was our teacher, too.

MISS LOUISA: Sheriff, I was hoping you or Ed would notice that the flag was down, and would remember that rule. Apparently my pupils remember *some* things that I teach them.

ANNABELLE (*Laughing*): Miss Louisa was just like Paul Revere's friend. She used a signal to tell about the enemy!

MISS LOUISA: That's right, Annabelle. And if Benjamin and Daniel were the slightest bit educated as to the ways of the weather, they would have known that cumulus clouds in the west rarely mean immediate rain.

BENNY: I had a hunch that we should have tied that teacher up in the closet the minute we came in!

DAN: Could *you* have tied her up?

BENNY: No, I guess I couldn't have at that. There's something about Miss Louisa. Well, you just can't imagine tying her up in a closet. (*Pauses*) She doesn't scare easy, and before you know it, you're half-scared of *her*.

MISS LOUISA: The proper grammar, Benjamin, is—*She doesn't scare easily*.

BENNY: Yes, Miss Louisa.

SHERIFF: Well, we'll take these scoundrels down to jail where they belong. You'll receive the hundred dollars' reward in a few days, Miss Louisa.

MISS LOUISA: Thank you. I believe it will be just enough money to take the children on an outing to the Dodge City music festival. (*Children cheer*.)

ED: Come on, you two. It's jail for you.

MISS LOUISA: And now, children, I believe that I will dismiss you for the rest of the afternoon.

CLASS: Hooray! Hooray for Miss Louisa!

NARRATOR: The children run noisily out the door—all except William and Theodore. Miss Louisa sits limply down at her desk. She holds her head in her hands. After a moment she looks up and sees the boys.

MISS LOUISA: Well, boys, why are you still here?

THEODORE: You asked us to stay and learn the first three stanzas of "Paul Revere's Ride," Miss Louisa.

MISS LOUISA: Oh, so I did. Well, I will excuse you just this once. You see, I'm feeling a bit shaky.

WILLIAM (*Thoughtfully*): Miss Louisa, you were afraid when the outlaws were here, weren't you?

MISS LOUISA: Oh, yes. Very much afraid. I did everything in my power to delay them, so that they might miss the train and be captured. Yet, I longed for them to leave before they decided to use those wicked guns on some of us.

THEODORE: Well, you didn't act scared. Not one bit!

WILLIAM (*Stoutly*): Naturally, she didn't! She behaved bravely when she was most afraid. That's *courage*. Remember?

MISS LOUISA: Perhaps I taught something today after all. Before you leave, boys, please take the flag and hoist it again. There are several hours yet until sundown. We must abide by the rules of the school, you know.

WILLIAM (*With admiration*): Yes, Miss Louisa.

THEODORE: Yes, indeed. Goodbye, Miss Louisa.

THE END

The Dangerous Game

Here is a play that takes place in a foreign country during wartime. In it, some young girls save a soldier's life, even though they are in great danger from the enemy.

When you read the play silently to yourself, think how the girls change during the play. Even though they are frightened, they do not let the enemy soldiers know their secret. Talk over the play together to be sure everyone understands how the girls hide Mike.

Choose parts and read the play together. Ask yourself these questions:

1. Did I come in at the right time?
2. Did I change my voice to show feeling?
3. Did I read smoothly, without delays or pauses?

When you think you are ready, find time to read the play to a group.

THE DANGEROUS GAME

by Stephanie Miller

Characters

(3 boys, 5 girls, and a narrator)

NARRATOR
HELGA ⎤
KATYA ⎬ *teen-age girls*
ANNA ⎦
GERDA, *Anna's younger sister*
MIKE, *a young airman*
SERGEANT ⎤
CORPORAL ⎦ *enemy soldiers*
MANYA, *Anna's older sister*

NARRATOR: It is wartime, in a country occupied by the enemy. The play takes place in an old barn in the countryside. It is empty except for a pile of straw and a heap of sacks. In one corner are some old crates and two overturned chairs. The remains of a scarecrow—a broomstick and crosspiece dressed in a large coat and hat—stand at one side. Suddenly, Helga and Katya run in. They are laughing and panting as they stop and look around in surprise.

HELGA: We're first after all, Katya. I thought we were late.

KATYA: Let's hide, Helga. Then when the others come we can jump out and frighten them.

HELGA: Good idea.

KATYA: Come on then, quickly, Helga, before they come.

HELGA: Mm-m-m—where?

KATYA: I'm going under these old sacks. Cover me up properly, will you?

HELGA: All right. Katya! Do stop wriggling, silly. How do you expect to stay properly covered when you're squirming around like an eel?

KATYA (*Giggling*): I can't help it. You're tickling.

HELGA: There, you're covered. Don't move now.

KATYA (*In a muffled voice*): No.

NARRATOR: Helga looks around for a hiding place. Then Katya sits up suddenly.

KATYA: Where are you going?

HELGA: For goodness' sake! Keep down and I'll cover you up again. There. Stay still! I'll get behind the crates.

ANNA (*Calling*): Helga—Katya!

HELGA: That's Anna.

KATYA: Quick! Are you hidden?

HELGA: Nearly. All right. Not a sound now, Katya. (KATYA *giggles*.) Hush, you'll spoil everything.

NARRATOR: The girls remain hidden and quiet. Then Anna and Gerda, who wears a red hat, burst in.

ANNA: Helga? Katya? There's no one here, Gerda.

GERDA: There must be. I saw them climbing the hill.

ANNA: Perhaps they went on into the woods.

GERDA: Without waiting for us?

ANNA: We were late.

GERDA: Only a few minutes.

ANNA: We needn't have run, anyway. Phew! I'm out of breath. I'm going to sit here on these sacks for a minute and rest.

KATYA: Yow!

ANNA (*Shrieking*): Oh, Katya! You little beast! You frightened the life out of me.

KATYA: And you nearly squashed the life out of me. You must weigh a ton.

ANNA: Don't be so personal. (GERDA *laughs*.)

KATYA: I don't know what you are laughing at, Gerda.

GERDA: If you were standing here, you would be laughing, too.

I don't know who frightened whom the most.

NARRATOR: Gerda leans back on the pile of crates where Helga is hidden.

GERDA (*Laughing*): You both looked so silly!

HELGA (*Shouting*): Boo!

GERDA: Helga! You wretch!

KATYA: Now who looks silly? (*Chanting*) Gerda is silly. Scaredy-cat Gerda.

GERDA: You wait!

NARRATOR: Gerda chases Katya, with Anna and Helga joining in, until they all fall to the ground, laughing and puffing.

KATYA: Enough! I give up!

HELGA: Why were you so late, Anna?

ANNA: We overslept.

KATYA: So did we.

ANNA: It was the planes. They kept us awake all night. Plane after plane, thundering over.

KATYA: Wasn't it exciting?

GERDA: Frightening, though! All the bombing. You could hear it even from here, and we are miles from the town.

HELGA: The planes come so often these days that surely the enemy soldiers will soon be driven out and our own country liberated.

ANNA: Oh, I hope so. I don't like the planes.

HELGA: And the fires! Did you see the sky all lit up?

ANNA: We saw the searchlights, too. And the flashes as they shot at the planes.

KATYA: I hope they missed.

GERDA: Not all of them did. We saw one plane shot down. It came spinning down with smoke and flames pouring out.

KATYA: Oh, the poor pilot! I hope he and all the crew bailed out.

ANNA: It wouldn't do them much good if they did. Not if they were caught. They'd probably be shot.

HELGA: But they'd be all right if they fell in the mountains or the forests. The partisans would find them, and look after them.

KATYA: And get them back to their own country, too. (*She sighs.*) I wish I were old enough to be a partisan.

GERDA: So do I. It would be marvelous to be able to help get rid of the beastly soldiers occupying our country.

ANNA: That's enough of that. It's dangerous to talk like that. If the enemy heard you it would mean the end for us all.

KATYA: But, Anna, how could they possibly hear us up here, in the old barn? We're miles from anywhere.

ANNA: That doesn't matter. If you talk like that here, you may make a mistake and do it in the village. You're such a little scatterbrain.

HELGA: All right, you two. We don't want another argument. Let's change the subject. What shall we play? Hunt the Thimble?

ANNA: How about I Spy? Or Forfeits?

KATYA: Oh, no. We can play all those when it's wet and we can't go out. There were storm clouds gathering over the mountains when we came up, and it'll probably rain hard before very long. Let's play something outside while we can.

ANNA: O.K. Hide and Seek then?

KATYA: Yes, lovely. I know some good hiding places in the woods.

HELGA: Who's going to hide?

GERDA: We'll pick straws. The shortest straw stays here and counts while the others hide. I'll get some straws.

HELGA: Only up to twenty, though, so the hiders can't get too far.

GERDA: Come on, pick a straw.

KATYA: Look, Anna's is the shortest. She's It.

GERDA: Hide your eyes, Anna, and don't begin to count until we are out of the door.

KATYA: Which door shall we go out of—back or front? Does it matter?

HELGA: All out the same one. Front one. Come on.

GERDA: Cover your eyes, Anna.

KATYA: And no peeking!

NARRATOR: The three hiders run out the front door of the barn. Anna covers her eyes and begins to count.

ANNA (*Very slowly*): One, two, three. (*Quickly, all in one breath*) Four-five-six-seven-eight-nine-ten. (*She counts rapidly to twenty, then calls out*) Coming!

NARRATOR: Anna runs out of the barn to find her friends. After a moment, a man appears at the back door of the barn. It is Mike, a young airman. He is wearing a ripped and blackened shirt and dirty trousers. His face is streaked with blood and oil. Mike's right arm is in a sling made from a scarf and he is limping badly. He stops just inside the barn, breathing heavily, and looks warily around. Then he drags himself to the pile of sacks. He lowers himself to the ground, and covers himself up with the sacks, before collapsing completely. Just then Anna, Helga and Gerda run in, laughing.

ANNA: I found you right away, Helga.

HELGA: How could you? I thought I was so well hidden.

ANNA: You forgot your feet. They were showing. And Gerda —you forgot your red hat. It shows up too well.

GERDA: Bother!

ANNA: I won! I won!

NARRATOR: Suddenly there is a crash of thunder, and Gerda runs to the door and looks out.

GERDA: We came back just in time. Katya was right. It's starting to pour.

HELGA: Where is Katya? Did you catch her?

ANNA: Not yet. I couldn't find her.

GERDA: If she doesn't turn up soon, she'll get soaked.

NARRATOR: Anna points to the pile of sacks. She nudges the others, putting her finger to her lips.

ANNA (*Whispering*): Look! I think she's hiding under the sacks. She must have crept in again by the back way.

NARRATOR: Anna tiptoes to the sacks and whips off the top one.

ANNA (*Shouting*): Found you! Oh, my goodness! A soldier!

NARRATOR: Mike sits up, still dazed, raising his good arm as though to ward off a blow.

GERDA: Who is he?

HELGA: I don't think he's an enemy soldier. Maybe he's one of the airmen shot down last night.

NARRATOR: As the girls gather around Mike, he lowers his arm and watches them warily. Anna kneels beside him.

ANNA: It's all right. We're friends. Friends. Do you understand?

MIKE: Yes. Thank you.

ANNA: You're hurt. Is it very bad?

MIKE: I'll be all right, if you'll just let me rest.

ANNA: Yes, of course! You are one of the airmen helping to liberate our country, aren't you? It's an honor to meet you. I am Anna. This is my sister, Gerda, and my friend, Helga.

MIKE: How do you do? My friends call me Mike.

ANNA: Then we shall, too! We shall be glad to be your friends.

MIKE: Thank you. You won't give me away, will you?

ANNA: Give you away? Never!

HELGA: We will help you!

GERDA: Please don't laugh at us. You may think we are only children, but we can help.

ANNA: Yes, indeed. Our sister Manya acts as a courier for the partisans. She knows where to find them. She will take a message to them, and they will come fetch you, and hide you safely until you are well enough to make the journey back.

MIKE: To my country?

GERDA: Certainly. The underground will help you.

MIKE: I don't know what to say.

ANNA: Say nothing. Just rest. Gerda! Run quickly and tell Manya what has happened.

GERDA: I will be back soon.

MIKE: What is this place? I didn't think anyone lived here.

GERDA: They don't. It's the Simons' farm. Or at least, it was. There's no one here now.

ANNA: They came one day and took Mr. and Mrs. Simons away—and the children, too.

MIKE: Who? The soldiers?

ANNA: No. The secret police.

HELGA: No one knows where they are or what happened to them.

GERDA: We don't even know if they are still alive.

ANNA: The next day the soldiers came with trucks and loaded up all the cattle and pigs, and the poultry, and took them away, too.

GERDA: So now there is no one here. We come here to play because it's so quiet and we can do as we like without people telling us not to make noise.

ANNA: Is your arm badly hurt? We can get some water from the pump outside, and I could tear up my petticoat for bandages.

MIKE: No, don't do that. I'll be fine. My leg was hurt when we were hit by flak on the way here—about half an hour before we were actually shot down. The rest of the crew fixed it up for me.

ANNA: The rest of the crew? What happened to them? Did they bail out, too?

MIKE: I don't know. The plane was on fire. The skipper ordered everybody to bail out. I was hurt, and a bit groggy, so the others pushed me out first. I remember falling, then the jerk when the parachute opened. After that it's all hazy. There was an explosion, then nothing—nothing until I hit the ground. I can remember dragging myself into some bushes, and then I must have passed out. But the others—I don't know.

HELGA: We are so thoughtless. Here you are, hurt and tired,

and all we can do is chatter like monkeys and ask questions. Lie down on the sacks and try to sleep. When Gerda comes back, she will have news for us. Until then, try to rest.

MIKE: That'll be easy. I feel as though I've been dragging through those woods for weeks.

NARRATOR: Mike lies back. Helga and Anna take off their coats and put them over him. Then they tiptoe quietly away and talk in whispers.

ANNA: Poor thing. He's exhausted.

HELGA: He needs some more clothes.

ANNA: Manya will see to it.

NARRATOR: Katya bursts into the barn.

KATYA: Guess what?

NARRATOR: The others try to quiet her, but Mike starts up in alarm.

ANNA: Katya! Why do you have to be so noisy? Now you've awakened him.

KATYA: Oh, no! He's not one of the airmen from the planes last night, is he?

HELGA: Yes, his name is Mike. Isn't it exciting?

KATYA: Oh, no! Whatever can we do?

ANNA: We've already done it. Gerda has gone to tell Manya—and he was having a rest until you burst in.

KATYA: This is terrible!

ANNA: Have you taken leave of your senses, Katya? Why all the fuss?

KATYA: Soldiers! That's what I came to tell you. They are searching the village. (HELGA *and* ANNA *gasp.*)

ANNA: Are you sure? They are really searching—it's not just a routine check?

KATYA: No. I met Jan in the woods. He told me. The enemy soldiers found a parachute a few miles away. So they know someone is hidden somewhere. They are searching the whole area. All the houses, the fields, the woods . . . the barns.

ANNA: Oh! What can we do?

KATYA: He must leave at once. Mike, you can reach the forest before they get here. I'll go with you. I know a big hollow tree where you can hide. They'll never find you there.

HELGA: It's no good, Katya. He has hurt his leg. He can hardly move at all, let alone climb a tree.

KATYA: Then where can he hide? (*Suddenly*) Under the sacks!

ANNA: That's the first place they will look.

HELGA: Except they won't *look*. I've seen them searching before. With piles of sacks, or straw or anything like that, they just jab their bayonets in, and if there is anyone hidden there . . . well . . .

KATYA: How horrible.

MIKE: You girls must go. At once. I'll be all right. You leave me here, then if they find me you won't be blamed for hiding me.

KATYA: We can't leave you.

ANNA: There must be some other way.

MIKE: Please don't be silly. I can't move away fast enough, and there is nowhere to hide.

ANNA: But they'll kill you.

MIKE: No, they won't. I shall be sent to a prisoner of war camp.

ANNA: Look at yourself. Only your shirt and trousers. No uniform. No identity papers. It will be the perfect excuse. They will say you are a spy, and you will be shot.

MIKE: Then go, and go quickly. If you are accused of harboring a spy, you will all be shot.

HELGA: There must be something we can do. Let me think. (*Slowly*) They will expect you to be hiding . . . so if you were right out where everyone could see you, you might be so obvious that they wouldn't notice you.

KATYA: Helga, what are you talking about?

HELGA: Hush, I'm thinking. There's an idea coming to me. (*She pauses.*) What do you expect to see when you come into this barn?

KATYA: I don't know. Nothing much.

HELGA: Come on—think.

KATYA: A pile of straw . . . the sacks . . .

HELGA: What else?

ANNA: The boxes . . . and the chairs . . .

KATYA: And the scarecrow.

HELGA: Yes! And what do you expect to see in the fields and yet never really look at?

ANNA (*Beginning to understand*): Scarecrows.

HELGA: Exactly. They are everywhere. Mike, could you sit still, completely still, without moving, for perhaps a long time?

MIKE: I think so, but I don't understand.

HELGA: Katya, fetch that chair and set it beside Mike.

KATYA: There. Will it work?

HELGA: I hope so. It's our only chance. Come on, Mike. Let me help you. Sit on the chair, please. You are about to become a scarecrow.

MIKE: What?

HELGA: Why not? Don't you see? The soldiers will have passed half a dozen scarecrows by the time they reach here. They'll be used to seeing them. An old scarecrow is the sort of thing they'll expect to find in a barn like this. So they won't think it odd. And if you are right out in view, not hidden at all, you'll be so obvious they won't think twice about you.

MIKE: It might work at that. But I can't let you try; it's too dangerous.

ANNA: Don't argue. You can't go away, and we won't. So you must do as you are told.

MIKE: You ought to be spanked . . . but, thanks. What do you want me to do?

HELGA: Absolutely nothing, except keep still. Quickly now, we've wasted enough time. We must hurry. Anna, get the coat from the old scarecrow. And the hat. Here, put your good arm through the sleeve and we'll fasten the coat over the other one. Katya, find some pieces of string, and tie the ends of the sleeves together so that his hands won't show.

ANNA: His feet. What about his feet?

HELGA: Oh, heavens!

ANNA: I know—sacking. I'll wrap them in sacking.

KATYA: Stick some bits of straw so that they will poke out. That'll make it look better.

ANNA: How are we going to disguise his face?

HELGA: Same as his feet. Sacking and straw.

NARRATOR: The girls work quickly, disguising Mike as a scarecrow. Katya runs to the door and looks out.

KATYA: Oh, hurry. I can see the soldiers coming across the field. They will be here any minute.

NARRATOR: Helga gets a large piece of sacking. She puts it over Mike's head and ties it around his neck with string. She puts a bundle of straw across the top of his head and jams the hat down over it so that the straw sticks out from under the hat like hair.

HELGA: He's almost ready. Give me your scarf, Anna, and I will wind it around his neck.

NARRATOR: Suddenly the enemy sergeant's voice is heard outside the barn.

SERGEANT: Squad, halt. Corporal!

CORPORAL: Sir!

SERGEANT: Take one man and guard the rear entrance. I will search inside.

CORPORAL: Yes, sir!

ANNA: Quickly, make a circle around Mike and join hands. All right, now, start singing "Here We Go 'Round the Mulberry Bush," and dance around.

ALL (*Singing*): "Here we go 'round the mulberry bush, the mulberry bush, the mulberry bush . . ."

SERGEANT: So!

ANNA: What do you want?

SERGEANT: So—this is your playground, eh?

ANNA: Yes.

SERGEANT: You come here often?

HELGA: Every day. Almost.

SERGEANT: You have been here all day?

HELGA: Yes.

SERGEANT: Tell me—who have you seen?

HELGA: No one—only us.

SERGEANT: Just you three?

ANNA: And my sister, Gerda.

SERGEANT: Your sister? Where is she now?

ANNA: She went home. She had some errands to do—for my mother.

SERGEANT: You have seen no one else?

ANNA: No one.

SERGEANT: Hah!

KATYA: Why? Are you looking for someone?

SERGEANT: Yes, and I will find him. An enemy airman is hiding somewhere in this area. He cannot get far. Never fear. I will find him, and when I do find him, it will be most unfortunate for anyone who is suspected of helping him. But, you do not seem to have him, so you will have no need to be sorry, will you? What is this? A scarecrow. Did you make him?

HELGA: Yes, we did.

NARRATOR: The sergeant stares at Mike, and the girls hold their breaths. Then the sergeant smiles and speaks in a softer tone.

SERGEANT: It reminds me of when I was a child. We lived on a farm. They were good days. My brothers and I used to make scarecrows. Yours is not bad. Not bad, but we made better ones. If you used a large turnip for the head, you could carve a face on it. Make it more lifelike. Here, find me a large turnip, we'll knock this one off, and I'll show you.

KATYA: Oh, no!

ANNA (*Quickly*): We aren't allowed to use turnips. We need them all to eat.

154 *THE DANGEROUS GAME*

HELGA: Food is hard to get. We can't waste any.

SERGEANT: No, of course, I was forgetting. (*In a sterner voice*) Shall I tell you what we of the Army use that kind of scarecrow for?

ANNA (*Fearfully*): What?

SERGEANT: Bayonet practice! (*The girls gasp.*) Yes. Would you like a demonstration?

KATYA: No! Oh no! You mustn't!

SERGEANT: What's that? You would give me orders?

ANNA: Please. Don't be angry with her. She's very young. She doesn't understand. She's never had dolls or toys. The scarecrow is the only plaything she's ever had, and he's like a real person to her.

SERGEANT: Then it's time she grew out of fancies like that. I will prove to her it's only sacking and straw.

KATYA: No!

ANNA: Please! You do not look unkind. You wouldn't want to make her cry, would you? Remember when you were small— how you felt about your scarecrows, the pride you took in them.

SERGEANT: Yes. (*He hesitates.*) Very well. I won't spoil your scarecrow.

KATYA: Thank you, thank you. I can't tell you how much it means to me.

ANNA: I knew you were kind.

HELGA: We are all so grateful to you.

SERGEANT (*Flattered*): That's all right. Remember what I told you now—you can make a much better head from a turnip.

HELGA: Yes, yes, we will.

SERGEANT: And remember also—if that airman comes here you are to report him immediately.

ANNA: Oh, we will. We will. If he comes.

SERGEANT: Very well. See that you do!

NARRATOR: The sergeant leaves. The girls move toward the

door and stand listening as the sergeant calls his men together outside.

SERGEANT: Corporal, bring the men back here.

CORPORAL: Yes, sir.

SERGEANT: Get in line here. March!

NARRATOR: The girls turn slowly in relief.

ANNA: They've gone.

HELGA: It worked. We did it!

KATYA: We fooled the enemy!

NARRATOR: The girls cling together, laughing, crying, and dancing. Anna breaks away and goes to Mike.

ANNA: We're forgetting Mike. Are you all right?

MIKE (*Mumbling*): Yes.

ANNA: Don't talk for a minute. We'll soon have you out. I'll take the sacking off his head. You two free his arms and feet.

HELGA: You might as well keep the old coat, Mike. It's not much, but it's warmer than nothing.

ANNA: How do you feel, Mike? Was it very bad?

MIKE: Phew! I don't think I'll ever be frightened of anything again. Not after that. I was petrified.

KATYA: I was so scared. I thought the sergeant was going to bayonet you.

MIKE: So did I. I almost moved then.

HELGA: It must have been dreadful, not being able to see anything.

MIKE: Come here. Let me look at you all. You were wonderful. I don't know how to begin to thank you.

HELGA: We were glad to help.

KATYA (*Airily*): Think nothing of it. Any time.

ANNA: Stop showing off, Katya.

MIKE: Let her. She deserves to. You all do. What a tale you'll have to tell your grandchildren.

NARRATOR: Suddenly there is a knock on the door. The girls quickly gather around Mike to hide him. Then Gerda and Manya come into the barn.

ANNA: Gerda!

HELGA: Manya!

MIKE: My heart nearly stopped beating.

HELGA: We thought you were the soldiers coming back.

MANYA: The soldiers have been here?

KATYA: Yes, but we fooled them.

MANYA: I don't understand . . . but tell me later. We have no time to spare now.

ANNA: This is Mike. Mike, this is Manya.

MANYA: We will introduce ourselves properly later. Now we must hurry. The enemy commander is sending for more soldiers to help in the search, and soon there will be a full-scale man-hunt, with dogs, too. We must get you away at once.

MIKE: You are risking too much for me.

MANYA: Nonsense. You have risked your life for us; it is only right that we should do something for you. I have a cart of hay outside and a pass from the soldiers to take it to feed the cattle we keep in the mountains. The cart has been searched once, so it should be safe, at least until the new troops arrive —and by then we should have reached the partisans. They will take you high, high into the mountains to their hideout. You will be safe there until you are well enough to travel.

MIKE: And they can really get me safely out of the country?

MANYA: There are ways and means. But come, we must hurry. There will be plenty of time for talk later. Let me help you.

MIKE: Goodbye—and thank you. Thank you—all of you.

ANNA: Good luck. Come back one day.

MIKE: I will. Don't worry, I'll be back. We all will.

THE END

Thirteen

This is a comedy-drama about superstitions. It has suspense and excitement, as well as humor.

Read the play through silently, and then discuss it with the group. Can you think of other superstitions besides the ones mentioned in the play? Are there any superstitions you believe in?

Choose your parts and read the play together. Remember that each girl must be sure to come in with her part on time. The play should be fast-paced and natural—as much like ordinary conversation as possible, but clear and distinct.

This would be a good play to tape-record so that you all can hear the way you sound. Ask yourselves as you listen whether the parts could be improved. Did everyone speak clearly? Were there unnecessary pauses? Did each character sound natural?

If you are not satisfied, practice reading the play until you are ready for an audience.

THIRTEEN

by *Anne Coulter Martens*

Characters

(12 girls and a narrator)

NARRATOR
SUSAN
ROBERTA
CAROL
PATTY
JOAN
EMMY   } *the Twelve Teens Club*
DIANE
MARGIE
LYNN
FRANNY
GINNY
BONNIE

NARRATOR: It is Friday evening, and Susan is sitting at the desk in her living room, making notes from several open books in front of her. Pages of notes are scattered all over the desk. She crumples a piece of paper and tosses it into an overflowing wastebasket, just as Carol comes in.

CAROL: Hi, Susan! Am I the first one here?

SUSAN: That's right, Carol.

CAROL (*Eagerly*): Have you heard from Bonnie? She's coming, isn't she? Do you think she suspects it's a surprise party? And tell me, did Roberta bring the birthday cake? (SUSAN *laughs*.) Well, say something!

SUSAN: Give me a chance, will you? Roberta should be here with the cake any minute.

CAROL: Oh, good!

SUSAN: And, yes, Bonnie's coming—I hope.

CAROL: What do you mean—you *hope?* Aren't you positive?

SUSAN: She promised to come. I tried to get her on the phone just now, but the line was busy.

CAROL: Oh, wouldn't it be awful if she changed her mind?

SUSAN: Relax, Carol, relax. Bonnie thinks this is just an ordinary meeting of the Twelve Teens Club. We can't make too much of a fuss, or she'll suspect something.

CAROL: I guess you're right. I brought the money we collected for her gift. Dad took our change and gave me a crisp ten-dollar bill.

SUSAN: That's fine. I saw some darling shoulder bags downtown. Bonnie can pick out just the kind she wants.

NARRATOR: Carol hands Susan an envelope, which she puts down on the desk. Susan then continues to go through her notes, crumpling some and tossing them in the wastebasket.

CAROL: What are you so busy about—homework?

SUSAN: A special report for English, about superstitions.

CAROL: Never walk under a ladder. (*Scoffing*) It might fall on you!

SUSAN: Make a wish when you see a load of hay pulled by a white horse. (*Laughs*) How often do I see a load of hay?

CAROL: Nobody believes those things anymore.

SUSAN: You'd be surprised what some people still believe.

CAROL: I'll be surprised if we can pull off this party without Bonnie's finding out.

SUSAN: It's not easy for eleven girls to keep a secret.

CAROL: You ought to empty that basket before it overflows.

SUSAN: I'll have to pretty soon.

NARRATOR: Susan gathers up the scattered papers and puts them in a large book, straightening up the desk. There is a knock on the door, and Roberta comes in, carrying a decorated cake, which she sets down on the coffee table.

CAROL: The cake has arrived. It's beautiful. Can I try the icing, Roberta?

ROBERTA: You sample that icing when all twelve of us are here, and not before.

CAROL: I can dream, can't I?

ROBERTA: Your dream had better not have sticky fingers. I have to dash. Mother's out front waiting for me in the car.

SUSAN: You're leaving?

ROBERTA: I promised to do a little errand with Mother. If I'm a few minutes late, try to stall things till I get back, will you?

SUSAN: Sure, we'll do that.

ROBERTA: Oh, I almost forgot. My cousin Grace is here for the weekend. Do you mind if I bring her along?

SUSAN: Of course not.

CAROL: We all like Grace. The more the merrier.

ROBERTA: O.K., then.

NARRATOR: Roberta opens the door to leave, and Patty comes in.

ROBERTA: Hi, Patty. See you later.

PATTY: Where's Roberta going?

SUSAN: She'll be back.

CAROL: Look, Patty—the cake!

PATTY (*Impressed*): Out of this world! Won't it be simply terrible if Bonnie doesn't come?

SUSAN: What makes you say that? Of course she's coming.

PATTY: I was talking to her on the phone just now.

SUSAN: No wonder her line was busy.

CAROL: What did she say?

PATTY: That the woman next door wants her to baby-sit.

CAROL: Oh, no—she can't do that tonight.

SUSAN: I'll go over to her house and talk her out of it. Come on, let's all go.

NARRATOR: There is a knock on the door, and the girls look at one another.

CAROL: Maybe it's Bonnie this time.

PATTY: Come on, cake. Let's go to the kitchen.

NARRATOR: Patty takes the cake to the kitchen as Susan opens the door. Bonnie is standing there. Patty returns and breathes a sigh of relief as she sees Bonnie.

PATTY: Thank goodness!

BONNIE: What's the matter?

SUSAN: We're just glad to see you, that's all.

PATTY: And glad that you're not going to baby-sit.

BONNIE: Oh, but I am. I just stopped in to ask if Mother may borrow your pinking shears. She's making a dress.

SUSAN: Of course, but, Bonnie, please don't baby-sit tonight. We want you at our meeting.

BONNIE: Honestly, I hate to miss it, but I need the money. I'm saving for a new shoulder bag.

SUSAN: Carol and Patty, you talk to her. I'll be right back.

CAROL: Everybody will be so disappointed if you don't come.

PATTY: Please, Bonnie.

BONNIE: Anything special going on?

CAROL *and* PATTY: Oh, no!

BONNIE: Then I'd better baby-sit. Anyway, the woman is counting on me now.

CAROL: Can't you get some other girl?

PATTY: Your sister. Ask your sister if she'll do it.

CAROL: Oh, do you think she would? Ask her, Bonnie. Please ask her.

BONNIE (*Weakening*): Well, all right.

NARRATOR: Susan returns with the scissors.

CAROL: Oh, Susan, she'll come!

BONNIE: If my sister will take over the baby-sitting job.

SUSAN: Oh, I'm so glad. Here are the shears. Take them home and then come right back.

BONNIE: Just a minute. A penny for you.

SUSAN (*Surprised*): A penny?

BONNIE: Because you're giving me something with a sharp edge. They say it keeps away bad luck. (*Knocks on wood*)

SUSAN: Listen to her—pennies, knocking on wood! I didn't know you were superstitious, Bonnie.

BONNIE: Maybe I'm just careful. (*Laughs*) Thanks for the shears.

SUSAN (*Anxiously*): You *will* ask you sister to do the baby-sitting, and you'll promise to come back?

BONNIE: I guess so.

SUSAN: Promise you will. Promise.

BONNIE: O.K., I will. 'Bye for now.

CAROL (*After a pause*): Gol-ly! Am I glad we straightened that out!

SUSAN: She really had me worried.

BONNIE (*Calling*): It's me, again! I forgot my purse.

CAROL: There it is on the chair.

NARRATOR: Bonnie picks up her purse, then begins to turn around, counting slowly.

BONNIE: One. Two. Three.

SUSAN: What in the world—?

BONNIE: If you forget something and have to go back for it, you turn around three times and then sit down. Bad luck if you don't. (*Knocks on wood*)

CAROL: Oh, Bonnie—really!

BONNIE: I *always* do it. See you later.

SUSAN: How can she possibly believe such nonsense?

PATTY: Just habit, I guess.

SUSAN: I'll burn these papers in the incinerator. Carol, I'm still worried. Suppose Bonnie changes her mind about coming back?

CAROL (*Worried*): Or suppose her sister won't take the baby-sitting job?

SUSAN: Why do things always go wrong at the last minute?

NARRATOR: Susan takes the wastebasket out, as Emmy and Diane come in.

EMMY: Hi.

DIANE: How's everything?

CAROL: Under control—we hope. Sit down, girls.

EMMY: When do you expect Bonnie?

CAROL: Pretty soon.

DIANE: I do hope she doesn't suspect anything.

CAROL: I'm pretty sure she doesn't.

EMMY: After all, her birthday's not till tomorrow.

CAROL: That part doesn't worry me. (*Sighs*)

DIANE: But something else does?

CAROL: Well, a little. (*Brightly*) But I guess it will work out all right.

NARRATOR: Margie, Lynn, and Franny come in, happy and excited. Susan returns with the empty wastebasket and puts it down by the desk.

MARGIE: Here we are!

SUSAN: Find yourself a chair or a cushion.

LYNN: I'm glad we got here before Bonnie.

FRANNY: This is going to be fun.

MARGIE: Is everybody coming?

CAROL: They all said so.

EMMY: How many more to come now?

SUSAN: Let's count how many are here. (*Counts*) Eight of us. Joan and Ginny still to come. That makes ten.

DIANE: Bonnie—eleven.

LYNN: And Roberta—twelve. All accounted for.

CAROL: Roberta's bringing her cousin Grace.

FRANNY: Oh, good! I'm glad Grace is coming.

NARRATOR: Joan and Ginny come in and join the group.

JOAN (*Looking around*): Bonnie isn't here yet?

SUSAN: She's coming any minute now.

GINNY: We practically ran all the way.

SUSAN: I hope you girls have kept the secret.

GIRLS (*Ad lib*): I have! Of course we have! Sure thing! (*Etc.*)

SUSAN: Remember, we won't say a word about her birthday till

Roberta and Grace get here. Then Patty can bring in the cake, and we'll all yell, "Surprise!"

CAROL: When you give the signal.

NARRATOR: There is a knock on the door, and Bonnie bounds in, with a sweater over her arm and an umbrella in her hand.

BONNIE: My sister put up a stiff fight—but I won! Hi! (*They greet her.*) Susan, I brought back the sweater I borrowed last week.

SUSAN: Thanks, Bonnie. No hurry.

PATTY: Hey, why the umbrella? Not a cloud in the sky.

BONNIE (*Laughing*): That's why I carried it.

CAROL: Say that again?

BONNIE: I set my hair, and you know how if you don't carry an umbrella, it always rains—and if you do carry one, it never does. Where do I sit?

SUSAN: Anywhere you can find room.

BONNIE: Is everybody here?

SUSAN: All but Roberta.

CAROL: And her cousin Grace.

BONNIE: Grace is coming? Good. (*Suddenly upset*) Oh, no!

SUSAN: What's the matter?

BONNIE: You're sure Grace is coming?

SUSAN: Positive.

PATTY: I thought you liked her.

BONNIE: Oh, I do.

CAROL: Then why all the fuss?

BONNIE (*Nervously*): There'll be thirteen of us!

SUSAN: That's right.

BONNIE (*Agitated*): Thirteen! And on a Friday, too.

CAROL: So?

BONNIE: I'm sorry, but I won't stay.

SUSAN (*Surprised*): Oh, Bonnie, don't be silly. As if thirteen means anything. (BONNIE *knocks on wood.*)

PATTY: There she goes, knocking on wood.

CAROL (*Impatiently*): Don't start that again.

BONNIE (*Upset*): I shouldn't even have come. As I was crossing the street, a black cat ran across my path.

CAROL: I like black cats.

BONNIE: *I* don't. My grandmother knew a woman who fell and broke her arm after seeing a black cat.

CAROL: Because she tripped over the poor animal?

BONNIE: No! (*Annoyed*) You don't believe me.

CAROL: I certainly don't think the black cat had anything to do with it. Or that thirteen is an unlucky number.

BONNIE: Oh, it is!

PATTY (*Cheerfully*): I'm not worried.

BONNIE: *I* am.

SUSAN: Not really?

BONNIE (*After a pause*): I'll take your sweater up, and then I'll go home and baby-sit after all.

PATTY: Oh, Bonnie—no!

JOAN: Honestly, nothing will happen.

DIANE: Nothing bad, anyway.

EMMY: Maybe even something good.

BONNIE: My grandmother knew a woman who had a dinner party for thirteen. They all seemed well and happy, but that night—

SUSAN: Stop it! Bonnie, you're staying here, and we don't want to hear any more nonsense.

BONNIE: Sorry, but I'm *not* staying.

NARRATOR: Bonnie goes out, and Susan runs after her to try to convince her to change her mind.

JOAN: If she leaves—there goes our party!

LYNN (*Excitedly*): We have to stop her from going.

FRANNY: But how?

GINNY (*Sighing*): Even if we tell her about the surprise, she might not stay.

MARGIE (*Slowly*): I suppose we could call Roberta and ask her not to bring Grace.

EMMY: And hurt Grace's feelings, when we all like her?

DIANE: We'd hurt Roberta, too.

LYNN: It wouldn't be *fair*.

MARGIE: You're right. We can't call Roberta.

CAROL: It would be giving in to superstition.

PATTY: We all know thirteen isn't unlucky, but how can we convince Bonnie?

EMMY: Instead of bad luck, *good* things are going to happen if she stays.

CAROL (*Thoughtfully*): Maybe we *can* prove that to her.

DIANE (*Eagerly*): How?

CAROL: Are any of you girls the least bit superstitious?

GIRLS (*Ad lib*): No! Not me! Of course not! (*Etc.*)

CAROL: Then we can do it! We'll deliberately invite bad luck.

PATTY: How?

CAROL: Quick. Tell me some easy superstitions.

PATTY: Breaking a mirror.

CAROL: You have one in your purse. When Bonnie comes in, drop it. And if it doesn't break—step on it!

PATTY: On purpose?

JOAN: Bonnie will have a fit.

CAROL: Let her, for a few minutes.

JOAN: I've heard it's bad luck to put new shoes on a table.

CAROL: Susan has a new pair. Joan, you get them and put them on this table!

PATTY: What else?

CAROL: Bonnie's umbrella!

PATTY: Poor Bonnie! I know just what you're going to do.

MARGIE: Now I catch on. Bonnie will see that in spite of everything, she has *good* luck.

CAROL: And that should cure her of all these silly superstitions.

PATTY: Carol, you're a genius.

CAROL (*Laughing*): Maybe I am, at that.

NARRATOR: Bonnie comes back and heads for the door.

BONNIE: Well, I'm on my way. Sorry I'll miss the meeting.

CAROL: You don't have to leave this minute. Only eleven of us are here.

BONNIE: Please don't be angry with me. I know you think I'm foolish—but—well, I won't stay with thirteen.

NARRATOR: Joan comes in, carrying a pair of shoes and reaches out as if to set them on the table.

BONNIE (*Quickly*): Don't do that!

JOAN (*Innocently*): Do what?

BONNIE: Never put new shoes on a table. It's bad luck. Oh, you've done it! (*Knocks on wood*)

JOAN: So I have.

BONNIE: Something will happen. Just you wait.

JOAN: Oh, I don't think so.

EMMY: Aren't there any *good* luck signs?

BONNIE: Oh, sure. The horseshoe—

CAROL: If it doesn't clonk you on the head.

BONNIE: And the four-leaf clover. A rabbit's foot brings good luck, too.

CAROL: But not for the poor rabbit. Looking for something, Patty?

PATTY: My mirror. Oh, I dropped it! And now I've stepped on it!

BONNIE (*Sharply*): Is it broken?

PATTY: Right in half! Too bad.

BONNIE (*Upset*): Oh, dear! (*Knocks on wood*)

CAROL: You really think Patty's going to have seven years of bad luck because she broke a mirror?

BONNIE: I hope not. (*Unhappily*) But that's what they say.

PATTY: Do I look worried?

BONNIE: Let's not talk about it. I'm leaving.

CAROL: Don't forget your umbrella. It's such a very pretty one. How does it look open?

BONNIE: Never open an umbrella in the house!

CAROL: I want to see how it looks.

BONNIE: Then don't hold it over your head!

CAROL: Bad luck? When does the sky begin to fall on me?

BONNIE: Oh, stop it! (*Suddenly*) I think you're all doing these things on purpose!

CAROL: Do you?

BONNIE: Now I know you are.

CAROL: I wondered how soon you'd catch on.

PATTY: We want to prove that these things don't really bring bad luck.

JOAN: Something *good* is going to happen.

BONNIE: Sorry, but I've stayed long enough.

DIANE: Don't go yet.

BONNIE: I really must.

CAROL: Stay just a few minutes longer.

PATTY: Oh, why doesn't Roberta come?

BONNIE: Goodbye.

LYNN: We can't let her go!

CAROL: Wait! Shall we tell her *why* we want her to stay?

GIRLS (*Ad lib*): Yes! Tell her! Hurry up! (*Etc.*)

CAROL: First, the envelope. Where did I put it?

SUSAN: On the desk, but I don't see it now.

CAROL: And neither do I. Where *is* it?

MARGIE: Look on the floor. Maybe it fell down.

SUSAN: I can't find it!

CAROL: But it simply must be here!

BONNIE: Why is the envelope so important?

CAROL (*Alarmed*): If it fell—oh, Susan—maybe it fell into the wastebasket!

SUSAN: Oh, my glory! I burned the papers without looking at them!

CAROL (*Near tears*): All our money—burned! (*Girls murmur in concern.*)

BONNIE: What is it? Tell me!

CAROL: I—can't. Oh, this is awful!

BONNIE (*Slowly*): Don't you see—this happened after Patty broke that mirror.

EMMY: That's right, it did.

DIANE: I wonder—?

CAROL: No! There simply couldn't be any connection.

PATTY (*Unhappily*): I'm beginning to be sorry I broke it.

CAROL: Patty, don't you go back on me! You know very well that Susan burned the papers quite a while ago.

NARRATOR: The telephone rings and Susan answers it.

SUSAN: Hello . . . For you, Joan.

JOAN: Me? Hello? . . . What is it, Johnny? . . . You want me right away? . . . (*Excitedly*) What happened? I'll be right home.

CAROL: What's the matter?

JOAN: My little brother says something's happened, and I have to go right away. Oh, dear! He wouldn't say what it was!

NARRATOR: Joan hurries out, and the girls look at each other in dismay.

BONNIE: Maybe it's an accident. I warned Joan not to put those shoes on the table.

LYNN (*Shivering*): This gives me a very funny feeling.

FRANNY: I'm getting scared, too.

GINNY: Oh, Carol, I wish you hadn't opened that umbrella in the house!

CAROL: I just won't believe in such stuff!

SUSAN: We'll have to call Roberta and tell her the bad news. Carol?

CAROL (*Unhappily*): You do it.

NARRATOR: Susan goes to the phone and dials a number.

SUSAN: Hello? Mr. Patton? May I speak with Roberta? . . . (*Startled*) What? Oh! When did she go? . . . Is it serious? . . . Oh, he hung up! Mr. Patton said her mother just took Roberta to the hospital!

PATTY: Oh, good heavens!

GINNY (*Excitedly*): Why?

LYNN: For an operation?

EMMY: Is it very serious?

DIANE: Poor Roberta!

MARGIE: That does it. I'm going home, too.

FRANNY: I guess I won't stay either.

BONNIE: Oh, Carol, why did you put that umbrella over your head?

GINNY: All our plans are ruined.

LYNN: The money gone—

EMMY: Roberta in the hospital—

DIANE: And goodness knows what's happened at Joan's house!

SUSAN: I hardly know *what* to think.

PATTY (*Reproachfully*): Breaking those superstitions was your idea, Carol.

CAROL: Have you *all* deserted me? But I only wanted to prove—

MARGIE: You proved it, all right. The wrong way.

CAROL: No! (*Upset*) Oh, I don't know. I'm all mixed up.

BONNIE: And I'm going home.

NARRATOR: Susan picks up the large book she had been taking notes from earlier and looks at it in a puzzled way. There is a knock on the door, and Roberta and Grace come in. Everyone gasps in surprise, and Susan drops her book, scattering the papers she had put in it earlier.

GIRLS (*Ad lib*): Roberta! She's here! Look! (*Etc.*)

PATTY: We thought you went to the hospital!

ROBERTA: I did. Why all the excitement? I told you I had an errand to do with Mother. She left some things there for a bake sale. (*Others murmur in relief.*)

SUSAN: Look, everybody! The missing envelope with all our money. The lost is recovered!

CAROL: Our money! Where was it?

SUSAN: In the book with my papers!

PATTY: Hooray!

NARRATOR: Joan hurries in. She is excited and happy. Patty goes out to the kitchen to get the cake.

JOAN: Girls, what do you think? Our Persian cat just had three kittens!

DIANE: Is *that* why your little brother called?

JOAN: Can you imagine? We're tickled pink.

NARRATOR: Patty comes in, carrying the birthday cake.

ALL: Surprise! Happy birthday, Bonnie!

BONNIE (*Excitedly*): For *me?* Oh! Oh, how nice of you! It's simply beautiful!

SUSAN: And here's some money to buy yourself a shoulder bag.

BONNIE (*Overwhelmed*): I—I don't know what to say. No wonder you tried so hard to make me stay. Thank you all so much.

CAROL: Now what about your silly superstitions? They don't mean a single thing!

BONNIE: I'm sorry I was so foolish.

CAROL: And you'll never be superstitious again?

BONNIE: Oh, never, never! Who cares about thirteen? Nothing can spoil our party now. (*Without thinking, she knocks on wood.*) Oh-oh. I did it again!

CAROL (*Laughing*): I give up. You're a hopeless case! (*They all laugh, then sing "Happy Birthday."*)

THE END

The Case of the Missing Masterpiece

This is a mystery play about a stolen painting. No one is supposed to know who the criminal is until the end of the play, so when you read it, be sure not to give away the surprise.

There are both older and younger people in the play. Would they speak differently? Read the play through silently to be sure you know what is happening, then discuss with the group how each of the parts should be read.

Have the boys read these lines of Clyde Fletcher's and see who sounds the most like "a mousy little salesman." Then choose the best one for the part.

CLYDE: Did I hear someone mention my name? The door was open so I took the liberty of coming up the back stairs. I hope you don't mind, Maud.

The rest of the group can then choose parts and read the play aloud together. Stop and discuss words you don't understand, and work for a fast, smooth pace. The play is a long one, and it should not drag.

Are you satisfied with your reading, or do you think there are parts that could be improved? If so, practice them until you are perfect.

Now read for a group, or read the play into a tape recorder so that you can listen along with the rest of the class to your reading. How would you rate your reading?

THE CASE OF THE MISSING MASTERPIECE

by Betty Tracy Huff

Characters

(3 boys, 6 girls, and a narrator)
NARRATOR
JOHNNY HERALD
KAY WYNDHAM
AUNT DEE
AUNT MAUD
BANNING STERN, *a gallery owner*
MRS. COLES, *an art collector*
CLYDE FLETCHER, *a salesman*
JESSICA VALE, *an art critic*
ESME PARISH, *an artist*

NARRATOR: This play takes place in an artist's studio on a cold winter evening. As it begins, the studio is dim and empty. Then a ray of light flashes around the dark corners, and from behind the model's platform comes a sinister hooded figure. Stealthily, with the aid of his flashlight, he looks at some of the canvases leaning against the walls and flashes his light on the large modern painting on an easel in the middle of the room. Suddenly, voices are heard from the hallway, and the hooded figure looks around wildly. Then, snapping off his flashlight, he drops down behind the model's platform. Kay Wyndham and Johnny Herald come in and Kay turns on the light.

KAY: I'm almost ashamed to show you Uncle Henry's studio with the light on, Mr. Herald. It's such a mess. All of poor Uncle Henry's painting things are still here—paints, palette,

palette knife. Everything is just the way he left it. I haven't wanted to come in here . . . since . . . since the murder.

JOHNNY: I understand, Miss Wyndham. But what's a little dust to a budding artist like me?

KAY: Of course I'll clean the place up if you decide to rent it. And anyway, it will look much better after the sale tonight, because most of the pictures will be bought and taken away. At least my aunts and I hope so!

JOHNNY: The place looks fine to me. It's just what I've been looking for. The only thing is, it's awfully cold in here.

KAY: Something's wrong with the furnace. We'll get it fixed tomorrow.

JOHNNY: Good. I'll take the place. I'd like to move in as soon as possible, if it's all right with you.

KAY: Anytime, Mr. Herald. I know my two aunts will be glad to have you.

JOHNNY: Won't you call me Johnny? I wish you would say, "Johnny Herald, the famous artist?"—but I know you won't. No one has ever heard of me.

KAY: No one ever heard of Uncle Henry either, until . . . until . . .

JOHNNY: It happened here?

KAY: As he finished painting that picture.

NARRATOR: Kay and Johnny stand together, looking at the painting on the easel. Behind their backs, the hooded figure rises noiselessly and takes the palette knife from the table, then ducks out of sight as they turn.

JOHNNY: And the police never did find the murderer?

KAY: No. Oh, Johnny, it was awful. This whole room was turned upside down, as if the murderer had been looking for something.

JOHNNY: And you don't know what he was looking for?

KAY: No, none of us has any idea. Ugh! This place makes me shudder. I feel as if someone were watching us. It's silly of me, I know, but sometimes in the dead of night I think I hear footsteps on the stairs, and the sound of someone searching, searching. Oh, dear! Now you'll be sorry you rented this dreadful old place.

JOHNNY: But it's just what I want. If you don't mind, I'll run down and get my things out of the car. That is, if having my stuff up here won't interfere with the sale of your uncle's work tonight.

KAY: Not a bit, Johnny. Only a few people are coming—just the ones who were really interested in Uncle Henry's pictures. You'll stay for the sale, won't you?

JOHNNY: I was hoping you'd ask. I'll get my things and be back in a moment.

KAY: Good. I'll tidy up the place a little.

NARRATOR: Johnny goes out. Kay begins to gather up the tubes of paint on the table. The hooded figure rises from behind the platform and Kay sees him and screams. The figure picks up the drapery on the model's platform, throws it over Kay's head, and makes his escape through the back entrance, as Kay screams again. Johnny, Aunt Dee and Aunt Maud rush in through the main door and help Kay untangle herself.

AUNT MAUD: Kay, Kay, my dear girl, whatever is the matter?

JOHNNY: It's all right, Kay.

AUNT MAUD: My goodness, Dee and I can't go out for a moment to do our shopping without something happening.

JOHNNY: What was it, Kay?

KAY: It was horrible! Someone . . . something was hiding in here. It threw the drapery over my head.

AUNT DEE: Nonsense, Kay. Somehow you got tangled up in the folds of that drape and your nerves did the rest.

KAY: You mean you don't think there was anyone here? I tell you, I saw him.

JOHNNY: There's no one here now.

KAY: But you haven't looked everywhere. I couldn't tell if he ran out or not. The cupboard—oh, what if he's hiding in there?

NARRATOR: Johnny strides over to the tall cupboard against the wall and flings the door open. A limp figure falls out and the women scream. Aunt Dee breathes a sigh of relief, picks up the figure and sets it on the model's platform.

AUNT DEE: It's only poor old Sebastian.

JOHNNY: Sebastian?

AUNT MAUD: Henry's artist's dummy. It's nothing but sawdust, straw and sackcloth! You remember, Kay. Your uncle used to use it instead of a live model, when he wanted to paint details of costumes.

AUNT DEE: Maybe you caught a glimpse of Sebastian, Kay, and thought he was real, and then you got bundled up in the drapery.

KAY: But I tell you I did see someone.

AUNT MAUD: Do you know, young man, since Henry's murder we've spent half our time jumping out of our skins.

KAY: Oh, I forgot, you haven't met Mr. Herald.

AUNT DEE: We introduced ourselves on the front stairs, just before you started screaming.

BANNING STERN (*Calling*): Miss Dee! Miss Maud! Anyone home?

AUNT MAUD: That's Banning Stern. He's come for the sale, I suppose. I'll go down and show him in.

JOHNNY: Banning Stern? The owner of the Stern Art Gallery?

AUNT DEE: We're hoping he might buy some of poor Henry's work, for old times' sake. Though everyone says poor Henry never did live up to his early promise as an artist.

KAY (*Alarmed*): The knife—Uncle Henry's palette knife. It's gone!

AUNT DEE: Are you sure? When did you see it last?

JOHNNY: It was here when I first came in this evening. I happened to notice it when Kay touched it.

AUNT DEE: Then someone really was in here. Kay did see something. Oh, dear—a murderer loose in this rambling old house—with a knife!

KAY: Oh, Johnny, I'm scared.

NARRATOR: Aunt Maud returns with Banning Stern.

AUNT DEE: Good evening, Banning! You'd better keep your coat and gloves on. Something's wrong with the furnace again. It's like the outside of an igloo in here.

BANNING: Dee, Maud, let's not waste any time. The Stern Gallery is prepared to make you a blanket offer for all of Henry's work.

NARRATOR: Mrs. Coles, an elegantly dressed woman wearing a fur stole and gloves, comes in with Jessica Vale in time to overhear Banning's remark.

MRS. COLES: Oh, no, you don't get away with all of Henry's work, Banning. I've been invited to this sale. Stern Gallery is not going to hog everything, especially after my coming here on such a cold night.

JESSICA: Good gracious, Mrs. Coles. You don't want to buy that stuff of Henry's. If I've said it in my column once, I've said it a dozen times, Henry's latest pictures were no good. And every other art critic in town agrees with me.

NARRATOR: Esme Parish, a young artist, comes bursting in.

ESME: Kay, be a dear and let me have some linseed oil. Oh, company! I'll go out and come in again later.

KAY: No, please stay, Esme. I'll see if there's some oil in the cupboard.

NARRATOR: Kay goes to the cupboard, as Esme turns to Johnny.

ESME: I know you. Let me see now—don't tell me. Now where was it?

JOHNNY (*Quickly*): You're making a mistake, Miss . . . Miss . . . er . . . I only moved in this evening.

AUNT DEE: Esme Parish has the studio next door, Johnny. Esme, this is Johnny Herald.

ESME: Johnny Herald—of course, now I remember. Trust an artist never to forget a face—though I only saw you for a second when you came bursting out of your office.

JOHNNY: Miss Parish, please. You're mistaking me for someone else.

ESME: No, I'm not. You run the detective agency downtown. The one with the picture of Little Boy Blue blowing his horn on the door. I painted it myself. Remember?

JOHNNY: I was robbed! You were supposed to paint a herald blowing a trumpet.

KAY: You, a detective, Johnny? Why did you pretend to be an artist?

JOHNNY: I thought people might be more ready to talk if they thought I was only an artist.

ESME: *Only* an artist? Well, I like that.

MRS. COLES: The Herald Detective Agency. Oh, dear! I don't want to get mixed up in anything. I mean, what would my bridge club say?

JESSICA: But you are mixed up in it, my friend. We all are. And it's no good pretending we're not.

MRS. COLES: Jessica, I don't know what you're talking about.

ESME: Now that I've stirred up such a pleasant little turmoil, I think I'll take my linseed oil and go home. You shall have this back as soon as Clyde Fletcher comes with my new supplies.

KAY: Clyde was due last week, wasn't he? Usually he's as regular as the clock. I wonder—

NARRATOR: Clyde Fletcher, a mousy little salesman, comes in.

CLYDE: Did I hear someone mention my name? The door was open, so I took the liberty of coming up the back stairs. I hope you don't mind, Maud.

ESME: I'm glad to see you. I need some more linseed oil.

AUNT MAUD: It's nice to see you, Clyde. But isn't it a bit late in the evening for you to be out selling supplies?

CLYDE: Oh, I'm not here to sell anything this time, Maud. I'm here to buy. Thought I might pick up a bargain when I heard about your sale.

JESSICA: Here for the same reason as everyone else, eh, Clyde? You've heard there's a Rembrandt going cheap.

CLYDE: I . . . I don't know what you mean.

JESSICA: That's strange. Everyone else does.

AUNT MAUD: Jessica, if this is some sort of a joke, I wish you'd explain.

AUNT DEE: I know about the Rembrandt being stolen, but what does that have to do with Henry?

JESSICA: Banning knows, don't you, Banning? After all, it was stolen from your gallery.

AUNT MAUD: Henry may not have been a great painter, but he was honest. I'm sure he wouldn't have anything to do with a stolen painting.

JESSICA: I'm sorry, Maud, if you didn't know about Henry's being involved in the robbery. I hear things at the newspaper office. I heard the police traced the Rembrandt to Henry. That's why you're here, isn't it, Johnny?

JOHNNY: The Central Insurance Company hired me to see if I could get a line on the missing painting.

KAY: So that's why Uncle Henry was murdered. That's why the studio was turned upside down. The killer was looking for the Rembrandt.

AUNT DEE: But there's nothing like that here. All the pictures were painted by Henry.

KAY (*With a sudden scream*): Look!

MRS. COLES: Oh, my goodness, whatever is wrong now?

KAY: The knife! Uncle Henry's palette knife! It's back.

JOHNNY: Then someone in this room was the one who frightened Kay. Perhaps the same person murdered Henry.

JESSICA: Well, don't look at me. Ask Mrs. Coles why she hated Henry. And everyone knows she'd give anything to have that Rembrandt in her collection.

MRS. COLES: All right, I did hate him! He cheated me. Sold me a fake Van Gogh he himself had painted. But I didn't kill him.

AUNT MAUD: I just can't believe Henry would do anything like that.

MRS. COLES: It's true. But Jessica has no right to talk, not feeling the way she did about Henry.

JESSICA: It's no secret that a long time ago he got me fired from the job I had. But Banning Stern's the man you want.

BANNING: Good gracious, are you accusing me?

JESSICA: They say at the paper that the robbery was an inside job. Maybe you and Henry had a deal, eh, Banning? And something went wrong.

BANNING: Why would I arrange to steal my own painting?

JESSICA: It's been done for the insurance before! Right, Johnny?

JOHNNY: I learn more by listening than by talking, Jessica. Please go on.

AUNT MAUD: Now I remember seeing a letter from Banning to Henry in the papers of Henry's that we've been sorting.

AUNT DEE: That's right! It sounded strange, but at the time we didn't think much about it.

BANNING (*Upset*): I didn't write anything to Henry that could prove anything was wrong.

JOHNNY: Then let's go get that letter and see what it says.

MRS. COLES: I'll be there as soon as I run down to the car. I left my purse there.

CLYDE: I think I'll go down and get that linseed oil for Esme. I'll see you in a few minutes.

BANNING: Enough of this talk. I want to see what letter you have.

NARRATOR: Banning follows Mrs. Coles and Clyde out. After a moment, the others leave. As Aunt Maud passes the light switch, she dims the lights. The room is still and empty for a few moments, then the hooded figure appears through the other doorway. He turns on his flashlight and begins looking at the pictures stacked against the walls. Suddenly he hears Kay's voice from the hallway.

KAY: I'll be back in a moment. I left the key to Uncle Henry's files in the studio, Johnny.

NARRATOR: The hooded figure looks around, then slips the dummy on the platform onto the floor and takes its place on the platform. Kay comes in and speaks to the hooded figure, thinking he is the dummy.

KAY: Hi, Sebastian! Boy, do you look real in this light! You're not sitting on the keys to Uncle Henry's file cabinet, are you?

NARRATOR: Kay reaches out, and the hooded figure moves and whispers something to her. Kay screams, and the figure rushes out. Johnny comes in the other door, turning on the light.

JOHNNY: Kay, what is it?

KAY: Sebastian, the dummy—spoke to me.

JOHNNY: Silly, here's the poor old thing on the floor. Look, he's perfectly harmless.

KAY: Oh, Johnny, it must have been the murderer sitting here. He ran out as you came.

JOHNNY: But no one passed me on the stairs.

KAY: You came up the front stairs. This old house has a back stairway, too, you know.

JOHNNY: So that's how he got away.

KAY: Johnny, I'm so frightened. It's as if the studio were haunted.

JOHNNY: It's all right, Kay, it's all right. I'm here with you. Tell me exactly what happened.

KAY: He—the figure—spoke to me. He asked where the missing Rembrandt was hidden.

JOHNNY: And do you know?

KAY: Of course not. Oh, Johnny, if only we could find out who killed Uncle Henry. It's all so weird. The knife disappearing and then coming back—Oh! I just thought of something! Wouldn't there be fingerprints on the palette knife?

JOHNNY: Everyone here tonight is wearing gloves, Kay. There wouldn't be any fingerprints.

NARRATOR: As they talk, the door to the back stairway opens a crack, and a gloved hand appears around it.

KAY: If only we knew where Uncle Henry had hidden the Rembrandt. If we had the painting, maybe it would bring the murderer out into the open.

JOHNNY (*Excitedly*): Kay, I've just thought of something. Give the knife to me, please.

KAY: What is it, Johnny?

NARRATOR: Johnny takes the knife and carefully scrapes a little paint from the corner of the painting on the easel.

JOHNNY: We should have thought of this before. Often when thieves want to ship a stolen painting out of the country, or to hide it for a while, they simply paint another picture over the original.

KAY: Of course. Why didn't I think of that?

NARRATOR: Kay turns and sees the gloved hand at the door. She grabs Johnny's arm, too scared to do anything but point at the hand. Johnny signals her to be quiet, and goes on talking as if nothing has happened, as he moves toward the door.

JOHNNY (*Loudly*): I suppose you've already made sure there's nothing in the cupboard? I'll have another look.

NARRATOR: Johnny dives toward the gloved hand, but the door slams shut. Johnny flings open the door and races down the back stairs.

JOHNNY (*Shouting*): Stop! Come back here!

KAY (*Calling after him*): Be careful, Johnny. He might come back up the other staircase.

NARRATOR: Kay paces nervously around the room, finally propping Sebastian the dummy against the wall near the main door to the studio. As she does so, the other door opens slowly and the hooded figure glides in. Kay sees him and turns to run; then he grabs her and she faints. He quickly puts Kay in the cupboard and shuts the door. The figure goes to the table and rummages around, and accidentally touches an open tube of paint. He looks at his paint-stained gloves, then tosses them on the model's platform as he hears Aunt Dee and Aunt Maud approaching, talking with Johnny. Then he ducks out down the back staircase.

JOHNNY: The murderer was here, but I lost him in the dark.

AUNT DEE: How frightening. Kay must have been terrified.

JOHNNY: She's all right. Aren't you, Kay? (*Worried*) Kay? Kay? Where are you?

NARRATOR: A faint sound comes from the cupboard. Johnny cautiously opens the door and Kay falls into his arms. He helps her sit on the model's platform.

JOHNNY: Kay, Kay, are you all right?

KAY: I think so. I guess I was so scared that I fainted.

JOHNNY: Did you see who locked you in the cupboard?

KAY: The same horrible, hooded figure. It's like an endless nightmare. (*Startled*) What's this?

JOHNNY: Gloves with paint all over them.

KAY: But I don't understand. All the paintings are dry.

JOHNNY: It must have come from one of the tubes on the table. Kay, don't you see what this means? These are the murderer's gloves!

KAY: And everyone is wearing gloves tonight except you, Aunt Maud, Aunt Dee and me.

AUNT DEE: That means whoever is not wearing gloves is the murderer!

AUNT MAUD: But which one of them could it be? These plain kid gloves could belong to anyone, man or woman.

JOHNNY: We'll soon know. I hear them now.

NARRATOR: Esme, Jessica, Mrs. Coles, Banning and Clyde come in together. Mrs. Coles has her hands buried snugly under her fur wrap, and Jessica's hands are hidden behind her large purse. Banning and Clyde have their hands in their pockets. Only Esme can be seen to be wearing gloves.

JESSICA: Where have you been? Did you find the keys?

JOHNNY: Not yet . . . but we've found something else.

BANNING: What do you mean?

JOHNNY: I'll show you in a minute.

JESSICA: It's freezing in here.

NARRATOR: Jessica's hands are gloveless as she fumbles with her purse. Kay gasps, then sighs with relief as Jessica takes her gloves from her purse.

MRS. COLES: It *is* cold in here.

NARRATOR: Mrs. Coles pulls her stole more closely around her with her gloved hands.

KAY (*Breathlessly*): Then it's Clyde or Banning.

JOHNNY: Banning, do you have any gloves?

BANNING: Certainly. You don't think I'd be fool enough to come here on such a cold night to this freezing, heatless hole without any, do you?

JOHNNY: Mind if I take a look at them?

BANNING: What's the idea, Herald? Why are you stalling? Strange. I can't seem to find them.

CLYDE: I'm glad I still have mine.

KAY: Banning! It was you who murdered Uncle Henry!

BANNING: Why, that's nonsense. Why pick on me? Anyone could have come up the back stairs that night and gotten rid of Henry!

JOHNNY: These paint-stained gloves belong to the murderer, Banning. And you're the only person here who does not have a pair of gloves at this moment.

BANNING: What possible motive would I have, Herald? Tell me that.

JOHNNY: The insurance money. You were in on the theft of the Rembrandt. As Jessica said, it was an inside job. The police have been on to you for weeks, Banning. My company was hoping you'd lead us to the stolen painting.

BANNING: All right, Herald, all right. I admit I was in on the robbery with Henry. It's true he refused to tell me where the painting was hidden, because he wanted the proceeds all for himself. But I didn't kill him.

CLYDE: Now that this is all getting settled, I'm going home. I'm tired. I've been on my feet all day. Goodnight, everyone.

JOHNNY: It's cold out, Clyde. You'd better put your gloves on.

CLYDE: Sure thing. Coldest night we've had this year.

NARRATOR: Nervously, Clyde tries to put the gloves on, but they are far too small for him. Johnny holds out the paint-stained gloves to him.

JOHNNY: Try the murderer's gloves on for size, Clyde.

CLYDE: You're joking, Herald.

JOHNNY: Maybe there's paint on your coat, too, Clyde.

CLYDE: There can't be! I wore a cloak. (*There is a moment of stunned silence from the group.*)

AUNT MAUD: You—Clyde—you, of all people!

ESME: Nice little mousy Clyde! I can't believe it!

CLYDE: Stand back, stand back, all of you!

AUNT MAUD (*Gasping*): He has a gun!

AUNT DEE: Clyde, why did you do it?

CLYDE: I knew Henry had the Rembrandt—one day when I came to Stern's gallery to sell supplies, I overheard Henry and Banning talking. I had to have that painting. Don't you see what it would have meant to me? All my life, always going from studio to studio with art supplies, wanting to be an artist myself and not having the talent. I thought once Henry was out of the way I could find the painting. I wanted one beautiful thing of my very own, just one beautiful thing!

AUNT MAUD: But Clyde, how . . .

CLYDE: I knew Henry had that painting, but I couldn't find it. Night after night I came here, searching!

KAY: Those were the footsteps I heard.

CLYDE: And then I heard about the sale. I was afraid that somehow the Rembrandt would be taken from here—or found. So I came here. I had to find it.

BANNING: And the gloves?

CLYDE: When I saw Herald was onto something, I took your gloves from your pocket, Banning. Don't come any nearer, Herald, I warn you! Stand back.

JOHNNY: Clyde, give yourself up.

CLYDE: Stand back, all of you.

NARRATOR: Clyde backs to the door, still holding the gun. He fumbles. behind him for the doorknob, steps backward, and stumbles over the dummy. Johnny catches him off balance and takes his gun.

JOHNNY: Maud, you'd better get the police. And you stay put, Clyde.

AUNT MAUD: I'll phone right away.

KAY: I don't suppose we'll ever know where Uncle Henry hid the Rembrandt.

JOHNNY: I think Sebastian can tell us that.

KAY: But how?

NARRATOR: Johnny reaches into the back of the dummy and draws out first some straw, and then a rolled-up canvas.

BANNING: My Rembrandt!

JOHNNY: Not so fast, Banning. You and the insurance company have to have a little talk.

BANNING: You can't prove anything.

JOHNNY: Yes, we can. You've admitted it yourself—and now it doesn't matter whether that letter has any incriminating evidence or not.

KAY: Johnny, you're wonderful. Whatever made you think of the picture being hidden in the dummy?

JOHNNY: Remember when we first came in here? There was straw on the floor. I wondered how it got there. Sebastian was the only answer. I knew he must have been opened up for some reason.

KAY: Why didn't I think of that? But now that everything is cleared up, I suppose you won't want to rent the studio after all.

JOHNNY: Oh, but I shall! Suddenly I find I'm tremendously interested in art. Strange, isn't it? I never was before. And don't forget, Kay, you and Dee and Maud will collect the reward for the recovery of the stolen picture.

KAY: Sebastian should really have it.

ESME: Sebastian, you're going to be rich. I must start being nice to you!

THE END

The Mystery at Tumble Inn

This is an exciting play about stolen jewels, a lonely old inn, and some teen-agers who help solve a mystery. It is filled with suspense up to the very end.

Read the play through silently so that you are sure you understand what is happening. Then discuss with your group how each character would sound. There are several different kinds of people in the play, and each one would speak differently.

Would Opal speak like the teen-agers? How would Duke sound? How would you show with your voice the difference between Lovella at the beginning of the play and at the end?

When you have a clear idea of what the characters are like, choose your parts and practice reading the play together. Work on the parts that are difficult, and help each other with words and phrases.

After you have read the play aloud, ask yourselves if it sounded dramatic and suspenseful. If it did not, practice until you are satisfied.

Now you can read the play to the class.

THE MYSTERY AT TUMBLE INN

by Elizabeth Lello

Characters

(4 boys, 5 girls, and a narrator)
NARRATOR
LOVELLA WICKWIRE, *owner of Tumble Inn*
DUKE, *handyman at Tumble Inn*
OPAL, *a maid*
MRS. TUSHINGHAM, *a traveler*
TERRY ⎤
LORI ⎟
GARTH ⎬ *teen-agers*
TOM ⎦
RADIO ANNOUNCER

NARRATOR: On a stormy September evening, in the living room of Tumble Inn, a few miles outside of Des Moines, Duke, the handyman, is reading a newspaper. The furniture is covered with sheets, because the Inn is closed for the season. Suddenly Duke looks up, as though hearing someone's approach. He folds the paper quickly, looks around for a place to hide it, then drops it on the seat of the chair, leaving a corner visible. He is arranging the sheet over the chair back as the maid, Opal, comes in and drops wearily onto the couch.

OPAL: What a storm! (*Pause*) Want to know something, Duke?

DUKE: What?

OPAL: All my muscles are saying "Ouch!"

DUKE: Same here. My charley horses think they're racing at Lincoln Park.

OPAL: Which one'll win?

DUKE: Neither. I'm just going to lead 'em to their stalls. I'm bushed.

OPAL: Don't go, Duke. Come over here and take a load off your feet.

DUKE: O.K. When's Miss Wickwire locking up the Inn?

OPAL: It's closed now. I've stripped all the beds, and the linens and blankets are put away.

DUKE: I hate to have the season end. Seems as though I just came.

OPAL: You did! A week isn't very long. (*Flirts*) Not long enough, Duke.

DUKE: You're a good kid, Opal.

OPAL: Thanks! What're you going to do now the Inn is closed?

DUKE: Move on, I guess. A handyman can always get a job. How about you?

OPAL: I have to go back to Missouri Valley and the farm! (*Suddenly frightened*) Oh-h! Thunder! I hate thunder!

NARRATOR: Duke starts to put his arm around Opal's shoulders, then changes his mind and rests it on the back of the couch.

DUKE: It won't hurt you. Lightning's worse.

OPAL: I hate it, too. Listen, it's pouring cats and dogs.

DUKE: Yeah.

OPAL: What'd you do before you came here?

DUKE: Worked at a couple of hotels in Des Moines and Chicago. (*As an afterthought*) I hopped cars in Los Angeles.

OPAL: Did you ever see any movie stars?

DUKE: No. Los Angeles is a big place, you know.

OPAL: Uh-huh. (*Sighs*) I've never been anyplace, except Des Moines, once. Oh! There goes the thunder again!

NARRATOR: Opal moves closer to Duke. Lovella Wickwire comes into the room, and stops when she sees Duke and Opal. She watches them, smiling, as Duke puts his arm around Opal's shoulders.

THE MYSTERY AT TUMBLE INN 191

DUKE: Thunder never hurt anyone. If you want to know the truth, I ordered it specially.

OPAL (*Pleased but embarrassed*): Oh, Duke.

LOVELLA: Well! Excuse me! Have you seen the Des Moines *Register*, Duke?

DUKE: No, ma'am, not today.

LOVELLA: Here it is! What does it say about the storm? (*Reads*) "Rain to continue."

NARRATOR: Her glance moves over the paper. She looks up, startled, looks at Duke, then back to the paper.

LOVELLA: That's strange!

OPAL: What?

LOVELLA: This picture.

OPAL: Let me see. Why, it does look like you, Duke!

DUKE: Me? Let me see it. Well, sort of, if you stretch your imagination.

OPAL (*Reading aloud*): "Jasper Collins, parolee, sought for the theft of the Vanderlip diamonds." Oh, Duke!

DUKE: Don't look at me like that! (*Laughs*) That's not my picture.

LOVELLA (*Suspiciously*): There's a strong resemblance.

DUKE (*Being very charming*): Miss Wickwire, don't you trust me?

LOVELLA (*Laughing*): I guess so. (*Playfully*) Shame on you for looking like a criminal! (*All laugh.*) Oh dear, there's someone at the door. We can't receive any guests tonight! Duke, just say that the Inn is closed for the season.

NARRATOR: Lovella leaves. Duke goes to the door, as Opal takes another look at the picture in the paper, then tosses it on the couch. Duke opens the door and Mrs. Tushingham rushes in, carrying a small suitcase.

DUKE: I'm sorry, the Inn is closed for the season.

MRS. TUSHINGHAM (*With great excitement*): They're after me! A car has been following me!

OPAL *and* DUKE: What?

MRS. TUSHINGHAM (*Breathlessly*): When I stopped, they stopped, too! A car with several people in it! Here, take my jewel case and put it in the safe!

OPAL: We don't have a safe.

MRS. TUSHINGHAM: No safe? Oh dear! Take a look outside. Are they still there?

NARRATOR: Mrs. Tushingham puts her jewel case in her purse and watches anxiously as Duke opens the door and looks out.

DUKE: I don't see anyone.

NARRATOR: Duke starts to close the door, but it is pushed open from outside by Terry. She comes in, dripping wet, followed by Lori, Tom and Garth.

TERRY: Am I soaked!

GARTH: Sorry to barge in like this.

LORI: Our car barely made it to the bottom of your hill!

TOM: The engine conked out.

TERRY: We were sure glad to see your lights!

MRS. TUSHINGHAM (*Indignantly*): Why were you following me?

GARTH: We weren't.

MRS. TUSHINGHAM: A car behind me stopped every time I stopped.

TOM: It wasn't us!

MRS. TUSHINGHAM: That's very queer!

LORI: What is this place? A hotel?

OPAL: This is Tumble Inn, but we're closed for the season.

LORI: Tumble Inn? That's a pretty good name for it.

TERRY: Lori!

LORI: I think it's groovy! It would be great for a Halloween party!

TOM: Don't mind her! Say, may we use your phone?

DUKE: I'm not in charge. Better call Miss Wickwire, Opal. Oh, here she is now.

OPAL: Oh, Miss Wickwire, these people just came . . .

MRS. TUSHINGHAM: I am Mrs. Cornelius Tushingham.

LOVELLA: Yes?

MRS. TUSHINGHAM: Your man said that your Inn is closed, but I would appreciate it if you would let me stay tonight.

TERRY: The roads are flooded.

LORI: Water's up to my knees!

TERRY: Not that high!

LORI: Almost! Anyway, it's like driving through a lake.

TOM: You can say that again!

LOVELLA: I'm sorry, but we aren't prepared to take guests.

MRS. TUSHINGHAM (*Indignantly*): Surely you'll let me stay until the rain stops! I insist.

LOVELLA: Our rooms are torn up. We've spent the whole day dismantling them.

OPAL: It's O.K., Miss Wickwire. We can fix up a room for her.

DUKE (*Protesting*): What?

OPAL: Have a heart, Duke. We can't send her out in the storm.

DUKE (*Disgusted*): Oh boy!

LOVELLA: All right, if you want to do the work.

MRS. TUSHINGHAM: Thank you, very much.

LOVELLA: Are you young people all together?

GARTH: Yes, we were on our way to a dance.

TOM: May we use your phone? Our car stalled.

LOVELLA: Yes. The phone's on the desk over there. Duke, you and Opal fix up No. 5 for Mrs. Tushingham, please.

DUKE: Yes, ma'am.

LOVELLA: You can register later, Mrs. Tushingham. The room will be ten dollars.

MRS. TUSHINGHAM: Thank you.

NARRATOR: Duke picks up Mrs. Tushingham's suitcase and goes out, followed by Mrs. Tushingham and Opal. Tom goes to the desk and picks up the phone.

TOM: Could you tell me the name of a garage near here?

LOVELLA: Lou's Service Station—but he doesn't stay open this late.

Tom: There's no dial tone.

Garth: Lines must be down.

Lori (*Wailing*): We'll never get to the dance!

Terry: We'll never get home! That's worse.

Garth: I'm supposed to have the car in the garage by one o'clock. If I don't, curtains!

Lori: What are we going to do?

Garth: Stay here until the telephone lines are fixed. That is, if you don't mind, Miss Wickwire.

Lori: At least we're inside a house, even if it is moldy.

Terry: Lori!

Lori (*Realizing her mistake*): Oh! I didn't mean your Inn was moldy, I meant—well (*Gives an embarrassed laugh*)—it's a lovely place.

Lovella (*Patiently*): Tumble Inn is noted for its age, not its beauty. It was here before the Civil War. Runaway slaves were hidden in the passages below.

Terry: They were?

Lovella (*Proudly*): It was part of the Underground Railroad. Tourists come from all over to see it.

Tom (*Impressed*): Could we take a look at the tunnels?

Lovella: No, the season's over. No one is allowed down there without a guide. Now, what am I going to do with you? Your car's stalled and the phone doesn't work. I suppose I'd better have rooms prepared for you. (*Calling*) Duke!

Duke (*As if from a distance*): Yes?

Lovella: Fix up No. 7 for the boys and put the girls in No. 3. Go along down the hall and Duke will take care of you.

Terry: Shouldn't we register, or something?

Lovella: Later. My register's put away.

Terry: How much will the rooms be?

Lovella: We'll discuss that later.

Garth: We're sort of, well, broke, you know, but our folks'll send you a check.

Lovella: That will be fine.

GARTH: Thanks a lot.

NARRATOR: Lovella watches the teen-agers leave, then paces for a moment, thinking. She picks up the newspaper again, looks at the picture and shrugs. She drops the paper on the couch and leaves the room. After a moment, Duke pokes his head in the door and sees that the room is empty. He goes to the window, raises the blind and lowers it, raises it and lowers it. Then he goes to the couch and picks up the paper. Opal returns and speaks to him with mock indignation.

OPAL: Well, Duke!

DUKE: I'm taking a breather.

OPAL: I could use one, too. Mind if I sit here with you? (*Sighs*) Where's the picture that looks like you?

DUKE: I don't know.

OPAL: Let me see. Here it is.

DUKE (*Without interest*): Uh-huh.

OPAL: Duke, it looks just like you!

DUKE (*Menacingly*): I'm a desperate criminal, and you'd better not tell the police, if you know what's good for you! (*Laughs.*) I'm only joking, Opal.

OPAL (*Laughing, relieved*): Stop it, Duke! Let me read what it says. (*She reads.*) "Reward of $1,000 offered for information leading to the arrest of Jasper Collins." Golly! (*Reading*) "Until his disappearance, he was employed by the Vanderlip family as a chauffeur."

DUKE (*Playfully*): Are you going to turn me in?

OPAL: Silly! Is your name really "Duke"?

DUKE: No.

OPAL: What is it?

DUKE (*Looking around*): Sh-h! I never say it out loud. Will you promise to keep it a secret?

OPAL (*Giggling*): Yes.

DUKE: Marmaduke!

OPAL: No! Marmaduke Wainright! Your mother sure had fancy ideas!

DUKE: How would you like to be stuck for life with that name?

OPAL (*Flirting*): Why, Duke, I didn't know you cared!

NARRATOR: Mrs. Tushingham rushes in.

MRS. TUSHINGHAM (*Agitated*): My jewel case is gone!

OPAL: What?

MRS. TUSHINGHAM: My small jewel case! You saw me put it in my purse!

DUKE: And it isn't there now?

MRS. TUSHINGHAM: I told you, it's gone! I was afraid someone would take it from my purse, so I hid it under the mattress in my room.

DUKE: Who could have taken it?

MRS. TUSHINGHAM: Probably one of those young people! You can't trust any teen-ager these days. I want them all searched! Here's Miss Wickwire. She'll take care of it. (*Upset*) Miss Wickwire, there is a thief, or thieves, among us! I had a very valuable piece of jewelry in my purse when I entered this Inn, and now it's gone!

LOVELLA (*Calmly*): I'm sure you have just misplaced it. Opal, are you and Duke finished?

OPAL: Just about. We were just catching our breath.

LOVELLA: Better get those young people taken care of.

DUKE: Yes, ma'am. Come on, Opal.

NARRATOR: Opal follows Duke, who takes the newspaper with him.

MRS. TUSHINGHAM (*Angrily*): This is no small matter, Miss Wickwire. The missing medallion is part of a collection of ancient Egyptian jewelry. You must search everyone in the Inn. (*Pauses*) If you don't, I shall call the police.

LOVELLA: That will be difficult with the phone out of order. Come now, sit down. I'm sure it will turn up. Are you from around here?

MRS. TUSHINGHAM: No, San Francisco. But my husband's

business keeps us traveling all the time. He buys and sells rare art. I should never have let it out of my hands!

LOVELLA: The medallion will turn up. (*Pause*) A dealer in rare art. What a fascinating occupation.

MRS. TUSHINGHAM: After a while the glamor wears off. Traveling becomes very tiresome. My husband is waiting for me in Chicago now. This medallion completes the collection which he is offering for sale. I simply cannot face him without it!

NARRATOR: Garth and Tom come in.

GARTH: May we try the phone again, ma'am?

LOVELLA: Surely.

GARTH: If I could only get through to my dad! It's still dead.

MRS. TUSHINGHAM: Please tell me when it's fixed. I'm going to phone the police! I'm going to my room now.

TOM: What's with her? Try the phone again, Garth.

GARTH: It's no use.

NARRATOR: Terry and Lori join Garth and Tom.

TERRY: Any luck?

TOM: Nope.

LORI: I wanted to go to the dance! Tommy, why don't you stand down on the road and flag someone going by?

TOM: That's bright! Who's going to be driving by in this flood?

LORI: We did! So did that lady—Mrs. Tushingham.

GARTH: The water wasn't so high then. Nobody's on the road now, Lori.

TERRY: Why don't *you* go down to the road, Lori?

TOM: No one's going down, so don't argue. Are there any other homes near here, Miss Wickwire?

LOVELLA: The Bartletts live down the road.

TOM: Their phone might be working.

LOVELLA: We're on the same line.

TOM: Oh.

LOVELLA: You're safe and dry, so be thankful and make the best of it. I'll be upstairs if I'm needed.

TERRY: What'll we do?

LORI: I have my transistor radio. Let's see what the weather report is.

RADIO ANNOUNCER: You are asked to report to the Des Moines police if a dark-haired man in his twenties should apply at your home for a job as chauffeur, gardener, or handyman. Such a man is being sought by the police . . .

TERRY (*Breaking in*): Can't you find any music?

LORI: I'm trying. All I get is static.

NARRATOR: Suddenly, there is a flash of lightning, followed by a crash of thunder, and the lights go out.

TERRY: What happened?

GARTH: The lights went out.

TERRY: I know that!

NARRATOR: As the teen-agers stand in the dark, a loud banging is heard which seems to come from beneath the floor.

TERRY: What's that banging?

LORI: It seems to be coming from underneath the floor. Oh, Tommy!

TOM: Relax. The lights will come on in a minute.

TERRY: Lori, where are you?

LORI: Here. (*Frightened*) Oh, Terry! Someone's down in those passages she told us about!

GARTH: Sh-h! Someone's coming!

TOM (*Bravely*): Who—who's there?

NARRATOR: Duke comes in, wearing a wet slicker. He shines his flashlight around the room.

DUKE: Don't be afraid. It's just me. The lights will be on in a minute. (*Aside*) Darned storm. It wrecks everything.

NARRATOR: The lights come on, and the girls fall on the couch, relieved.

LORI: We thought you were a prowler!

DUKE: I've been outside, taking a look at your car, and I came up through the basement.

TERRY: Were you knocking?

DUKE: Knocking? No. Oh, yes, I was pounding a door shut.

NARRATOR: Suddenly Opal runs in.

OPAL (*Exasperated*): Duke! Where have you been?

DUKE: Checking on the kids' car.

OPAL: I looked everywhere for you. The lights went out.

DUKE: I know.

OPAL: Mrs. Tushingham's hysterical. She thinks someone's after her, personally.

DUKE: I'll see if I can calm the old girl. Here, you kids take my flashlight in case the lights go out again.

TERRY: O.K. Thanks.

OPAL: Come on, Duke. What a night!

TERRY: What a night is right! Try the phone again, Tom.

TOM: O.K. . . . Still dead.

LORI: This is weird! What are we going to do?

TERRY (*Gleefully*): I know what I'm going to do!

LORI: What?

TERRY: Investigate the tunnels!

LORI: You wouldn't dare!

TERRY: Sure I would! I have a flashlight. What is there to be afraid of? Let's go down.

GARTH: Great! Lead the way.

LORI: No, sir! I'm not going down in an old dark tunnel.

TOM: Come on, let's go!

LORI: No! Stop it, Tommy! No!

TOM: O.K., stay then!

NARRATOR: Terry and Garth go out, and Tom starts to follow them.

LORI: Tom! Don't leave me alone!

TOM: Come on, then!

LORI: No.

TOM: Have it your way! I'm going.

LORI (*Calling*): Tommy! I'm afraid! Come back! Please. (*There is no answer.*)

NARRATOR: Duke comes in quickly.

DUKE: What's the matter?

LORI: Well—er—nothing.

DUKE: Why are you yelling?

LORI: The kids went off and left me.

DUKE: Where did they go?

LORI: To the kitchen, I guess. No place. It doesn't matter. I just don't like to be left alone.

DUKE: I'll bet you're not left alone very much, a pretty girl like you.

LORI: Oh, I'm not so popular.

DUKE: Don't tell me that! Any time you're afraid you just call on me. What's the matter, Lori? You aren't afraid of me, are you?

LORI: I—I think I'll go find the others.

NARRATOR: Lori runs off. Duke shrugs and starts to leave as Mrs. Tushingham appears in the doorway.

MRS. TUSHINGHAM: You're just the one I want to see. If I don't find my jewel case and its contents, I want you and the maid to be my witnesses that I had it when I came to this Inn.

DUKE: I can swear you had the case, but it may have been empty for all I know.

MRS. TUSHINGHAM (*Exasperated*): Oh!

DUKE: You didn't open it and show us, did you?

MRS. TUSHINGHAM: No. Why won't that Wickwire woman have everyone searched?

DUKE: You have to be careful when you accuse people, you know. They could turn around and sue for defamation of character.

MRS. TUSHINGHAM: I suppose they could. I'll search my room once more.

DUKE: Yes, do that.

NARRATOR: Mrs. Tushingham leaves the room. Duke checks to see that no one is around, then takes Mrs. Tushingham's jewel case from his inside pocket. He opens it and takes out a medallion on a chain. He looks at it a moment, then returns it to the jewel case. Moving quickly to the window, he holds the shade out cautiously and peeks out. Terry, Lori, Tom and Garth come in, and Duke straightens up and turns quickly. Garth is carrying a newspaper-wrapped package.

DUKE: Where have you been?

TERRY: Down in the dungeons!

DUKE: That's dangerous. The tunnels might have been flooded. Miss Wickwire will be angry if I tell her.

GARTH: We didn't hurt anything.

TOM: Let's see what you found, Garth.

DUKE (*Quickly*): Where did you find that package?

GARTH: Just a minute! Don't get grabby! This little item was way back on a shelf in a cubbyhole. I'm going to unwrap it.

LORI: Maybe it's been there for more than a hundred years, since before the Civil War!

GARTH: The paper's only three months old!

LORI (*Disappointed*): Oh!

DUKE: Anything you found down there belongs to Miss Wickwire, you know.

TOM: Don't worry, we'll give it to her.

GARTH: What do you know! A jewel case!

TERRY: Open it!

TOM: Wow! A necklace! Those look like real diamonds!

TERRY: Oh, Garth! It's gorgeous!

GARTH: Man! These stones didn't come from a dime store!

LORI: Who does it belong to?

DUKE (*With authority*): I'll take the necklace.

GARTH: I don't know about that.

TERRY: Better give it to Miss Wickwire.

DUKE: I'll see that she gets the necklace. Give it to me, please.

GARTH: Well, O.K. Here. There's something funny about this.

DUKE: Thanks. I'll see that it gets to the right party. In the meantime—

NARRATOR: Mrs. Tushingham rushes in, very upset.

MRS. TUSHINGHAM (*Interrupting*): It's definitely disappeared, vanished! Where did you find that jewel case?

TERRY: We found it in the basement. Is it yours?

MRS. TUSHINGHAM: No. My jewel case is much smaller.

LORI: Maybe it grew!

TERRY: Did you lose your jewel case?

MRS. TUSHINGHAM (*Suspiciously*): Yes.

TERRY: This is the only one we found.

MRS. TUSHINGHAM: What's inside?

TOM: A diamond necklace. At least they look like diamonds.

MRS. TUSHINGHAM: May I see?

NARRATOR: As Duke opens the jewel case, Lovella comes to the doorway and watches, unnoticed by the others. Mrs. Tushingham holds up the necklace.

MRS. TUSHINGHAM: Oh! Beautiful! These diamonds are worth a fortune.

LOVELLA: Indeed they are. Give them to me, if you please.

DUKE: I don't think so, Miss Wickwire.

NARRATOR: As he speaks, he reaches inside his coat and draws a gun. All gasp and draw back. Opal comes in and stops, amazed.

OPAL: What's going on?

LOVELLA (*Angrily*): Shut up, Opal.

DUKE (*Calmly*): Hands up, Lovella Wickwire. All the way! That's better, Lovella. One of the best fences in the business, aren't you? Garth, reach in my coat pocket, will you? Go ahead, I just want you to pull out my credentials.

GARTH (*Reading*): "James Kendrick, Des Moines Police Department." This is his picture all right.

LORI: Is he a policeman?

TERRY: Sh-h!

DUKE: Now if you'll reach in my other pocket, you'll find a pair of handcuffs. Put them on her, please.

GARTH (*Hesitating*): Do I have to?

DUKE: Please.

GARTH: Sorry, ma'am.

DUKE: Don't give us any trouble, Lovella. Go on, Garth.

LOVELLA: You rat! You dirty, rotten rat!

DUKE: Now we can relax. At last we've got the fence.

LORI: What's a "fence"?

TOM: Someone who gets rid of stolen goods for thieves.

MRS. TUSHINGHAM: And I walked in here and asked her to hide my medallion! What has she done with it?

DUKE: Here it is.

MRS. TUSHINGHAM: Well! And you called *her* a thief! Thank heavens it's safe!

DUKE: I had to check it out. You might have been her accomplice, you know.

MRS. TUSHINGHAM (*Offended*): Well, thank you very much!

OPAL: What is all this about? The Vanderlip diamonds?

DUKE: There aren't any Vanderlip diamonds. This necklace is part of the famous Roth jewel collection which was stolen several months ago.

OPAL (*Puzzled*): But the newspaper said—

DUKE: That story about the Vanderlip robbery was a fake. It was put in the paper as part of the plan to catch Lovella. I wanted her to think that I was a jewel thief so she would confide in me.

OPAL (*Still puzzled*): I guess I see.

DUKE: Tom, there's a police car behind some bushes at the end of the road. Will you go down and tell the officers in the car that I've caught Lovella with the goods? Tell them to get up here right away.

TOM: Sure! Sir, could we use the police car radio to get help for our car?

DUKE: Certainly.

TOM: Thanks. Hey, it's stopped raining!

LORI: Good! We'll all go with you. Come on, Terry, Garth!

OPAL: Was it the police car that was following Mrs. Tushingham?

DUKE: Yep! This place has been covered for weeks. I'll bet you never suspected that, Lovella.

LOVELLA: You double-crosser!

DUKE: Now, Opal, take Miss Wickwire to her room and help her pack a bag. As soon as the officers get here, she's going on a little trip.

OPAL (*Frightened*): You want *me* to take her? (DUKE *laughs*.)

DUKE: O.K., Opal. I'll come with you to protect you. Let's go, Lovella.

THE END

All Hands on Deck

This is an historical play—about the old sailing ship days in Salem, Massachusetts.

In this play, you will find that there are many different kinds of characters. They will not ,all speak the same way. Read the play silently, and then discuss with the group how you think each character should sound.

The language the girls and their great-aunt use is a little different from the kind of English we speak today. And the pirates and Ramu Singh also speak in a different way.

Choose your parts and read the play aloud together. The play has plenty of action, so everyone should study his or her part carefully and practice the difficult places. You will find some unfamiliar words which you may need help with. Do you know the meaning of the following words?

memsahib	scuttle
schooner	ransom
intrusion	guffaws
genteel	*en garde*
galumphing	hamper

If not, ask your teacher for help with them and any others you do not understand.

Be sure you read without pauses or delays; when you read for the class, you will want everyone to feel the surprise and excitement.

ALL HANDS ON DECK

by Claire Boiko

Characters

(6 boys, 5 girls, and a narrator)

NARRATOR
ASIA BRISTOW ⎫
EUROPA BRISTOW ⎬ *a sea captain's daughters*
INDIA BRISTOW ⎭
AUNT PATIENCE BRISTOW, *their great-aunt*
BETTY APPLE, *the maid*
RAMU SINGH, *a young Indian prince*
CAPTAIN DREAD, *a pirate*
MATEY ⎫
SQUID ⎬ *his men*
NAVAL OFFICER
SAILOR

NARRATOR: On a summer afternoon in 1830, the three Bristow sisters, Asia, Europa, and India, and their great-aunt Patience are sitting in the parlor of Captain Bristow's home in Salem, Massachusetts. Heavy curtains are drawn across the large window that looks out on the harbor. Aunt Patience is seated in her rocking chair, embroidering. The girls are at her feet, each embroidering a section of a small coverlet. As they work, the maid, Betty Apple, is dusting the mantel, bookcases, and a long cradle that stands in a corner of the room.

AUNT PATIENCE (*Reciting*): Up . . . down . . . knot the little knot.

GIRLS (*Reciting in unison*): Up . . . down . . . knot the little knot.

INDIA: Aunt Patience, this is all such a jumble. What *are* we embroidering?

AUNT PATIENCE: Can't you see, India? 'Tis your father's own flag, the very flag his ship carries so bravely at sea. It will be a most appropriate coverlet for your new baby cousin's cradle. Now, India, hold it up so I can see how much you have done.

ASIA: Oh, India! You're holding the flag upside down!

AUNT PATIENCE: That is certainly *not* appropriate for a baby!

INDIA: And why not?

AUNT PATIENCE (*Horrified*): India Bristow! The daughter of a great sea captain should know that a ship's flag hung upside down is a distress signal. Turn it right-side-up at once.

EUROPA (*Laughing*): That's better, India.

AUNT PATIENCE (*Sharply*): That is quite enough, girls. Back to work. Think of it, girls. Your new cousin will rest his head in the cradle you slept in. Betty Apple, did my nephew say when his servants would come to fetch the cradle to his home?

BETTY APPLE: Yes, ma'am. He did, ma'am. They will come this afternoon, ma'am.

AUNT PATIENCE: Gracious, Betty Apple, you need not curtsy so much. You'll make us all seasick.

BETTY APPLE: Yes, ma'am. (*Girls laugh*)

AUNT PATIENCE (*Sharply*): Girls! Young ladies do not guffaw in the parlor. You must try to make a pretty picture. I remember a time in 1776—or was it '77? 'Twas during the Revolution, at any rate, and General Washington said—India! Are you a great gaping fish, to yawn so?

INDIA: No, Auntie. (EUROPA *and* ASIA *giggle.*)

AUNT PATIENCE: Ladies do not yawn in the parlor. Now, while you work, I shall read you tidbits from the *Chronicle*. Ladies should strive to be well informed. (*Shocked*) Oh! Upon my soul! How dreadful!

ASIA: What is it, Auntie? Not bad news about Father's ship, is it?

EUROPA: His ship is not due in Salem until next week.

INDIA: Has there been a storm at sea?

AUNT PATIENCE: No, 'tis not about your father, thank heaven. But none of us is safe. There are pirates abroad! Listen!— (*Reads*) "A wicked deed by foul pirates has been reported to this paper. Some months ago the young prince, Ramu Singh, was taken from his father's palace in Delhi, India, and placed aboard a three-masted schooner. A note demanding ransom was sent to the Raja, his father. It is believed the pirate ship set sail for New England."

GIRLS: New England!

AUNT PATIENCE (*Reading*): "Merchant men and coastal frigates are warned to beware of any unmarked ship resting in hidden coves, and to report any such to the Admiralty at Salem."

BETTY APPLE: Pirates! Oh, I shall stay away from hidden coves.

ASIA: Poor little prince. I hope they find him soon.

AUNT PATIENCE: Indeed. Ah, me. I feel quite exhausted. I think I shall go to my room and take a short nap. My cane, India. Good afternoon, girls. I trust you will finish the coverlet this afternoon and engage yourselves in profitable conversation. During the Revolution we had the most stimulating conversation. I remember General Washington said—or have you heard that tale?

ASIA: Many times, Auntie. 'Twould tire you to tell it again.

AUNT PATIENCE: True. Now, no idle gossip. And no loud guffaws!

GIRLS (*Meekly*): Yes, Auntie.

NARRATOR: The girls bend their heads obediently over their needlework as Aunt Patience leaves the room. When she is out of sight, India flings down the embroidery and does a hornpipe. Europa takes a large spyglass out of the sewing basket, and goes to the window. She opens the spyglass and draws back the curtain to look out at the harbor.

INDIA: Avast, you lubbers! She's shoved off, at long last.

ASIA: Poor Aunt Patience. She means well, truly she does. But she doesn't realize that this is 1830—not 1776. Girls aren't china dolls any more.

INDIA: Indeed not. They are China clippers. Hoist your mainsail!

EUROPA: Hush, India. I can't think. Why, there's a new ship in the harbor. The *Pearl of the Sea*, she's called, under Dutch colors with a new flag. Three-masted, too.

ASIA: How very strange. I know every ship that plies these waters and I never saw that one before.

EUROPA (*Excitedly*): Oh, some men have come ashore from the schooner with a great hamper. Look, Asia!

ASIA: Why, they're heading up our street!

BETTY APPLE: Perhaps they're coming to the inn next door. (*Fearfully*) There's strange goings-on there these days. Why, the serving girl told me how a great, fierce stranger with a black beard took rooms there this week, and he keeps his door locked all the time.

ASIA: Hush, Betty Apple. Don't go worrying us with tales of fierce strangers.

INDIA: Let me look, Asia. (*Pause*) Oh, help! They're coming to our very door with that hamper.

EUROPA: I know! It must be a present from Father. He sent it by a fast ship, to reach us before he came home.

ASIA: Of course. Father has often sent us gifts before he came himself.

NARRATOR: There is a heavy knock on the door, which startles the girls, who draw close together.

EUROPA (*Fearfully*): It *must* be from Father.

MATEY (*Shouting*): Ahoy, inside there—open up! (*Girls gasp.*)

ASIA (*In a loud whisper*): Answer the door, Betty Apple.

NARRATOR: Asia, Europa, and India hide behind the curtains, as Betty Apple walks hesitantly to the door and opens it. Matey and Squid, two rough-looking sailors, push in a large hamper.

MATEY (*Roughly*): Be you the serving girl?

BETTY APPLE: I am.

SQUID: Here's the hamper, then. Hands off, if you know what's good for you.

BETTY APPLE: Oh! You're rude, you are.

MATEY: Now, now, Squid. Don't upset the maid. 'Tis only odds and ends, girl. Come on, Squid. We've done our bit. Now let's shove off.

NARRATOR: Matey and Squid leave, and the girls come out from behind the curtains and gather around the hamper.

ASIA: Are you all right, Betty Apple? I never saw such rude sailors. I shall report them to Father. Odds and ends, indeed!

EUROPA: Open it, Asia. It's Paris hats, I know it!

INDIA: No, it's miles and miles of Chinese silk. Oh, hurry, Asia.

ASIA: On a count of three I'll open it. Then we'll all see at the same time. Ready? One . . . Two . . . Three . . .

NARRATOR: Asia throws back the lid of the hamper. Ramu Singh, wearing a turban and a brocaded tunic, jumps up, his hands over his face. The girls gasp in amazement.

INDIA: Upon my soul, it's a boy. A real, live boy!

EUROPA: What a jolly idea of Father's to send us a playmate. Do come out, boy. Let us look at you.

RAMU SINGH: Please . . . please to help me.

ASIA (*In dismay*): This is no ordinary boy!

INDIA: Of course not. Father wouldn't send us an ordinary boy.

ASIA: He's wearing a turban . . . jeweled rings . . . silks. Boy, what is your name?

RAMU SINGH: Ramu Singh is my name, memsahib.

ASIA: Ramu Singh! The Indian prince Auntie just read about.

EUROPA: 'Tis unbelievable!

INDIA: 'Tis marvelous!

RAMU SINGH: I beg you, memsahib, hide me! I am in great danger. Those men who brought me here are pirates. They have kept me prisoner for many months. Let me stay with you. Please!

INDIA: Of course you may stay with us. But, Asia, why do you suppose those men left him here, at our house?

BETTY APPLE: I think I know, miss. 'Twas a mistake. He was meant to be left next door, at the inn. With that strange, fierce man.

ASIA: That must be it. And if it's true, we have to work quickly. Those seamen will come back here for the prince when they discover their mistake. Europa, go to the window and keep a sharp lookout. Now, Betty Apple, you put some books in the hamper and close it fast. Perhaps those seamen will take it without looking too closely.

NARRATOR: Betty Apple hurries to the bookcase, takes an armload of books and dumps them into the hamper, then closes it.

ASIA: Now, where to hide you, little prince?

INDIA: In the grandfather clock?

ASIA: Too small.

INDIA: In Auntie's room, under the bed?

ASIA: No, if Auntie wakens, there will be a most dreadful fuss.

EUROPA (*Gasping*): They're coming back, and they're bringing a great fierce man with them. He has a beard black as ink!

RAMU SINGH: It is Captain Dread! Oh, he is a wicked man, memsahib. He is a shark who makes men walk the plank or sets them adrift without oars. Hide me! Hide me!

BETTY APPLE: Oh, Miss Asia, they are at the door!

INDIA: I have an idea. Come, Ramu, lie down in the cradle. Don't move. I'll stay by you.

NARRATOR: Ramu climbs into the cradle and India covers him with a blanket. The girls then sit down and take up their sewing. Europa rocks the cradle. The pirates knock loudly on the door.

BETTY APPLE: Oh, they'll break the door down!

ASIA: Answer it, Betty Apple, quickly.

BETTY APPLE: Oh, Miss Asia! My knees don't want to hold me up. (*In a quavering voice*) Come in, if it please you.

NARRATOR: Captain Dread swaggers in and makes a low bow.

Matey and Squid come in behind him and stand with their arms folded.

CAPTAIN DREAD: Pardon this intrusion, ladies. I be the captain of the schooner you may see from your window—*Pearl of the Sea*. These are Dutch seamen come to help me fetch a hamper they left here by mistake. Just odds and ends, it is.

ASIA (*Coolly*): Your hamper is here, Captain. Pray take it as soon as you can. We are ladies and we do not care for odds and ends in our parlor.

CAPTAIN DREAD: Up with it, you scurvy dogs. When we are outside, the cat-o'-nine-tails will give you a lesson in reading addresses.

NARRATOR: Squid and Matey start to push the hamper toward the door. Matey stumbles and overturns the hamper, spilling out the books.

MATEY: Shiver me timbers! It's full of books!

GIRLS: Oh!

CAPTAIN DREAD (*Unpleasantly*): So it is. An educated family of genteel ladies, I see. And to think I was planning to say farewell to these learned lassies. Now, Matey and Squid, what do you say we settle down here for a while? Perhaps they can teach us something. Tell me, my pretty little dears, what do you know about princes, eh? What have you done with our property, eh?

ASIA (*Bravely*): Captain, I must ask you to leave. I do not like the tone of your voice.

CAPTAIN DREAD (*Snarling*): Oh, you don't, don't you? I'm Captain Dread, the pirate, and these are my men. Don't any of you cross me, or you'll find your bones feeding the fishes. My ship is the terror of the sea and she flies the Jolly Roger. Now, where is the boy? (*The girls remain silent.*) Matey, search the room, and you, Squid, guard the door. I'll give you ladies just five minutes. If you don't produce my property by then, I'll *scuttle* ye!

BETTY APPLE: Oh, I don't want to be scuttled!

MATEY: What's this in the cradle? A baby! Now isn't that sweet.

INDIA: Stay away from our baby!

MATEY: Aw, now I mean him no harm. I just want to chuck him under his little chin.

INDIA: Stop! Do you know what happened to the last man who chucked him under the chin? The baby bit him!

MATEY (*Indignantly*): All right, then. It's a sad world when little babies are unfriendly. Here's another room, off here.

ASIA: 'Tis our great-aunt's room. I pray you, do not disturb her. She is over eighty and she'll do you no harm.

CAPTAIN DREAD: Leave her. If she gives us trouble, Squid can take care of her.

SQUID: Hist, Cap'n. I can hear voices outside.

CAPTAIN DREAD: One of you girls go to the window and see who it is. If they are coming here, tell them to go away.

NARRATOR: The girls hesitate, then Europa runs to the window, taking the coverlet they have been sewing.

EUROPA: 'Tis servants from my uncle's house. They've come for—for—a piece of furniture that was promised to him.

CAPTAIN DREAD: Wave them away. Go on. Do as I say.

NARRATOR: Europa looks at the coverlet in her hands, then leans out the window and waves it.

EUROPA (*Calling out*): You, down there. Go away. 'Tis not ready. Come back tomorrow.

NARRATOR: When she turns back, she no longer has the coverlet.

BETTY APPLE (*In a loud whisper*): Miss Europa, the coverlet— what have you done with it?

EUROPA: Sh-h! I can't tell you now.

CAPTAIN DREAD: You two. Stop that whispering.

BETTY APPLE: Oh, yes, sir. Yes, sir. I'll just get on with the dusting.

RAMU SINGH: Ah-h-h-choo!

MATEY: What was that?

INDIA (*Quickly*): 'Twas just the baby. Betty Apple's dusting made him sneeze. (RAMU SINGH *sneezes again.*)

CAPTAIN DREAD: The baby, heh? What a very large sneeze—for such a very small baby.

NARRATOR: Captain Dread pulls the blanket from Ramu Singh. The captain seizes him and pulls him from the cradle.

RAMU SINGH: Help, help, memsahib!

CAPTAIN DREAD: Some baby, eh, mates? Worth a prince's ransom. It's back to the ship with you, boy, and this time I'll put you in the hold with the bilge water. Matey, put him in the hamper.

SQUID: What'll we do with the girls, Cap'n?

CAPTAIN DREAD: Take them with us. They know too much, so we can't leave them here to set the Navy after us. We'll set sail with the tide in an hour, and once we're on the high seas (*Laughs evilly*), we'll take care of them.

MATEY: The plank, Cap'n?

CAPTAIN DREAD: Aye. The dear little ladies will walk the plank. Now, ladies, move quickly, all of you. Act as if we were your kindly old uncles, taking you for a stroll. Put the prince in the hamper, Matey.

NARRATOR: Aunt Patience, cane in hand, enters the room briskly, and looks at the scene, bewildered. Ramu Singh quickly hides behind the hamper.

AUNT PATIENCE: Girls, what is going on out here? I heard loud guffaws. Oh! Who are these gentlemen?

INDIA: Oh, Auntie, Auntie, they aren't *gentlemen!*

GIRLS: They're pirates!

AUNT PATIENCE (*Gasping*): Pirates! In my parlor? Oh, mercy!

ASIA: Auntie, please don't faint. Not now.

AUNT PATIENCE (*Recovering herself*): Faint? Of course I shan't faint. I didn't faint during the Revolution when General Burgoyne put a cannon right on my front lawn. Here, you pirates, you're trespassing. Begone!

CAPTAIN DREAD: Put that cane down, old lady, or I'll scuttle ye.

AUNT PATIENCE: Girls, remember that you are daughters of a fighting sea captain. Battle stations, girls. All hands on deck and don't give up the ship! *En garde*, pirate!

NARRATOR: Aunt Patience, using her cane as a sword, begins to fence with Captain Dread, who backs away. Betty Apple thrusts her feather duster into Matey's face and backs him into a corner while the girls surround Squid, push him into the rocker and quickly tie him with ribbons from the sewing box. Aunt Patience forces the captain to the wall and pins him against it with her cane.

CAPTAIN DREAD: This old lady fences like a French champion!

AUNT PATIENCE: Of course. 'Twas Lafayette himself who taught me, back in 1776—or was it '77? Now stay there or I'll scuttle *you!*

NARRATOR: A naval officer and a sailor run in.

OFFICER: Ahoy, Miss Bristow, the Navy is here.

AUNT PATIENCE: And just in time. We have three pirates ripe and ready for the brig. Oh, I haven't had such a jolly time since the Boston Tea Party.

OFFICER: Upon my soul—Captain Dread. And Matey and Squid. Congratulations, ladies. You've captured the three most notorious pirates since Captain Kidd. Ho, seaman, put them in irons.

SAILOR: Aye, aye, sir.

CAPTAIN DREAD: One favor, one favor I beg ye.

OFFICER: What's that?

CAPTAIN DREAD: If it's all the same to you, don't tell anyone how we were captured.

MATEY: That's right. We'll never live it down. The "terrors of the sea" we used to be called—and now look at us.

SQUID: Done in by little girls and an old lady. Oh, the shame of it!

OFFICER: Ha, ha! But of course I'll tell the tale of these gallant ladies. You invited yourselves here, now take the consequences. Seaman, stow them in the brig.

SAILOR: Aye, aye, sir.

OFFICER: 'Twas a lucky thing we sighted your distress signal, ladies.

AUNT PATIENCE: Distress signal? What distress signal?

OFFICER: The ship's flag, hung upside down from your window —the seamen's distress signal.

EUROPA: I did it, Auntie.

BETTY APPLE: Oh, Miss Europa, what a clever notion!

INDIA: If you please, sir, we have an even bigger surprise than those old pirates. You can come out of hiding now, Prince.

RAMU SINGH: I am here, memsahib.

INDIA: May I introduce Prince Ramu Singh, formerly of Delhi, India, now the guest of the Bristows of Salem?

AUNT PATIENCE: A prince! Oh, nicely introduced, dear India.

OFFICER: Ramu Singh. It is! Upon my word, the entire Admiralty has been scouring the coast for this child. Are you all right?

RAMU SINGH: I am most happy now. Thank you, memsahibs. I will not forget you when I return to Delhi. My father, the Raja of Singh, will reward you with the greatest gift a Raja can give.

INDIA: Oh, lovely. We adore gifts. What might it be, pray?

RAMU SINGH: The largest—

GIRLS (*Eagerly*): Yes?

RAMU SINGH: And the noblest—

GIRLS: What? What?

RAMU SINGH (*Triumphantly*): Sacred elephant! (*Girls squeal with joy.*)

AUNT PATIENCE: An *elephant?* Mercy, mercy! A great galumphing elephant? Girls! You are not to let that elephant *in my parlor!* (*All laugh.*)

THE END

Treasure Island

This story is a tale of hidden treasure and danger. You may already know it. This play adaptation includes the most exciting scenes from the book.

The pirates do not speak ordinary English. In the play, many of the words are spelled to show the way they should sound. Everyone in the group should read the play through silently to be sure each one knows their meanings. Each member of the group should practice reading aloud these lines of Long John Silver:

"Ye'll be sicker of it afore I give the word to mutiny. Ye'll work proper, speak soft, and keep sober. When we get to the Island, then we'll get the map—and the treasure."

"An honest sea cap'n sticks in me gullet. Why, I'll break his bones with me bare hands!"

"The devil himself would have been afeared to go to sea with us."

Choose the best one for the part of Silver, then assign the other parts. This is an exciting play, so be sure to keep it moving. The narrator and Jim explain much of what is happening, so they should read their lines clearly and distinctly.

Your teacher may like to have you read for the class when you are ready, and then the class can discuss the people and events in the play.

TREASURE ISLAND

by Robert Louis Stevenson
adapted by Marjorie Ann York

Characters

(*9 boys and a narrator*)
NARRATOR
JIM HAWKINS
LONG JOHN SILVER
MORGAN
HANDS
DOCTOR LIVESEY
CAPTAIN SMOLLETT
SQUIRE TRELAWNEY
BEN GUNN
SAILOR

SAILOR (*Singing loudly*):
Fifteen men on the Dead Man's chest—
Yo-ho-ho, and a bottle of rum!
Drink and the devil had done for the rest—
(*Fading*) Yo-ho-ho, and a bottle of rum!
NARRATOR: *Treasure Island* . . . by Robert Louis Stevenson. And here's Jim Hawkins, cabin boy aboard the *Hispaniola*—bound out of England for Treasure Island.
JIM: I really started this whole adventure. You see, I was given a map by an old sea dog—the treasure map of the famous pirate, Flint. So I'll get one-third of the treasure along with my friends and partners, Doctor Livesey and Squire Trelawney.
NARRATOR: Between them, the three partners bought and out-

fitted a schooner, the *Hispaniola*. They were lucky to find a fine sailor, Captain Smollett, to navigate the ship for them. And they hired a crew—a rough lot, but they gave no trouble, until a few things began to happen.

JIM: Our mate, Mr. Arrow, fell overboard one dark night. Then a few weeks later I went below to get an apple from one of the barrels. It was after sundown, and supplies were so low, I couldn't see into the barrel, so I climbed inside it to take my pick. Just as I got inside I heard the voices of Hands and Morgan, two of the crew . . . and Long John Silver, our one-legged cook . . . coming toward me.

SILVER: And that's what I say. So what's ailing ye now, Morgan?

MORGAN: We're sick of holding off, Silver.

SILVER: Ye'll be sicker of it afore I give the word to mutiny. Ye'll work proper, speak soft, and keep sober. When we get to the Island, then we'll get the map—and the treasure.

HANDS: Will they just sit while we cut their throats and take the map?

MORGAN: We crewmen took a vote. Didn't we, Hands?

SILVER: Shiver me timbers! You mean there was a fo'c's'le council?

HANDS: Aye, Silver. Fo'c's'le council. Pirate rights. We know the rules.

SILVER: I make the rules! First one agin them and I'll open him with me knife. We'll do as I say. At the Island, we'll slit every honest throat aboard. Then the map is ours and we'll take this ship home piled with treasure. I claim only one thing—Cap'n Smollett. An honest sea cap'n sticks in me gullet. Why, I'll break his bones with me bare hands!

MORGAN: You're a man, Long John. Good as Cap'n Flint.

SILVER: Aye. Flint's crew were always the roughest. The devil himself would have been afeared to go to sea with us. And Flint was the flower of the lot. Now I'm Flint—I'm taking over where he left off.

SAILOR (*Calling from distance*): Land ho! Land ho!

NARRATOR: The plotters went running up the ladder. Everyone was rushing around the decks. Jim climbed out of the barrel and ran forward to report to his friends. In the captain's quarters Jim told the story to the doctor, the squire, and the captain. The doctor was the first to speak.

DOCTOR: What do you suggest, gentlemen?

JIM: We just have to give them the map, Doctor Livesey. They'll slit our throats for it, won't they, Captain Smollett?

CAPTAIN: Indeed they will, lad. It breaks my bones to command a ship of pirate scum.

SQUIRE: I agree with you, Captain. Now that they know there's treasure—

DOCTOR: But they don't know where, Squire Trelawney.

JIM: Why not give 'em a map—any map? By the time they figure it out we could have the treasure and be gone.

DOCTOR: Capital idea, Jim. We could mark up our sailing chart showing the treasure on the opposite side of the Island.

CAPTAIN: You've hit it! We'll be gone by the time they learn the difference.

SQUIRE: I say we try it. We've a few faithful hands aboard. And we'll beat Silver's crew at their own trickery.

DOCTOR: We may as well force the issue right now, gentlemen, and save ourselves a neck slitting.

CAPTAIN (*Shouting*): Mister Anderson, pipe all hands. (*In his normal voice*) We'll go out together and face that bunch. But stick close, gentlemen, shoulder to shoulder. And don't turn your backs to the likes of them.

NARRATOR: Led by the captain, the friends went up on deck where the crew had assembled.

CAPTAIN: My lads, this is the place we've been sailing to. You've done good duty aloft and below. And to show appreciation, I'm passing out double rations of grog.

SILVER (*Loudly*): Double grog and more!

CAPTAIN (*Loudly*): What say you, Silver? Come up and speak out.

SILVER: We'll take the grog and the treasure.

CAPTAIN: What treasure?

SILVER: Don't fool with me. We know this be a treasure ship. We want our share. You'll not stand in our way.

CAPTAIN: Mutiny, eh? I'll have you in irons.

SILVER: Not so, I say. The crew is with me.

MORGAN *and* HANDS: Aye!

CAPTAIN: Oh? Well, speak your mind.

SILVER: Ye have a map showing where the treasure is hid. We want it.

CAPTAIN: I'll see you stretched from a yardarm first!

SILVER: Ye'll not live to see it! Forward, lads!

DOCTOR: Wait! If we give you the map, will you take an oath you'll not harm us?

SILVER: The map, Doctor Livesey. Then I'll promise.

DOCTOR: Give it to them, captain.

CAPTAIN: Why I'd rather—well, if you say so, doctor. Before I hand it over to you, Silver, will you and your men promise not to harm anyone aboard?

SILVER: Aye. Hand it over.

CAPTAIN: And your men?

SILVER: They're with me.

CAPTAIN: Well, here's your map. Much good it may do you.

HANDS: We have the map. Now let's slit their throats.

SILVER: Back, ye fool! I've a better plan. No doubt ye know, Cap'n Smollett, we were Flint's crew. That being the way the wind blows, we do nothing that's not our right. That gold on the Island is rightly ours. I'd let yer blood for pleasure. But the gold is more important. We'll have that afore we slit yer throats.

CAPTAIN: Stand back, I warn you!

SILVER: Ha! Ye've only a handful of men. I've nineteen on my side.

SQUIRE: You'll hang, you scoundrel!

SILVER: I think different, ye landlubbing squire.

SQUIRE: You may win now, but you'll hang.

SILVER: Not while I can make a trade.

CAPTAIN: A trade? What's in your scurvy mind now?

SILVER: Belay that gab! It's the young 'un. His life for mine.

DOCTOR: Jim? You wouldn't dare!

SILVER (*Laughing*): I'll not kill him, doctor. At least not now. But come with yer hanging talk and I'll slit him for sure.

SQUIRE: You can't. You wouldn't. Jim's only a boy.

SILVER: He's only a hostage. Get over here, young lad.

DOCTOR: Leave the boy alone.

SILVER: He'll not be harmed less'n he doesn't run here fast.

JIM: I'm not afraid, Doctor Livesey.

SILVER: All right, Hawkins, ye go with us.

CAPTAIN: The saints preserve you if harm comes to that lad, John Silver.

NARRATOR: Jim boarded the long boat and went ashore with the pirates. They landed near a bunch of trees and Jim hid there while Silver and his men beached the boat. Then he ran far into the woods. Suddenly Jim ran into something that looked like a great white shaggy animal. It turned out to be a man—Ben Gunn, a buccaneer marooned years ago on the Island by Long John Silver.

JIM: I told Ben Gunn my story. He said Silver was a bad one and agreed to help us against the pirates. He wanted me to promise that we'd take him back to England with us. I couldn't speak for my friends, but I told him they were fair-minded men. And I told him that we'd need his help to sail the ship home. Suddenly we heard gunfire.

BEN: Do ye hear the firing? It's coming from Flint's Stockade. He built the fort when he buried the treasure.

JIM: My friends must be in trouble. Can you show me the way to the Stockade?

BEN: Follow me.

NARRATOR: Ben led Jim through the trees to the clearing at the edge of the Stockade. When they got there, they saw that the Union Jack was waving in the breeze and Jim's friends were defending the fort against the pirates.

JIM: Ben decided to hide among the trees until I found out if my friends would take him in. I ran like mad for the Stockade. Doctor Livesey saw me coming and let me through the heavy gates.

DOCTOR: Praise heaven you're safe, Jim!

CAPTAIN: Good work, lad! How did you manage to escape Silver?

JIM: I hid soon as we beached. They never even missed me. Then I met a marooned man. Said he was Ben Gunn. He knows a way to help us against the pirates. Why, he used to sail with them.

SILVER (*From a distance*): Ahoy, log house, ahoy!

CAPTAIN: That swine Silver himself—

DOCTOR: With a flag of truce.

CAPTAIN: Watch for trickery, men. Shoot if you spot anyone moving.

SILVER (*Calling*): Flag o' truce. Silver to come aboard and make terms.

CAPTAIN (*Shouting*): Any tricks will be on your side, Silver. Hold your fire, men, and one of you help him over the stockade.

SILVER (*Calling*): As ye say, Cap'n Smollett. (*Closer*) Morning, gentlemen, my respects. Well, Jim, we missed ye, lad.

DOCTOR: Enough of that! What do you want?

SILVER: That was a nice trick, sending me off with a fake map.

CAPTAIN: Fake map?

SILVER: Don't act innocent. You've the Stockade, but we have the ship. Just look yonder and see the skull and crossbones at the masthead. (*Pauses*) I though that would make ye look a bit different. (*Laughs*) We not only have the ship but the stores and the ammunition, too. And we want the treasure. We aim to get that treasure.

CAPTAIN: Along with our lives, no doubt.

SILVER: No, we'll leave ye them. They're worthless to us. Just give us the map, and we'll give you a choice. Come along with us, and once the treasure is found, I'll give ye my word of honor to clap you somewhere safe ashore.

CAPTAIN (*With sarcasm*): Naturally, you're to be trusted!

SILVER: If that's not to your fancy, then ye can stay here. We'll divide stores with ye, man for man. I'll give ye my word as before to speak to the first ship I sight and send 'em to pick ye up. Handsomer talking ye couldn't look to find. (*Raising voice*) And I hope all hands here overhear my words.

CAPTAIN: Is that all?

SILVER: Every last word, by thunder! Refuse and ye've seen the last of me but musket balls.

CAPTAIN: Very good. Now hear me. If you'll come up, one by one, unarmed, I'll engage to clap you all in irons and take you home to a fair trial in England.

SILVER: Ye dare make terms!

CAPTAIN: I've flown my sovereign's colors and I'll see you all with Davy Jones before I'll sail under the Jolly Roger. You can't find the treasure, and there's not a man among you fit to sail the ship. I tell you so and they're the last good words you'll get from me. By Heaven, I'll put a bullet in your back when next I meet you.

SILVER: Before an hour's out, I'll stove in yer old blockhouse.

CAPTAIN (*Angry*): Bundle out of here, hand over hand, double quick, Silver!

SILVER (*Fainter*): Before the hour's out . . .

CAPTAIN: Double quick, I say.

SILVER: I'm going. (*As if from a distance*) Just remember, them that die'll be the lucky ones.

NARRATOR: The pirates launched a furious attack at once.

But it was over soon. Jim and his friends had the best shots inside the fort, so they beat the pirates off. Something had to be done fast, though. If only they could reach the *Hispaniola* and beach it where the pirates couldn't find it!

JIM: The more I thought about it, the more I figured I could do it. Ben Gunn had told me about a boat he'd made. With that I could reach the ship, cut her adrift and let her go ashore where she fancied. I decided to slip out without telling anyone my plan.

NARRATOR: Jim found Ben Gunn's boat hidden on the beach. The tide was with him so he made it to the *Hispaniola* quickly. He cut her rope and the vessel swung free. She turned on her keel, spinning across the current.

JIM: I was almost swamped. Then my little boat lurched and changed course. I was whirled along in the wake of the *Hispaniola*. The schooner turned twenty degrees and found a quiet bay. My little boat continued to be beaten to and fro upon the billows. For hours I was showered by flying spray until a great weariness grew upon me. I lay in my sea-tossed bed and dreamed of home.

NARRATOR: It was day when Jim awoke, tossing at the southwest end of Treasure Island. There was a great swell upon the ocean. But he was very near land so he sat up and paddled. Then the sea mounted and pulled him toward the *Hispaniola* in her bay. Lapping alongside her, Jim crawled along the bowsprit and tumbled headfirst on her deck.

JIM: The few pirates left aboard were all below. I struck the Jolly Roger and hoisted the Union Jack. The ship was ours again! A few minutes later I had her sailing easily before the wind along the coast of Treasure Island. I headed her straight for the shore. She hit . . . staggered . . . and ground in the sand. I jumped clear and hurried to tell my friends. It was very dark, but with the moon to help, I sighted a campfire. Surely that would be Ben Gunn. I ran joyfully toward it.

SILVER (*Calling*): Who goes?

JIM (*In a whisper*): Silver! I tried to retreat and not even breathe, but it was too late.

SILVER: Come here, I say! Hands, go fetch him and bring your prize to the firelight. Let's see what ye caught. (*Closer*) Well, bless my bones—Jim Hawkins. (*Laughs*) Come to call, lad? Now that's right friendly. So ye come to join us now we got the real map.

JIM: You—the real map?

SILVER: Aye, lad. Ye sound like a parrot. Doctor Livesey did a bit of trucing.

JIM: He wouldn't!

SILVER: Batten down yer hatches til yer spoken to! As I was saying, the doctor came to terms. Says he, "Cap'n Silver, let's bargain. We're beaten. You can have the map." Silver has beaten ye, lad!

JIM: Have you? Where's the *Hispaniola*? It's gone.

SILVER: By thunder, ye lie!

MORGAN: Enough of this! I'm for slitting Hawkins.

SILVER: Avast there, Morgan! Shiver me timbers! Where's the ship? Right out there on the—Why, I can't see it on the water.

JIM: You won't, either. The ship is lost. So's the treasure. So are all of you. Marooned here with us. And I did it all.

SILVER: Why, you—I'll take a cutlass to you, I will!

HANDS: Run the young 'un through.

SILVER: Avast, ye swabs, I say. Maybe ye think you're cap'n here. By the powers, I'll teach ye better. Take a cutlass, him that dares, and I'll see the color of his insides. I'm the best man here by a long sea mile, and I like the boy. He's more a man than any pair of rats of you.

MORGAN: Your pardon, sir. You're pretty free with the rules.

SILVER: Say it all, Morgan. Pipe up or lay to.

MORGAN: This crew's dissatisfied. We have rights. I say you be cap'n, but I claim my right to step outside for a council.

HANDS: Aye! Fo'c's'le council!

SILVER: Run, ye scurvy dogs. Council if you like. Ye don't scare Long John.

JIM (*Whispering*): What's happening?

SILVER (*Whispering*): You're within a plank of death, lad, and so am I. They'll slip me the Black Spot for sure.

JIM: The Black Spot?

SILVER: Aye. That's a summons. It means the cap'n has to do the crew's bidding. You're my last card, Jim Hawkins, and by the living thunder, I'm yours. I'll save my witness and you'll save my neck.

JIM: You mean all's lost?

SILVER: Aye, by gum. I do. Ship's gone—neck's gone—that's it. I see no schooner. I'm tough, but I've given out. That lot at council are fools and cowards. I'll save your life, but tit for tat, Jim. Ye'll save Long John from swinging.

JIM: I'll do what I can. They're coming.

MORGAN: Here be our decision at council.

SILVER: Well, step up, Morgan. Hand it over. I know the rules, I do. Ah, the Black Spot! I thought so. Where'd ye get the paper? (*Pauses*) Ye fools! What dog of ye cut a Bible? 'Tisn't lucky. Ye'll swing for this.

HANDS: Belay that talk, John Silver. This crew tipped ye the Black Spot at full council. You're deposed.

SILVER: The Black Spot's not worth a biscuit. I have the map and the boy as hostage. I'm still cap'n.

HANDS: We want Flint's map. Then we find the treasure. And we're gonna dig for it now.

SILVER: So that's it, Hands. Well, shovels it is then. We'll find the treasure. Hawkins, here, will lead us to the ship or he'll walk the plank for it. Are ye with me? (*The pirates cheer.*)

JIM: The pirates were now in good humor. Picking up shovels, we went treasure hunting. Silver led the way. They dragged me along as they struggled through the trees. But as we got near the treasure the crew began to sing and leap to and fro. Morgan found the spot first and let out a great yell.

MORGAN (*Angry*): There's a hole here already. The treasure's gone. There's nothing here but a piece of old wood with Flint's name on it. We'll keelhaul ye for this, Silver. Ye and Hawkins! I'll have the lad's heart.

SILVER: Avast! First scum of ye makes a move to me'll be sorry. I'll split ye with me cutlass.

DOCTOR (*Calling*): Don't anyone make a move!

JIM: Doctor Livesey! Am I glad to see you! And Ben Gunn.

SILVER: By thunder—Ben Gunn!

GUNN: Aye, Mister Silver. The same ye marooned long ago.

DOCTOR: Are you all right, lad?

JIM: I am now, sir.

SILVER: Aye, doctor. Ye came in about the nick for me and Hawkins.

DOCTOR: No one addressed you, Silver. I'd not care if we found you dead.

SILVER: That's unkind, seeing that I saved the boy's life.

DOCTOR: Is that true, Jim?

JIM: It is, sir.

DOCTOR: So you double-crossed your crew, Silver.

SILVER: In a manner of speaking, no. I just like the lad.

DOCTOR: And especially your own neck, no doubt.

JIM: I promised to save him from swinging, doctor.

DOCTOR: So that's it. Well, as much as I hate to do it, you're free, Silver.

JIM: That's tit for tat, Silver. But how did you ever find me, doctor?

DOCTOR: We've Ben Gunn to thank for that. He's been watching.

JIM: But the treasure's gone.

GUNN: Aye. I have it. 'Tis how I spent my time. Digging it up.

SILVER: You have the treasure?

GUNN: 'Tis what I said. The doctor's seen it.

SILVER: Ben—Ben, old shipmate—to think it's ye that done me.

GUNN: Aye. Pretty well, too, I think.

SILVER: But, Ben, old friend—

GUNN: 'Tis not the way ye said it afore. Jim and the doctor are me friends. I know ye not at all, Mister Silver.

NARRATOR: So they returned to the *Hispaniola*. Jim's friends had found it and were standing guard. Captain Smollett wanted to put Silver in irons. Jim told them about his promise but they didn't care. Doctor Livesey talked the captain and the squire into letting Jim keep his promise. For saving Jim's life, Silver was let aboard as a free man. The captain just ignored him, but Squire Trelawney had to speak his mind.

SQUIRE: John Silver, you are a terrible villain and an impostor, but I'm told I am not to prosecute you, so I will not.

SILVER: Thank ye kindly, sir.

SQUIRE: I dare you to thank me! You should swing from a yardarm. Now stand back.

NARRATOR: Those were the last words anyone aboard the *Hispaniola* spoke to Long John Silver. Three days later the gold, a huge fortune, was all aboard. They weighed anchor, and before noon the highest rock of Treasure Island had sunk into the blue round of the sea.

JIM: In a few days Long John Silver escaped in one of the boats, taking a sack of coins with him. But it was well worth it to get rid of him. We finally landed in Bristol. Ben went through his part of the treasure like water. Captain Smollett retired from the sea. The Squire, Doctor, and I settled comfortably back to our lives, glad to be rid of that accursed Island. All is fine but at night when I hear the surf pounding on the coast, I sit upright in bed and hear far off the sound of Flint's men and their cutthroat song.

SAILOR (*Singing*):
Fifteen men on a dead man's chest—
Yo-ho-ho, and a bottle of rum!

THE END

Sherlock Holmes and the Red-Headed League

Sherlock Holmes is one of the most famous detectives ever to appear in fiction. This play is taken from one of the best-known stories about him.

After you read the play to yourself, discuss with the group the crime Holmes solves. Did you understand the clues, or, like Watson, did you have to wait until the end for an explanation?

What kind of a person is Watson? How does Holmes treat him?

Does it matter that you cannot really see the red-haired Mr. Wilson? Do the words make him seem real without your seeing him?

Choose parts. Read the play aloud. How did you sound? Did you understand all of the words? This play should move along, with no unnecessary pauses. Ask yourself if you made your part as interesting as possible. Did you really *sound* like the character you are playing?

If you think you can improve with more practice, read the play again. Then try reading it into a tape recorder and listening to the tape. How did you sound? Ask your teacher if you can read for the class.

SHERLOCK HOLMES AND
THE RED-HEADED LEAGUE

by A. Conan Doyle
adapted by Lewy Olfson

Characters

(6 boys and a narrator)
NARRATOR
SHERLOCK HOLMES
DR. WATSON
JABEZ WILSON
VINCENT SPAULDING
DUNCAN ROSS
LANDLORD

NARRATOR: Dr. Watson, opening the door of Sherlock Holmes' Baker Street rooms, finds Holmes seated beside a man with the reddest hair he has ever seen. . . .

HOLMES: Ah, Watson, you could not have come at a better time. Here is a gentleman I should like you to meet. Mr. Wilson, this is Dr. Watson, my partner and helper in many of my most successful cases, and I have no doubt that he will be of the utmost use to me in yours also. Watson, this is Mr. Jabez Wilson.

WATSON: How do you do, Mr. Wilson?

WILSON: I'm so glad to meet you, Dr. Watson.

HOLMES: Try the settee, Watson. You know, since in the past you have shown such extraordinary interest in everything that is outside the conventions and humdrum routine of everyday life, I'm sure you will particularly enjoy the details of this case.

WATSON: Ah, Holmes, you know your cases have been of the greatest interest to me. But what is this particular case about?

HOLMES: Mr. Wilson here has been good enough to call upon me this morning, and to begin a narrative which promises to be one of the most singular which I have listened to for some time. Perhaps, Mr. Wilson, you would be kind enough to begin your tale again because my friend, Dr. Watson, has not heard the beginning of the tale.

WILSON: I shall be happy to do so, Mr. Holmes.

HOLMES: Can you find the advertisement you spoke of in that newspaper again?

WILSON: Yes, I have it now. Here it is. This is what began it all, Dr. Watson. Here. Just read it for yourself.

WATSON (*Reading aloud*): "To the Red-Headed League. On account of the bequest of the late Ezekiah Hopkins, of Lebanon, Pennsylvania, U.S.A., there is now another vacancy open which entitles a member of the League to a salary of four pounds a week for purely nominal services. All red-headed men who are sound in body and mind, and above the age of twenty-one, are eligible. Apply in person on Monday, at eleven o'clock, to Duncan Ross, at the offices of the League, 7 Pope's Court, Fleet Street."

HOLMES: Curious, is it not?

WATSON: Well, what does it mean?

HOLMES: That is what we must find out. But before I ask Mr. Wilson to relate any more, I ask you, Watson, to note the paper and the date.

WATSON: It is the *Morning Chronicle* of April 27, 1890. Just two months ago.

HOLMES: Very good. Now, Mr. Wilson?

WILSON: It is just as I have been telling Mr. Sherlock Holmes. I have a small pawnbroker's business at Coburg Square. Of late years it has not done more than give me a bare living.

HOLMES: Do you work in it alone?

WILSON: No, I have an assistant—though, to tell the truth, I should not be able to employ him if he did not agree to work for such low pay.

HOLMES: What is his name?

WILSON: His name is Vincent Spaulding, and I should not wish a smarter assistant. He could earn better money elsewhere—but, if he's satisfied, I'm not the one to put ideas in his head. He has his faults, too. Never was such a fellow for photography. Snapping away with his camera, and then diving down into the cellar to develop his pictures. That is his main fault, but on the whole he's a good worker.

WATSON: He is still with you, I presume, sir?

WILSON: Yes, he is. We live very quietly, the two of us—for I'm widowed, with no family—and we keep a roof over our heads and pay our debts if we do nothing more. The first thing that interrupted our dull and quiet lives was this advertisement. As a matter of fact, it was my assistant, Vincent Spaulding, himself, who called it to my attention.

HOLMES: How was that?

WILSON: Vincent Spaulding came into the office just this day eight weeks ago with this very paper in his hand, and he said . . .

SPAULDING (*A young, vigorous voice*): Mr. Wilson, I wish that I were a red-headed man.

WILSON: Why should you wish that, Vincent?

SPAULDING: Why, here's another vacancy in the Red-Headed League. It's worth quite a little fortune to any man who qualifies, and I understand they can never find enough men with hair of just the right shade. Why, if my hair would only change to the same color that your hair is, I could step into a nice fortune.

WILSON: I've never heard of it. What is it then?

SPAULDING: I wonder that *you* don't know of it, for you're eligible yourself for one of the vacancies, what with your flaming red hair.

WILSON: What are the vacancies worth?

SPAULDING: Merely a couple of hundred pounds a year—but the work is slight, and wouldn't interfere with other occupations.

WILSON: Tell me about it. A couple of hundred a year would certainly come in handy.

SPAULDING: As far as I can make out, the League was founded by an American millionaire who was very peculiar in his ways. He was himself of red hair, and wanted to make life easier for those who were like him. From all that I hear, it is splendid pay and very little to do.

WILSON: There would be millions of red-haired men that would apply.

SPAULDING: Not so many as you might think. You see, it is confined to grown men, from London, which was the American's native city. And as for color, why, the man's hair must be bright, blazing, fiery red like yours . . .

WILSON: "Bright, blazing, fiery red like yours." Yes, Mr. Holmes and Dr. Watson, those were the very words he used. You can readily see for yourselves that my hair is of a full, rich color, so I decided, upon Spaulding's urging, that I would have a try at it.

HOLMES: What happened after that, Mr. Wilson?

WILSON: Well, sir, I went to the specified address at the appointed time, accompanied by my assistant, Spaulding. Let me say that I never hope to see a sight such as that again. From all corners of London had come every man who had a shade of red in his hair. I didn't think there were so many in the whole country as were brought together by that advertisement. Every shade of color, they were—straw, lemon, orange, brick, Irish-setter, liver, clay—but, as Spaulding pointed out, none was as bright as my own. Well, sir, we pushed and pulled and jammed our way forward, and finally found ourselves next in line at the office door.

HOLMES: Your experience has been a most entertaining one, Wilson.

WATSON: Indeed, yes! Pray continue your story!

WILSON: The office itself was a small one—nothing particular about it. Behind the desk sat a man whose hair was redder than mine—a Mr. Duncan Ross, he told me later. As we entered the office, he shut the door, and said . . .

ROSS: Your name, sir?

WILSON: Mr. Jabez Wilson, and willing to fill a vacancy in the League.

ROSS: You are admirably suited for it, Mr. Wilson. I cannot recall when I have seen a red head so fine. May I take hold of your hair, sir?

WILSON: Certainly, if you like.

ROSS (*As if pulling*): Ugh! Mph! No, it's yours all right. I am sorry to have had to take this precaution, but we have twice been deceived by wigs, and once by dye.

WILSON: Oh, no, sir. My hair is my own.

SPAULDING: Indeed it is, sir.

ROSS: Well, then, Mr. Wilson. My name is Duncan Ross, and I am myself one of the pensioners upon the fund left by our noble benefactor. I am pleased to tell you that the position is yours. When shall you be able to enter upon your new duties?

WILSON: It is a little awkward, for I have a business already.

SPAULDING: Never mind that, Mr. Wilson. I shall look after that for you.

WILSON: What would the hours be, Mr. Ross?

ROSS: From ten to two.

WILSON: A pawnbroker's business—for that is my trade—is done mostly at night. So I suppose I can trust my shop to my assistant here. Yes, yes, Spaulding, you're a good man. Yes, ten to two would suit me very well. And the pay?

ROSS: Four pounds a week.

WILSON: And the work?

ROSS: The work is to copy out the *Encyclopaedia Britannica*. Don't ask me why: it is the terms of the will. You must provide your own pens, paper and ink, but we provide the table and chair. Also, you forfeit the position if you once leave the building during the hours of ten to two. Will you be ready tomorrow?

WILSON: Certainly.

Ross: Then goodbye, Mr. Jabez Wilson, and let me congratulate you once more on the important position which you have been fortunate enough to obtain. And welcome to the Red-Headed League . . .

WILSON: With those words, gentlemen, he bowed me and my assistant out of the room. I was, at the same time, both pleased and puzzled.

WATSON: Pleased and puzzled? How so?

WILSON: Well, you see, Mr. Watson, I was pleased with my new source of income, but puzzled over why anyone should want me to copy out the encyclopedia. In fact, by nightfall I had almost convinced myself that it was all a great hoax.

HOLMES: Did it prove to be a great hoax?

WILSON: On the contrary. The next day, when I reported for work, there was the encyclopedia laid open upon the table, the page at letter "A." Mr. Duncan Ross was there, and he started me off, then left. At two o'clock he returned, complimented me upon the amount that I had written, bade me good day, and locked the door of his office after me.

HOLMES: How long did this procedure continue?

WILSON: This went on day after day, Mr. Holmes, and on Saturday, the manager came in and plunked down four golden sovereigns for my week's work. It was the same the next week, and the same the week after. Every morning I was there at ten, and every afternoon I left at two. Eight weeks passed away like this, and I had written about Abbots and Archery and Armour and Architecture and Attica, and hoped that with diligence I might get on to the B's before very long. It had cost me something for paper, but it was worth it. Then suddenly—

WATSON: Yes?

WILSON: The whole business came to an end.

HOLMES: To an end!

WILSON (*A bit puzzled*): Yes, sir. This very morning. I went to my work as usual at ten o'clock, but the door was shut and locked, with a little square of cardboard hammered onto the middle of the panel with a tack. Here it is, and you can read it for yourself.

HOLMES: Hm, how curious.

WATSON: What does it say, Holmes?

HOLMES: "The Red-Headed League is dissolved. June 22, 1890." (WATSON *laughs, and* HOLMES *joins in.*)

WILSON (*Indignantly*): I cannot see that there is anything very funny. If you can do nothing other than laugh at me, I can go elsewhere.

HOLMES: Oh, no, no, I shouldn't miss your case for the world. But you must admit that it has a slightly comical side to it. Pray, what steps did you take when you found this card on the door?

WILSON: I was staggered, sir. I did not know what to do. Then I called at the landlord's, and asked if he could tell me what had become of the Red-Headed League. He looked at me, astonished, and said . . .

LANDLORD (*Puzzled*): Red-Headed League, you say? I never heard of such a body.

WILSON: Well, then, can you tell me what happened to Mr. Duncan Ross?

LANDLORD: What happened to whom?

WILSON: Duncan Ross.

LANDLORD: Ross? I know of no one of that name.

WILSON: Well, then, what happened to the gentleman who rented number four?

LANDLORD: Oh, you mean the red-headed man. His name was William Morris. He was a solicitor and was using my room as a temporary convenience until his new premises were ready. He moved out yesterday.

WILSON: Where could I find him, sir?

LANDLORD: He's at his new offices. Let me see; he did tell me the address. What was it now? Ah, yes. 17 King Edward Street, near St. Paul's. . . .

HOLMES (*Muttering*): 17 King Edward Street. I'll make a note of that, Mr. Wilson. It may help us.

WILSON: Well, I already checked there, but there was no one there of either the name of William Morris *or* Duncan Ross. It was a manufacturer of artificial knee-caps. Well, at that, I knew not what to do, so decided to take the advice of my assistant, Spaulding, who said simply to wait. But I got impatient, sir, and hearing that Sherlock Holmes was very clever at such things, I decided to come here for aid.

HOLMES: And you did wisely, Mr. Wilson. From what you have said, I think it is possible that a far more serious issue may be at stake than might at first appear.

WILSON: The issue is quite serious enough as it is. I have lost four pounds a week!

HOLMES: Mr. Watson and I will do our best to help you, Mr. Wilson. But first, a few questions. This assistant of yours who first called your attention to the advertisement—how long has he been with you?

WILSON: He'd been with me about a month at that time. He answered an advertisement that I placed in the paper.

HOLMES: Was he the only applicant?

WILSON: No, I had a dozen.

HOLMES: Why did you pick him?

WILSON: Because he was intelligent and handy, and would come at half wages, in fact.

WATSON: What is he like, this Vincent Spaulding?

WILSON: Small, stout-built, very quick in his ways, no hair on his face—though he's not short of thirty. He has a white splash of acid upon his forehead.

HOLMES (*Excitedly*): Acid, you say? Yes, I thought as much. Have you ever observed that his ears are pierced for earrings?

WILSON: Yes, sir. He told me that a gypsy had done it for him when he was a lad.

HOLMES: Hm-m. He is still with you?

WILSON: Oh yes, sir; I have only just left him. But I must be on my way. Will there be anything else you require to ask of me, gentlemen?

WATSON: Not for my part, Wilson.

HOLMES: Yes, I have one more question. All the mornings that you were out—did your assistant attend to your business in your absence?

WILSON: Yes, sir, and he's honest and careful enough. Nothing to complain of, sir. There's never very much to do of a morning.

HOLMES: I believe you have given us all the information we shall need, Mr. Wilson. I shall be happy to give you an opinion on the subject in the course of a day or two. Today is Saturday, and I hope that by Monday we may come to a conclusion. Good day, Mr. Wilson.

WILSON: Good day, Dr. Watson, Mr. Holmes.

HOLMES (*After a pause*): Watson, what do you make of it all?

WATSON: I make nothing of it. It is a most mysterious business.

HOLMES: As a rule, the more bizarre a thing is, the less mysterious it proves to be. But we must be prompt over this matter.

WATSON: What are you going to do, then?

HOLMES: We are going to the pawnbroker's shop of Mr. Jabez Wilson.

WATSON: Whatever for?

HOLMES: To investigate, my dear Watson. To investigate!

NARRATOR: Holmes and Watson set out at once for Jabez Wilson's shop. After leaving their cab a short distance away, they stroll down the street.

HOLMES: There, Watson. See the three gilt balls? That is the place.

WATSON: Yes, Wilson's name is painted over the door. But now that you are here, what are you going to do?

HOLMES: First, an experiment.

NARRATOR: Holmes pounds his walking stick on the pavement.

WATSON (*Taken aback*): Pounding your stick on the pavement?

HOLMES: And now, to knock on the door. I hope that Spaulding fellow answers.

SPAULDING: Won't you step in, gentlemen?

HOLMES: Thank you, but I only wished to ask you how one would go from here to the Strand.

SPAULDING: Oh. Third right, fourth left, sir. Good day.

HOLMES: Smart fellow, that. He is, in my judgment, the fourth smartest man in London, and for daring I am not sure that he has not a claim to be third. I have known something of him before.

WATSON: Evidently Mr. Wilson's assistant counts for a good deal in this mystery of the Red-Headed League. I am sure that you inquired your way merely that you might see him.

HOLMES: Not him. The knees of his trousers.

WATSON: And what did you see?

HOLMES: What I expected to see.

WATSON: Why did you beat the pavement before knocking on the door?

HOLMES: My dear doctor, this is a time for observation, not for talk. We are spies in an enemy's country. We know something of this city square. Let us now explore the parts which lie behind it.

NARRATOR: Holmes and Watson continue on down the street and around the block. Holmes observes carefully each building they pass.

HOLMES: Let me see. I should just like to remember the order of the houses here. There is the tobacconist's, the little newspaper shop, the Coburg branch of the City and Suburban Bank, the restaurant, and the carriage-builder's. That carries us right onto the other block, on which stands the pawn-broker's establishment of our friend, Jabez Wilson. This business of Wilson's is serious. A considerable crime is in contemplation. I have every reason to believe that we shall be in time to stop it. But today being Saturday rather complicates matters. I shall want your help tonight, Watson. Will you come to Baker Street at ten? Goodbye for now, then, Dr. Watson.

NARRATOR: Promptly at ten, Watson arrives at Baker Street, and he and Holmes take a carriage, and set off into the night. Watson questions Holmes about the adventure as the carriage drives them through the city . . .

WATSON: Will you not tell me, Holmes, where we are going, or whom we seek?

HOLMES: I shall gladly do both. We are now going to the Coburg branch of the City and Suburban Bank. The man we seek is none other than John Clay.

WATSON: John Clay! You mean the thief and forger who has escaped the police so many times?

HOLMES: The same, and you may add murderer to your list. His brain is as cunning as his fingers, and though we meet signs of him at every turn, we have never known where to meet the man.

WATSON: Why, all of London has been on his trail for years!

HOLMES: I hope that I may have the pleasure of introducing you to him tonight!

NARRATOR: Leaving the carriage some distance away, Holmes and Watson cautiously enter the bank with a key that Holmes produces without an explanation. They descend to the cellar . . .

HOLMES (*Softly*): Here, Watson. Through here. Righto!

WATSON (*Quietly*): Is this the cellar of the bank, then?

HOLMES: It is. We must act quickly, for time is of the essence. I perceive that the ceiling is thick enough. We are not vulnerable from above.

WATSON: Nor from below. The floor seems . . . why, dear me! A hollow sound!

HOLMES: I must really ask you to be a little more quiet. Sit down on one of those boxes while I shade the light.

WATSON: What is in these great packing-cases, Holmes?

HOLMES: The 30,000 napoleons of French gold from the Bank of France.

WATSON: What!

HOLMES: It has become known that this gold was being stored, completely packed, in the cellar where we now find ourselves. The directors of the bank began to have misgivings about leaving so large a quantity of gold about, and now it appears that their fears were well justified. The bank is to be robbed tonight, if I am not mistaken.

WATSON: How so? And only the two of us to stop the thieves?

HOLMES: I have ordered an inspector and two officers to be at the one possible retreat—the front door.

WATSON: How, then, will the thieves enter?

HOLMES: Through a hole in the floor.

WATSON: What!

HOLMES (*Whispering*): Huddle in the shadows! One of the stones is moving! They are coming. Hush!

NARRATOR: There is a chink of stones, and then Vincent Spaulding's voice is heard faintly, talking to another . . .

SPAULDING: It's all clear. Have you the chisel and the bags?

HOLMES (*Suddenly*): I have you, John Clay!

SPAULDING (*Calling out*): Run, Archie! I'm caught!

HOLMES: It's no use, John Clay. You have no chance at all. You did not reckon with Sherlock Holmes. It is no use!

SPAULDING: So I see. I fancy my friend has escaped though. At least my struggle with you gave him that chance. You are not totally successful.

WATSON: The door was guarded. There are three men waiting for him.

SHERLOCK HOLMES AND THE RED-HEADED LEAGUE 243

SPAULDING: Oh, indeed. You seem to have done the thing completely. I must compliment you.

HOLMES: And I you. Your red-headed idea was very clever.

WATSON: Ah, Clay, you'll be seeing your friend soon—in court, you scoundrel!

SPAULDING (*With dignity*): I beg your pardon. You may not be aware that John Clay has royal blood in his veins. Have the goodness when you address me always to say "sir" and "please."

HOLMES (*Laughing*): As you wish, John Clay. Well, would you please, sir, march upstairs, sir, where we can please to get a cab, sir, to carry Your Highness to the police station—sir?

NARRATOR: A short time later, back at Baker Street, Holmes explains to Watson . . .

HOLMES: It was obvious from the start that the purpose of the Red-Headed League was to get our friend, Jabez Wilson, out of the way for a few hours every day. The plot was suggested, I'm sure, by Wilson's own hair. The four pounds a week was a lure—and who could not afford four pounds who was gambling on thirty thousand? They put in the advertisement. One accomplice posed as Duncan Ross, the other insured that Wilson would apply. From the time I heard that the assistant had come for half wages, I knew he had some strange motive for securing the station.

WATSON: How could you guess what the motive was?

HOLMES: Wilson's business is very small. It must be, then, the house itself that was of value. When I thought of the assistant's fondness for photography and his vanishing constantly into the cellar, I realized at once that that was it.

WATSON: Yes, I remember now. Wilson mentioned that.

HOLMES: The description of the assistant convinced me that it was the notorious Clay himself. But what could he be doing in the cellar of a pawnbroker, I asked myself. Why, digging a tunnel, of course, each day over a period of months.

Then I wondered, what building could he be tunneling into? Our visit to the actual scene itself showed me that. Remember I observed that the bank was right around the corner from Wilson's?

WATSON: Now that you mention it, I do indeed.

HOLMES: I surprised you, I recall, by tapping my stick on the pavement. That was to determine whether the cellar extended to the front of the buildings. Then I paid a call on John Clay himself—at that time known to us as Spaulding, the assistant.

WATSON: Yes. You said you wanted to observe his knees. What did you see?

HOLMES: You yourself must have noticed how worn, wrinkled and stained they were—which was a natural consequence of his burrowing. All my conclusions assembled, I called Scotland Yard and the bank, and secured permission and a key for our admittance.

WATSON: How could you tell that they would make their attempt tonight?

HOLMES: When they closed their League offices, that was a sign that they cared no longer about Mr. Jabez Wilson's presence—in other words, that they had completed their tunnel. But it was essential that they should use it soon, as it might be discovered. Saturday would suit them best, as it would give them two days for their escape. For all these reasons I expected them to come tonight.

WATSON: Ah, you reasoned it out beautifully. It is so long a chain, and yet every link rings true. It was indeed remarkable, Sherlock Holmes. Remarkable.

HOLMES: On the contrary, it was elementary, my dear Watson. Elementary!

THE END

The Wizard of Oz

This is an adaptation of a well-known book, so you may be familiar with it, and know it is a fantasy. The things that happen in it are not like real life.

Read the play through to yourself. The group can then choose parts and talk about the characters in the play. How would the different witches sound? Two of them are good and one is wicked. There are talking animals, a scarecrow and a woodman in the play. You should discuss how these characters should sound. Should they talk like people or would you make them sound different?

In this play, you have a chance to act a part very unlike yourself. Try to do a good job so your listeners will really believe you are a lion or a winged monkey or whatever your part is.

The part of Dorothy is important, and you should decide what sort of a girl she is. Is she unusual, or just an ordinary girl?

Work on the play scene by scene, making sure everyone understands all the words. Are you paying attention to punctuation and varying your tone of voice to show different feelings?

Practice the places you think need improvement. Then when you are ready, read the play for the class. Did the play hold their interest? If not, how can you improve your performance?

Note to the teacher: The class may read the play silently, then split up into groups as follows: Scene 1: narrator, 3 boys, 2 girls; 3 boys or girls; Scenes 2 and 3: narrator, 6 boys, 2 girls; Scenes 4 and 5: narrator, 4 boys, 2 girls.

THE WIZARD OF OZ

by L. Frank Baum
adapted by Lynne Sharon Schwartz

Characters

(6 boys, 4 girls, 3 boys or girls, and a narrator)
NARRATOR
DOROTHY
WITCH OF THE NORTH
THREE MUNCHKINS
SCARECROW
TIN WOODMAN
COWARDLY LION
SOLDIER
WIZARD OF OZ
WICKED WITCH OF THE WEST
KING OF THE WINGED MONKEYS
GLINDA, *the Good Witch of the South*

SCENE 1

NARRATOR: Once upon a time there was a little girl named
Dorothy, who lived in Kansas with her Uncle Henry, who
was a farmer, and her Aunt Em, and her dog, Toto.

One day they heard a low wail of the wind, and they saw
the long grass bowing in waves; they heard a sharp, whistling
sound in the air, and they knew that a cyclone was coming.
Uncle Henry ran out to take care of the cattle, and Aunt Em
ran to a trapdoor in the floor, calling to Dorothy to follow
her. But at that moment Toto jumped out of Dorothy's arms
and hid under the bed. As Dorothy reached to get him, the

house shook so hard that she lost her footing and fell down on the floor. Then the house whirled around two or three times and rose slowly through the air, and Dorothy felt as if she were going up in a balloon. The house was in the exact center of the cyclone, and it was carried miles and miles up into the air. The wind was shrieking loudly, but the house was very still, and Dorothy crawled into her bed and fell asleep. When she awoke, she found herself in a strange place. There she was in the middle of a field, with her house, which had two silver shoes sticking out from under it, beside her.

DOROTHY: I wonder where I am! All I can remember is whirling around and around.

NARRATOR: Dorothy hugged Toto, as she looked around fearfully. The Witch of the North and a group of Munchkins were coming across the field toward her.

WITCH OF THE NORTH: You are welcome, most noble Sorceress, to the land of the Munchkins. We are grateful to you for having killed the Wicked Witch of the East, and for setting our people free.

DOROTHY: You are very kind, but there must be some mistake. I have not killed anyone.

WITCH OF THE NORTH (*Laughing*): Your house did, anyway, and that is the same thing. Look there! There are her two feet, sticking out from under the house.

DOROTHY (*Dismayed*): Oh, dear! The house must have fallen on her. Whatever shall we do?

WITCH OF THE NORTH: There is nothing to be done. She was the Wicked Witch of the East, and she made the Munchkins her slaves. Now they are set free, and are grateful to you.

DOROTHY (*Puzzled*): Who are the Munchkins?

WITCH OF THE NORTH: They are the people who live in this land of the East. These are my Munchkin friends with me. I am the Witch of the North.

DOROTHY (*Doubtfully*): Are you a real witch?

WITCH OF THE NORTH: Yes, indeed. But I am a good witch, and the people love me.

DOROTHY: I thought all witches were wicked.

WITCH OF THE NORTH: Oh, no, that is a great mistake. There were four witches in all the land of Oz, and two of them—the Witch of the North and the Witch of the South—are good witches. The other two—the Witch of the East and the Witch of the West—are wicked witches. Now that you have killed the Wicked Witch of the East, there is but one Wicked Witch left—the Wicked Witch of the West.

1ST MUNCHKIN: Look! Look! Her feet have disappeared.

WITCH OF THE NORTH: She was so old that she dried up quickly in the sun. That is the end of her. But the silver shoes are yours, Dorothy, and you shall have them. Put them on.

2ND MUNCHKIN: There is some charm connected with these silver shoes, but what it is, we never knew.

DOROTHY: Thank you for the shoes. Can you help me find my way back to Aunt Em?

3RD MUNCHKIN: There is a great desert all around this land, and no one can cross it and live.

WITCH OF THE NORTH: I am afraid, my dear, that you will have to stay here with us.

DOROTHY (*Starting to cry*): But I want to go back to Kansas.

WITCH OF THE NORTH: Perhaps we will get a magic message from inside my cap to help us. (*Reading*) It says, "Let Dorothy go to the City of Emeralds." Is your name Dorothy, my dear?

DOROTHY (*Controlling her tears*): Yes. Where is the City of Emeralds?

WITCH OF THE NORTH: It is in the center of the country, and is ruled by Oz, the Great Wizard.

DOROTHY: Is he a good man?

WITCH OF THE NORTH: He is a good *Wizard*. Whether he is a *man* or not I cannot tell, for I have never seen him.

DOROTHY: How do I get there?

WITCH OF THE NORTH: It is a long journey, through a country that is sometimes pleasant and sometimes dark and terrible. However, I will use all the magic arts I know of to keep you from harm. I will also give you my charmed kiss. No one will dare injure a person who has been kissed by the Witch of the North. The road to the City of Emeralds is paved with yellow brick, so you cannot miss it. When you reach Oz, tell the Great Wizard your story and ask him to help you. Goodbye, my dear.

DOROTHY: Goodbye, and thank you all. I shall start on my journey right away.

WITCH *and* MUNCHKINS: Goodbye!

NARRATOR: Dorothy waved goodbye to the Witch and her friends. She looked around helplessly until she noticed the beginning of a road made of yellow bricks. Remembering the Witch's advice, she started down the road, with Toto following behind her. After walking for what seemed like hours, she came upon a scarecrow in a field beside the road.

DOROTHY: I'm sure I saw that Scarecrow wink at me, but it just couldn't be. After all, he's made of straw.

SCARECROW: Good day.

DOROTHY (*Surprised*): Did you speak?

SCARECROW: Certainly. How do you do?

DOROTHY: I'm pretty well, thank you. How do you do?

SCARECROW: I'm not feeling well. It's very tedious being perched up here night and day to scare away crows.

DOROTHY: Can't you get down?

SCARECROW: No, because this pole is stuck up my back. If you will please take away the pole, I shall be greatly obliged to you.

NARRATOR: Dorothy helped the Scarecrow down off his pole. He stretched and yawned, then looked at Dorothy.

SCARECROW: Who are you, and where are you going?

DOROTHY: My name is Dorothy, and I am on my way to the

Emerald City to ask the great Oz to send me back to Kansas.

SCARECROW: Where is the Emerald City? And who is Oz?

DOROTHY: Why, don't you know?

SCARECROW (*Sadly*): No, indeed. I don't know anything. You see, I am stuffed with straw, so I have no brains at all.

DOROTHY: Oh, I'm awfully sorry.

SCARECROW: Do you think that if I go to the Emerald City, with you, Oz would give me some brains?

DOROTHY: I cannot tell, but you may come with me if you like.

SCARECROW: I think I shall. You see, I don't mind my legs and arms and body being stuffed, because I cannot get hurt. But I don't like to be thought a fool. Well, let's be on our way.

NARRATOR: Dorothy and the Scarecrow started down the yellow brick road. After a while, they passed a Tin Woodman, standing beside the road, his ax raised. He groaned loudly.

DOROTHY: I'm sure I heard someone groan. Look! A woodman made of tin! Did you groan, sir?

TIN WOODMAN: Yes, I did. I've been groaning for more than a year.

DOROTHY (*Sympathetically*): What can I do for you?

TIN WOODMAN: Get an oilcan and oil my joints. They are rusted so badly that I cannot move them at all. You will find an oilcan on the ground beside me.

DOROTHY: Here it is. Where shall I put the oil?

TIN WOODMAN: Oil my neck, first. Now oil the joints in my arms. (TIN WOODMAN *sighs*) This is a great comfort. I have been holding that ax in the air ever since I rusted in a rainstorm, and I'm glad to be able to put it down at last. Now, if you will oil the joints of my legs, I shall be all right once more. Thank you so much! I might have stood there forever if you had not come along. How did you happen to be here?

DOROTHY: We are on our way to the Emerald City to see the great Oz. I want him to send me back to Kansas, and the Scarecrow wants him to put a few brains into his head.

THE WIZARD OF OZ 251

Tin Woodman: Do you suppose Oz could give me a—a heart?

Dorothy: Why, I guess so. It would be as easy as giving the Scarecrow brains.

Tin Woodman: True. If you will allow me to join your party, I will also go to the Emerald City and ask Oz to help me.

Scarecrow: Come along. We'd be pleased to have you. But if I were you, I should ask for brains instead of a heart, for a fool with no brains would not know what to do with a heart if he had one.

Tin Woodman: I shall take the heart, for brains do not make one happy, and happiness is the best thing in the world.

Narrator: The Cowardly Lion was suddenly upon them with a loud roar. After knocking over both the Woodman and the Scarecrow, the Lion made a rush at Toto. Dorothy snatched up Toto and slapped the Lion on his nose.

Dorothy: You ought to be ashamed of yourself, a big beast like you, biting a poor little dog!

Lion: I didn't bite him.

Dorothy: No, but you tried to. You are nothing but a big coward.

Lion: I know it. I've always known it. But how can I help it?

Dorothy: I'm sure I don't know. To think of your striking a poor, stuffed Scarecrow!

Lion: Is he stuffed?

Dorothy: Of course he's stuffed.

Lion: That's why he went over so easily. Is the other one stuffed also?

Dorothy: No, he's made of tin.

Lion: Then that's why he nearly blunted my claws.

Scarecrow: What makes you a coward?

Lion: It's a mystery. I suppose I was born that way. All the other animals in the forest naturally expect me to be brave, because a lion is considered the King of Beasts. I learned that if I roared very loudly, every living thing was frightened and got out of my way. (*Confidingly*) Actually, if the elephants and the tigers and the bears had ever tried to fight me, I should have run myself—I'm such a coward.

SCARECROW: But the King of Beasts shouldn't be a coward.

LION (*Tearfully*): I know it. It is my great sorrow. But whenever there is danger, my heart begins to beat fast.

TIN WOODMAN: You ought to be glad of that, for it proves you have a heart. I have no heart at all, so it cannot beat fast or slow. But I am going to the great Oz to ask him for one.

SCARECROW: And I am going to ask him to give me brains, for my head is stuffed with straw.

DOROTHY: And I am going to ask him to send Toto and me back to Kansas.

LION (*Timidly*): Do you think Oz could give me courage?

SCARECROW: He can give you courage just as easily as he can give me brains.

TIN WOODMAN: Or me a heart.

DOROTHY: Or send me back to Kansas.

LION: Then, if you don't mind, I'll go with you, for my life is simply unbearable without even a bit of courage.

DOROTHY: You will be very welcome, for you will help to keep away the other wild beasts. I think it will be a long and difficult journey.

* * * * *

SCENE 2

NARRATOR: It was a long and difficult journey, but the four friends finally arrived at the end of the yellow brick road, in the Emerald City of Oz. They made their way through the city to the door to Oz's throne room, which was guarded by a soldier, to whom they gave their message to Oz.

DOROTHY (*Wearily*): I am so glad to be here. I thought we would never arrive.

TIN WOODMAN: Let us hope that the great Oz will see us. They say that no one has asked to see Oz in many, many years.

DOROTHY: Excuse me, sir, have you seen Oz and asked him about us?

SOLDIER: Oh, no! I have never seen Oz, but I speak to him—and I gave him your message. When I mentioned your silver shoes, he was very much interested. He said he would grant you an audience, but if you have come on an idle or foolish errand, he may be angry and destroy you all in an instant.

SCARECROW: But it is not a foolish errand, nor an idle one. It is *very* important.

SOLDIER: Very well, then. But each of you must enter his presence alone.

NARRATOR: The soldier escorted Dorothy to the door, and her friends watched as she entered alone. The throne room of the great Oz was all green, from ceiling to floor and end to end. Dorothy walked hesitantly toward the large green throne, but instead of a person, there was an enormous head hanging in the air above it. She watched in awe as the great head began to speak.

OZ (*In a booming voice*): I am Oz, the great and terrible. Who are you and why do you seek me?

DOROTHY: I am Dorothy, the small and meek. I have come to you for help.

OZ: Where did you get the silver shoes?

DOROTHY: I got them from the Wicked Witch of the East, when my house fell on her and killed her.

OZ: What do you wish me to do?

DOROTHY: Send me back to Kansas, where my Aunt Em and Uncle Henry are. I am sure Aunt Em will be dreadfully worried over my being away so long.

OZ: Why should I do this for you?

DOROTHY: Because you are strong and I am weak; because you are a Great Wizard, and I am only a helpless little girl.

OZ: But you were strong enough to kill the Wicked Witch of the East.

DOROTHY: That just happened. I could not help it.

Oz: Well, I will give you my answer. You have no right to expect me to send you back to Kansas unless you do something for me in return.

Dorothy (*Hesitantly*): I will if I can. What is it?

Oz: You must kill the Wicked Witch of the West!

Dorothy: But I cannot!

Oz: You killed the Wicked Witch of the East, and you wear the silver shoes, which have a powerful charm. There is now but one Wicked Witch left in all this land, and when you can tell me she is dead, I will send you back to Kansas—but not before.

Dorothy (*Beginning to weep*): I never killed anything, willingly, and even if I wanted to, how could I kill the Wicked Witch? If you, who are great and terrible, cannot kill her yourself, how do you expect me to do it?

Oz: I do not know, but that is my answer, and until the Wicked Witch of the West dies, you will not see your uncle and aunt again. Remember that the Witch is wicked—tremendously wicked—and should not live. Now go, and do not ask to see me again until you have done your task.

Narrator: Dorothy backed out of the throne room and rejoined her friends. Each one in turn entered the mysterious throne room, and each returned to report that Oz had promised to give what each desired—if they killed the Wicked Witch of the West. But each saw something different when he looked at Oz.

Scarecrow: Oz promised me brains. His form was like a lovely lady.

Tin Woodman: The Oz who promised me a heart looked like a horrible beast.

Lion: No, Oz is a huge ball of fire. He will give me courage if—

All: We kill the Wicked Witch of the West!

* * * * *

NARRATOR: The next morning the four friends met and marveled at the many forms the Great Wizard of Oz could assume. Then together they started for the castle of the Wicked Witch of the West. At night, Dorothy and Toto and the Lion lay down to sleep, while the Scarecrow and the Tin Woodman kept watch.

Now, the Wicked Witch of the West had an eye that was as powerful as a telescope and could see everywhere. As she stood in front of her castle, she looked out and saw Dorothy lying asleep with her friends around her. She was furious to find them in her country, and tried many ways to capture them, but was unsuccessful. But she thought of one last idea.

WICKED WITCH: The only way left to destroy these strangers is with the Golden Cap. This must be my last command to the Winged Monkeys, for I have commanded them twice already. I'll put the cap on and summon them. Ep-pe, pep-pe, tak-ke! Hil-lo, hol-lo, hel-lo! Ziz-zy, zuz-zy, zik!

KING OF THE WINGED MONKEYS: You have called the Winged Monkeys for the third and last time. What do you command?

WICKED WITCH: Go to the strangers within my land and destroy them all, except the Lion. Bring that beast to me, for I shall harness him like a horse, and make him work.

KING: Your commands shall be obeyed.

NARRATOR: The Winged Monkeys flew to Dorothy and her friends. First they seized the Tin Woodman and dropped him in a valley covered with sharp rocks, where he lay battered and dented. Then they caught the Scarecrow and pulled the straw out of his clothes. They made a small bundle of his hat and clothes and threw it into the branches of a tall tree. Next they captured the Lion and tied him to a stake. Then the King brought Dorothy and Toto to the Wicked Witch.

KING: We have obeyed you as far as we are able. The Tin Woodman and the Scarecrow are destroyed, and the Lion is tied up in your yard. The little girl we dare not harm, nor the dog she carries with her, for the Witch of the North has kissed her forehead and left her mark. Your power over our band is now ended. You may keep the girl.

WICKED WITCH: Aha! I have tried many ways to capture you, little girl, and at last I have you for my slave. See that you mind everything I tell you, for if you do not I will make an end of you. You will clean the pots and kettles and sweep the floor and tend the fire.

DOROTHY: You are a very wicked witch for destroying my friends and tying up the Lion, but your power cannot last long. I have a special charm in the silver shoes I took from the Wicked Witch of the East, and it will help me to get rid of you.

WICKED WITCH: The silver shoes! Give them to me!

DOROTHY: No!

NARRATOR: As the Wicked Witch started to pull off the silver shoes, Dorothy seized a bucket of water standing by the hearth and dashed it over the witch, who began to shrink away to nothing.

WICKED WITCH (*In muffled voice*): See what you have done? In a minute I shall melt away.

DOROTHY (*Frightened and astonished*): I'm very sorry, indeed.

WICKED WITCH (*Weakly*): Didn't you know water would be the end of me?

DOROTHY: Of course not. How could I?

WICKED WITCH: Well, in a minute I shall be all melted, and you will have the castle to yourself. I have been wicked in my day, but I never thought a little girl like you would ever be able to melt me and end my wicked deeds. (*Faintly*) Look out— here I go!

DOROTHY: And now I shall take her Golden Cap. It fits perfectly! Now I must go back to the Emerald City for my reward. But how can I save the Scarecrow and the Tin Woodman and the Lion? And I am afraid I am hopelessly lost. What can I do? Oh, look! There's a charm in the cap! It's a magic rhyme. Maybe it will help me. Ep-pe, pep-pe, tak-ke! Hil-lo, hol-lo, hel-lo! (*Louder*) Ziz-zy, zuz-zy, zik!

KING OF MONKEYS: What is your command? We can take you anywhere within the Land of Oz in a moment's time.

DOROTHY: I wish to rescue my friends and take them with me to the Emerald City.

KING: Have no fear. We will carry you there. We'll find your friends, and take them with us.

* * * * *

SCENE 4

NARRATOR: The Monkeys rescued Dorothy's friends, and brought all four back to the Emerald City. But when they entered the throne room, the throne was empty. Suddenly Oz's voice boomed out.

OZ: I am Oz, the great and terrible. Why do you seek me?

DOROTHY: Where are you?

OZ: I am everywhere, but to the eyes of common mortals I am invisible.

DOROTHY: We have come to claim our rewards, O Great Oz.

OZ: What rewards?

DOROTHY: You promised to grant us all our wishes when the Wicked Witch was destroyed.

OZ: Is she really destroyed?

DOROTHY: Yes, I melted her with a bucket of water.

OZ: Dear me, how sudden. Well, come to me tomorrow, for I must have time to think it over.

TIN WOODMAN: You've had plenty of time already.

SCARECROW: We won't wait a day longer.

DOROTHY: You must keep your promises to us. (LION *lets out a great roar.*)

NARRATOR: As the Lion roared, Toto jumped from Dorothy's arms in alarm and knocked over a screen beside the throne, revealing a little old man with a bald head—the great Oz!

TIN WOODMAN: Who are you?

OZ (*Fearfully*): I am Oz, the great and terrible (*Pleading*), but don't strike me—please don't—and I'll do anything you want me to.

DOROTHY (*Dismayed*): I thought Oz was a great head.

SCARECROW: And I thought Oz was a lovely lady.

TIN WOODMAN: And I thought Oz was a terrible beast.

LION: And I thought he was a ball of fire.

OZ: No, you are all wrong. I have been making believe. I'm supposed to be a Great Wizard, but I'm just a common man.

SCARECROW: You're not even that. Why, you're a humbug, a fake!

OZ: Exactly! But don't speak so loudly or you will be over-heard, and I shall be ruined.

TIN WOODMAN: But this is terrible. How shall I ever get my heart?

LION: Or I my courage?

SCARECROW: Or I my brains?

OZ: My dear friends, I pray you not to speak of these little things. Think of me, and the terrible trouble I'm in now that you have found me out.

DOROTHY: Doesn't anyone else know you're a humbug?

OZ: No one but the four of you.

DOROTHY (*Bewildered*): But I don't understand. How was it that you appeared to me as a great head?

OZ: That was one of my tricks. Everything I've done has been a trick.

SCARECROW: Really, you ought to be ashamed of yourself for being such a humbug.

OZ: I am—I certainly am—but it was the only thing I could do. You see, I was born in Omaha—

DOROTHY: Why, that isn't very far from Kansas!

OZ: No, but it's far from here! I worked in a circus as a balloon-ist—that's a man who goes up in a balloon on circus day, to draw a crowd. One day the ropes of my balloon got twisted, and I floated miles through the air until I landed in this strange and beautiful country. The people here, who saw me come down from the clouds, thought I was a great wizard. They promised to do anything I wished, so to keep the good people busy I ordered them to build this city and my palace. Because the country was so green and beautiful, I called it the Emerald City. I have been good to the people, and they like me. But one of my greatest fears was the Witches. That is why I was so pleased to hear that your house had fallen on the Wicked Witch of the East, and why I was so willing to promise anything if you would do away with the other Witch. But I am ashamed to say now that I cannot keep my promises to you.

DOROTHY (*Angrily*): I think you are a very bad man.

Oz (*Contritely*): Oh, no, my dear. I'm really a very good man, but I'm a very bad wizard, I must admit.

SCARECROW: Can't you give me brains?

Oz: You don't need them. You are learning something every day. A baby has brains, but it doesn't know much. Experience is the only thing that brings knowledge, and the longer you are on earth the more experience you are sure to get.

SCARECROW (*Sadly*): That may all be true, but I shall be very unhappy unless you give me brains.

Oz: Then I will try to give you brains. I cannot tell you how to use them, however. You must find that out for yourself. Let me put this powder on your head. The main ingredient is bran. Hereafter you will be a great man, for I have given you a lot of bran-new brains!

SCARECROW: Oh, thank you, thank you. And I'll find a way to use them, never fear.

DOROTHY: How do you feel?

SCARECROW: I feel wise indeed.

LION: Now, how about my courage?

Oz: You have plenty of courage, I am sure. All you need is confidence in yourself. There is no living thing that is not afraid when it faces danger. True courage is facing danger when you are afraid, and you have plenty of true courage.

LION: Perhaps I have, but I'm scared just the same. I shall really be very unhappy unless you give me the sort of courage that makes one forget he is afraid.

OZ: Very well, I will get some for you. Drink the liquid in this bottle.

LION: What is it?

OZ: Well, if it were inside you, it would be courage. You know, of course, that courage is always inside a person, so this really cannot be called courage until you have swallowed it. Therefore, I advise you to drink it as soon as possible. How do you feel now?

LION (*Happily*): Full of courage!

TIN WOODMAN: How about my heart?

OZ: Why, as for that, I think you are wrong to want a heart. It makes most people unhappy. If you only knew it, you are in luck not to have a heart.

TIN WOODMAN (*Firmly*): That must be a matter of opinion. For my part, I will bear all the unhappiness without a murmur, if you will give me a heart.

OZ: Very well. Here is an elegant paper heart I'll pin on your chest. Isn't it a beauty?

TIN WOODMAN: It is, indeed. But is it a kind heart?

OZ: Oh, very kind. It is a heart that any man might be proud of.

TIN WOODMAN (*Happily*): I am very grateful to you, and shall never forget your kindness.

DOROTHY: And now—how am I to get back to Kansas?

OZ (*Sighing*): I shall have to think about that for a while.

* * * * *

SCENE 5

NARRATOR: Oz thought for several days, and finally decided that he and Dorothy should leave in a balloon. At the moment they were to take off, she realized that she had lost Toto. She hurried through the crowd looking for him, but by the time she found him the balloon was already sailing overhead, and Oz could not bring it back. She was very sad, and cried because she thought she would never get back to Kansas. Finally, a soldier who felt sorry for Dorothy told her that Glinda, the Good Witch of the South, might help her. Glinda was the most powerful of all the Witches, and ruled over the Quadlings. The road to her castle was full of dangers to travelers, but Dorothy decided to go, nevertheless, because it was her last hope, and her faithful friends went along to protect her.

DOROTHY: This must be Glinda's castle. Isn't it beautiful?

TIN WOODMAN: She must be an especially good Witch, and I know she will help you, Dorothy.

GLINDA: I am Glinda, the Good Witch of the South. I have heard of how you landed here on the cyclone, child. What can I do for you?

DOROTHY: My greatest wish is to get back to Kansas, for Aunt Em will certainly think something dreadful has happened to me.

GLINDA: I am sure I can help you. But if I do, you must give me the Golden Cap.

DOROTHY: Willingly, for it will be of no use to me now.

GLINDA: I think I will need it just three times. What will you do when Dorothy has left us, Scarecrow?

SCARECROW: I will return to the Emerald City, for Oz has made me its ruler, and the people like me. The only thing that worries me is how to cross the tremendous mountain bordering your land. On our journey here the Winged Monkeys carried us over the mountain.

GLINDA: By the Golden Cap I shall command the Winged Monkeys to carry you again to the gates of the Emerald City, for it would be a shame to deprive the people of so wonderful a ruler. What will become of you when Dorothy leaves, Woodman?

TIN WOODMAN: The Winkies, in the land of the West, were very kind to me. After the Wicked Witch of the West was melted, they wanted me to rule over them. If I could get back there again, I should like nothing better than to be their ruler forever.

GLINDA: My second command to the Winged Monkeys will be that they carry you safely to the land of the Winkies. Your brains may not be as large as those of the Scarecrow, but you are really much brighter than he is when you are well polished. I am sure you will rule the Winkies wisely and well. Now, Lion, when Dorothy has returned to her home, what will become of you?

LION: The beasts in the forest on the outskirts of your land have made me their king, because during our journey here I saved them from a wicked monster. If only I could get back to them, I should pass my life there very happily.

GLINDA: My third command to the Winged Monkeys shall be to carry you to your forest. Then, having used up the powers of the Golden Cap, I shall give it to the King of the Winged Monkeys, so that he and his band may be free forever after.

SCARECROW, TIN WOODMAN, LION (*Ad lib*): Thank you. You are so kind to us. (*Etc.*)

DOROTHY: You are certainly as good as you are beautiful. But you have not yet told me how to get back to Kansas.

GLINDA: Your silver shoes have wonderful powers. They can carry you across the desert, or anywhere in the world. In fact, if you had known their power, you could have gone back to your Aunt Em the very first day you came to this country.

SCARECROW: But then I should not have had my wonderful brains. I might have passed my whole life in the farmer's cornfield.

TIN WOODMAN: And I should not have had my lovely heart. I might have stood and rusted in the forest till the end of the world.

LION: And I should have lived a coward forever, and no beast in all the forest would have had a good word to say about me.

DOROTHY: That is all true, and I am glad I was of use to these good friends. But now that each of them has what he most desired, and a kingdom to rule besides, I think I should like to go home.

GLINDA: All you have to do is knock your heels together three times and command the shoes to carry you wherever you wish. They will take you in only three steps, each step made in the wink of an eye.

DOROTHY (*Joyfully*): I shall command them at once. Goodbye, goodbye, everyone. You have all been such good friends, and I will never forget you.

SCARECROW, TIN WOODMAN, LION (*Ad lib*): Goodbye, Dorothy. We shall always remember you, too. (*Etc.*)

DOROTHY: I am so grateful for your kindness, Glinda. (*Solemnly*) Shoes, take me home to Aunt Em! (*After a pause*) Good gracious, here I am in Kansas! And there is Uncle Henry's new farmhouse, and there are the cows in the barnyard. Oh! I've lost the silver shoes. They must have fallen off in the air. There's Aunt Em. Here I am, Aunt Em! I've been in the land of Oz. And here is Toto, too. And, oh, Aunt Em, I'm so glad to be at home again!

THE END

Oliver Twist

This play is adapted from Charles Dickens' novel about a poor orphan who has many adventures before he finds a happy home.

The play has many short scenes, and you can work on them one by one. But first the group should read the play through silently to be sure you know what is happening. Then discuss these questions together:

What sort of people are Fagin, the Artful Dodger, Charley, and Bill Sikes? How are they different from Oliver?

What about Mr. Brownlow and Mr. Grimwig? How do you think they would sound?

Nancy works with the gang of thieves, but she is different. What kind of a person do you think she is? How is she like Rose?

Are there any words you find difficult? If so, discuss them with the group to be certain everyone knows what is happening.

Choose parts and read the first scene. Did it go smoothly? Practice it again if necessary. Now go on to the second scene and do the same, and so on for the whole play. Those who do not have parts in a scene should listen carefully and make suggestions for improvement.

This is a good play to read for a tape recorder and to listen to with the whole class.

Note to the teacher: Because of the large cast, starred parts may be doubled, or the entire class can read the play silently, then split up into groups as follows: Scenes 1 and 2: narrator, 7 boys, 3 girls; Scenes 3 and 4: narrator, 7 boys, 1 girl; Scenes 5 and 6: narrator, 7 boys, 3 girls; Scenes 7, 8, and 9: narrator, 6 boys, 3 girls. Starred parts may be doubled.

OLIVER TWIST

by Charles Dickens
adapted by Joellen Bland

Characters

(12 boys, 5 girls, and a narrator)
NARRATOR
OLIVER TWIST, *an orphan boy*
MR. BUMBLE, *a parish officer**
MRS. CORNEY, *matron of the workhouse**
BOY*
OLD SALLY, *an old woman**
THE ARTFUL DODGER, *a young pickpocket*
CHARLEY BATES, *a young pickpocket*
FAGIN, *leader of a gang of thieves*
BILL SIKES, *a robber*
NANCY, *a member of Fagin's gang*
MR. BROWNLOW, *a gentleman*
BOOKSELLER
POLICE CONSTABLE*
MAN*
MR. GRIMWIG, *a friend of Brownlow's*
ROSE MAYLIE, *a young lady*
MRS. BEDWIN, *Mr. Brownlow's housekeeper*

SCENE 1

NARRATOR: Long ago in England, in the 1830s, poor unwanted
orphan boys were often placed in workhouses, where they
were housed and fed, but lived in misery. In one such workhouse, young Oliver Twist was placed. He suffered along
with the other boys until one day when Mr. Bumble, the

parish officer in charge of the workhouse, was making a tour of inspection. Accompanying Mr. Bumble as he inspected the ragged boys in the dirty dining hall was Mrs. Corney, the matron, while Old Sally, a pauper woman working at the workhouse, hovered in the background. . . .

MRS. CORNEY (*Sternly*): All right! Eat up and be quick about it! Mr. Bumble and I haven't got all night to be standing here while you orphans gorge yourselves!

BUMBLE: For this bountiful meal before you, and for all the blessings given to penniless workhouse orphans, may you ever be humble, grateful, and obedient!

BOY (*Whispering*): Go on, Oliver. We drew straws and you got the short one. Raise your hand.

BUMBLE (*Fiercely*): Well, boy, what do you want?

OLIVER (*In a shaking voice*): Please, sir, I want some more to eat.

BUMBLE: *What?*

OLIVER: Please, sir, I . . . I want some more.

BUMBLE (*Angrily*): More? Mrs. Corney, do my ears deceive me? Did Oliver Twist ask for more?

MRS. CORNEY: Indeed he did, sir!

BUMBLE: Well, he won't do it again! Here! Lock him up! To-morrow I shall see if someone . . . perhaps the undertaker . . . will take this ungrateful young sinner off our hands! You'd like to be a coffinmaker's apprentice, wouldn't you, Oliver?

OLIVER (*Frightened*): No, sir.

BUMBLE: But you *will* like it! Yes, the undertaker can surely be persuaded to take you for, shall we say, five pounds? Take him away, Mrs. Corney. I shall be along directly to honor him with a sound thrashing!

OLD SALLY: Wait, mistress! Don't be hard with the boy. I know something about him that—

MRS. CORNEY: Be quiet, old Sally! Get back to your work!

OLD SALLY: But, mistress, I was at the bedside of this boy when he was born. And before his poor young mother died, she gave me something to keep for—

OLIVER: My mother? Did you know my mother?

MRS. CORNEY: Your mother! She was a pauper! We found her in the street, and a regular, downright bad one she was, if I ever saw one!

OLIVER (*Angrily*): That's not true! Don't you talk about my mother like that!

MRS. CORNEY (*Outraged*): Mr. Bumble! Did you hear how he spoke to me?

BUMBLE: I did, ma'am, and I shall make certain he doesn't do it again.

OLD SALLY: Run, boy! Run for your life!

MRS. CORNEY: Stop him! He's running away! Stop him!

* * * * *

SCENE 2

NARRATOR: So Oliver ran, to the cheers of the workhouse boys and old Sally. He ran and ran until he reached London. The city was big and strange to him, but tired as he was, he could not help but look about him in amazement. And as he stared about him, someone was watching him—a young pickpocket called by his friends the Artful Dodger. . . .

OLIVER: What a big city London is! And so far away from the workhouse. Mr. Bumble will never find me here, and maybe . . . I can make my fortune.

DODGER: Hello, my covey! What's the matter?

OLIVER: I've been walking for seven days, and I'm very tired and hungry.

DODGER: Walking for seven days! Running away from home, I suppose?

OLIVER: I don't have a home.

DODGER (*Thoughtfully*): I see. First time in London?

OLIVER: Yes.

DODGER: Parents living?

OLIVER: No.

DODGER: Got any relations?

OLIVER: None that I know of.

DODGER: Money?

OLIVER: Not a farthing.

DODGER: That's *un*-fortunate! I suppose you want some grub and a place to sleep tonight?

OLIVER: I haven't slept under a roof since I left the country.

DODGER: Well, don't fret your eyelids on that score. I happen to know a respectable old gentleman who'll give you lodgings for nothing and never ask for the change.

OLIVER: That's very kind of him. Are you sure he won't mind?

DODGER: Not if any gentleman he knows introduces you. And does he know me? (*Playfully*) Oh, no! Not in the least! What's your name?

OLIVER: Oliver Twist.

DODGER: Mine's Jack Dawkins, although among my intimate acquaintances I'm better known as the *Art*-ful *Dodg*-er. It's dark enough now. Let's be off!

NARRATOR: The Artful Dodger led Oliver through dingy alleys and narrow streets until they reached the lodgings the Dodger had promised. Oliver found himself in a big room with a few pallets on the floor and general disorder all about—dirty dishes, a line of handkerchiefs hanging above the fireplace, old clothes scattered about. Not a very welcoming place, but Oliver saw a group of boys with an older man toasting sausages over the fireplace. The Dodger went immediately to the man and whispered a few words in his ear, then introduced him to Oliver as Fagin.

DODGER: Here he is, Fagin, my new friend, Oliver Twist.

FAGIN: Well, Oliver, I hope I may have the honor of your intimate acquaintance.

OLIVER (*Politely*): Thank you, sir.

FAGIN: And here are my boys.

CHARLEY: I'm Charley Bates, Oliver. Allow me to empty your pockets for you before you sit down to supper!

FAGIN: That's enough for now, boys. We are very glad to see you, Oliver. Dodger, take off the sausages. Ah, you're staring at the pocket-handkerchiefs, eh? We've just hung 'em out ready for the wash, haven't we, boys? Ha! Ha! I hope you've all been hard at work today!

CHARLEY: Hard as can be, Fagin.

FAGIN: What have you got, Dodger?

DODGER: A couple of pocketbooks.

FAGIN: Not so heavy as they might be, but very neat and nicely made. Ingenious workman, isn't he, Oliver?

OLIVER: Yes, sir.

FAGIN: And what do you have, Charley?

CHARLEY: Handkerchiefs!

FAGIN: They're very good ones, but the marks will have to be picked out with a needle. We'll show Oliver how to do it. You'd like that, wouldn't you, Oliver?

OLIVER: Oh, yes, sir. Will you teach me, sir?

FAGIN: Of course! You'll be one of us in no time! I tell you what, we'll show you a little game we play. Come, boys! Now, Oliver, I'm going to pretend that I'm one of those absent-minded old gentlemen who wander about Clerkenwell Square peering into the shop windows.

NARRATOR: Fagin took a chest from the cupboard and removed several pieces of jewelry, watches and other items and placed them in his pockets. As he walked about the room, humming and slapping his pockets, the boys bumped into him, distracting him, and slyly took everything from his pockets. While Oliver watched, two other friends of Fagin's came into the pickpockets' den—Nancy and Bill Sikes. . . .

DODGER: You're a poor man, Fagin.

FAGIN: Ah, so I am. Good boys! There, you see what a jolly time we have at this game, Oliver?

OLIVER (*Laughing*): Yes, sir.

FAGIN: You shall learn to play it, too. Just make the Dodger your model.

DODGER: Hello, Nancy!

NANCY (*Cheerfully*): Hello, boys! Why, what's this, Fagin? You've got a new boy?

FAGIN: Yes, my dear. Oliver, I want you to meet Miss Nancy.

OLIVER: How do you do, miss?

NANCY: He's not like the others. He has manners. I'm pleased to meet you, Oliver.

FAGIN: And Oliver, this is Mr. Bill Sikes. I have quite a useful family, Oliver. Very thoughtful and generous. Ha, ha! Now! Is my handkerchief hanging out of my pocket?

OLIVER: Yes, sir.

FAGIN: See if you can take it away without my feeling it. Is it gone?

OLIVER (*Delighted*): Yes, sir. Here it is.

FAGIN: Ah, you're a clever boy! In a few days you can go out to work with Charley and the Dodger. Now you can go to bed over there with the boys. Good night.

OLIVER: Good night, sir. And thank you for being so kind to me. I think I'm going to feel right at home here.

* * * * *

SCENE 3

NARRATOR: So Oliver settled down in Fagin's Den, learning to pick out the marks from stolen handkerchiefs and, without realizing what was happening, picking up the tricks of the pickpockets. After a few days, Fagin sent him out with Charley and the Artful Dodger. The boys strolled through Clerkenwell Square, stopping by a bookstall where Mr. Brownlow, a prosperous-looking gentleman, was browsing through a book. The bookseller's back was turned, the other customers paid the boys no attention. The Dodger pulled Charley and Oliver to one side. . . .

OLIVER: What's the matter?

DODGER: Hush! Do you see that old gentleman by the bookstall?

OLIVER: The one who is reading? Yes, I see him.

CHARLEY: He'll do!

OLIVER: Do for what? Does he make handkerchiefs, too?

DODGER: Keep your eyes open, Oliver. You may learn a thing or two.

NARRATOR: The Artful Dodger and Charley moved cautiously toward Mr. Brownlow. Oliver watched horror-stricken as the Dodger neatly removed a handkerchief from the gentleman's back pocket and handed it to Charley. Then both boys slipped out of sight behind the bookstall, and Mr. Brownlow's glance fell upon Oliver. . . .

MR. BROWNLOW: Here, what's this? My handkerchief! Here, boy, give me my handkerchief! Stop! Thief! Thief!

NARRATOR: Oliver turned in panic and started to run, but a man at the bookstall easily captured him and dragged him to Brownlow. The police constable came at a run.

MAN: Here he is, sir. I've got him. Took your handkerchief, did he?

CONSTABLE: Here, let me through! A young pickpocket, eh? Don't try to escape, you little villain!

BROWNLOW: Oh, don't hurt him, Constable. He's quite frightened, poor fellow. And he doesn't seem to have my handkerchief after all.

CONSTABLE: No matter, sir. He'll have to go before the magistrate. Come along!

OLIVER: But I didn't take the handkerchief! It was another boy, sir.

BOOKSELLER: Wait! Don't take that boy away. He's innocent!

CONSTABLE: Who are you?

BOOKSELLER: I keep the bookstall where the robbery took place, Officer. I saw what happened. An older boy took this gentleman's handkerchief, then disappeared into the crowd. This boy watched it all in perfect amazement.

CONSTABLE: Are you certain this boy is innocent?

BOOKSELLER: Absolutely, sir!

CONSTABLE: Very well. There's no need to trouble the magistrate.

BROWNLOW: Poor lad! Where do you live, my boy? Don't be frightened.

BOOKSELLER: No doubt he's an orphan, sir, or he wouldn't be around the streets in such a sorry condition.

BROWNLOW (*Kindly*): My name is Mr. Brownlow. I'll take you home with me, and my housekeeper will see that you get a warm supper and a clean bed.

* * * * *

SCENE 4

NARRATOR: When Brownlow thanked the bookseller and departed with Oliver, the Artful Dodger and Charley were watching. They knew well that Fagin would be displeased to hear of these events, and hurried to his den to report. They found him there with Nancy and Bill and the other boys. . . .

FAGIN: What? Only two of you? Where's Oliver? Where's the boy? Speak out, or I'll throttle you!

DODGER: A rich old gentleman took a liking to him, and that's all there is about it. He's gone!

FAGIN (*Furiously*): Gone? I told you to look after him! Oliver knows all about us! He could say something that will get us into trouble!

SIKES: Hah! That's very likely. You could be found out, Fagin. (*With a sneer*) And hanged.

FAGIN: I'm afraid, Bill, if the game is up with me, it might be up with a good many more besides. And I think it would come out worse for you than it would for me.

SIKES: Then somebody's got to find him and get him back. You can do it, Nancy. Nobody suspects you.

NANCY: The boy's better off out of this company. Let him be.

SIKES (*Roughly*): If he blabs to the police, it's the end for you as well as the rest of us! She'll go, Fagin. Won't she?

NANCY: All right, Bill. All right.

DODGER: Oliver can't be too far away. The old gentleman *walked* out of Clerkenwell Square.

FAGIN: You'd better start right away, my dear. You can wear a white apron and a bonnet. Then you'll look like a perfectly respectable young woman when you walk into the better neighborhoods. Just make some tearful inquiries, my dear, about your lost little brother.

NANCY (*Reluctantly*): I'll see what I can do. But it may take time.

FAGIN: Ah, she's a clever girl, Bill.

SIKES: Aye! Here's to her! She'll find the boy!

* * * * *

SCENE 5

NARRATOR: At Mr. Brownlow's home, Oliver did not know that the thieves were looking for him. He fell ill with a fever that lasted a month. Now, well again, Oliver and Rose Maylie, a young woman, are sitting in Mr. Brownlow's parlor, looking at a book, while Mr. Brownlow discusses the boy with Mr. Grimwig, a lawyer and close friend.

GRIMWIG: So that's the boy you found in the street a month ago, eh, Brownlow? That's the boy who's had the fever?

BROWNLOW: That is the boy, Grimwig.

GRIMWIG: Boy! How are you now, boy?

OLIVER (*Politely*): A great deal better, thank you, sir.

BROWNLOW: Yes, you are coming along very well now, aren't you, Oliver?

OLIVER: Yes, sir. You've been very good to me.

BROWNLOW: And I promise I shall never desert you, my boy, unless you give me cause.

OLIVER: I never, never will, sir!

BROWNLOW: I'm sure you won't. Rose, will you have the goodness to step downstairs and tell Mrs. Bedwin we are ready for tea?

ROSE: Of course. Come and help me, Oliver.

GRIMWIG (*After a pause*): Do you know what you're doing, Brownlow? Where does that boy come from? Who is he?

BROWNLOW: I've made a number of inquiries after him, but I haven't yet received a satisfactory answer. I've even put an advertisement in the papers in hopes of learning something about his past. I'm strangely drawn to him, Grimwig, and the thing that strikes me most about him is his remarkable likeness to that portrait of Rose's sister. He's quite fond of it.

GRIMWIG: Nonsense! You found this boy in the street and that's where he'll end up! He will, or I'll eat my head, sir! And have you no better occupation for Miss Rose Maylie than to set her fussing over that young guttersnipe?

BROWNLOW (*Trying to be patient*): You know that Rose is always welcome here for the sake of my old acquaintance with her family. She and Oliver have become close friends, and I'm certain her careful attention has helped him to recover.

NARRATOR: Mrs. Bedwin, the housekeeper, comes in with a plate of muffins, followed by Rose with a tea-tray and Oliver, who carries some expensive-looking books.

BROWNLOW: Ah, here is our tea.

GRIMWIG (*Suddenly cheerful*): Ah, muffins! You always make the most excellent muffins, Mrs. Bedwin!

MRS. BEDWIN: Thank you, sir.

OLIVER: The boy from the bookstall has just brought these books, sir.

BROWNLOW: Oh, but there are some books to go back.

ROSE: I'm afraid the boy has gone, sir.

BROWNLOW: Well, I'm sorry for that. I wanted to return these books tonight.

GRIMWIG (*With a sneer*): Why don't you send Oliver with them?

OLIVER: Oh, yes, do let me take them for you, sir.

MRS. BEDWIN: I don't think he's well enough to go into the streets, sir.

GRIMWIG: Nonsense! He looks perfectly well and willing to me.

BROWNLOW: Well, I don't know . . . (*As* GRIMWIG *coughs loudly*) Very well, you may go, Oliver. It isn't far. Here are the books and a five-pound note to pay my bill.

OLIVER: I won't be gone ten minutes.

NARRATOR: Oliver and Mrs. Bedwin go out, with Mrs. Bedwin giving him a list of instructions. . . .

MRS. BEDWIN: Let me tell you the quickest way to go, my dear. And you must button your jacket and put on your cap.

BROWNLOW: He should be back before dark.

GRIMWIG: Indeed! You expect him to come back, do you?

ROSE: Why, of course he'll come back. Why shouldn't he?

GRIMWIG: He has a new suit of clothes on his back, a set of valuable books under his arm, and a five-pound note in his pocket. He'll join his old friends in the streets and laugh at you all!

ROSE: Dear Mr. Grimwig! I've nursed Oliver these past weeks, and I assure you he is a gentle and grateful child, sir.

GRIMWIG: Miss Maylie, I am sorry to say it, but if that boy ever returns to this house again, I'll eat my head!

* * * * *

SCENE 6

NARRATOR: Oliver makes his way quickly to the bookstall. There is no one about as he nears the bookstall, but then

Nancy, wearing her bonnet and apron, comes in. Seeing Oliver, she rushes up to him and takes him by the hands.

NANCY: Oliver! At last I've found you!

OLIVER (*Alarmed*): Let me go! Why are you stopping me? Why, it's you, Nancy.

NANCY: Yes, Oliver. Now do be quiet and come with me.

OLIVER: But I don't belong with you. I live with Mr. Brownlow and Mrs. Bedwin now.

NANCY (*Nervously*): But you must come with me, Oliver. I won't harm you.

OLIVER: No! You'll take me back to Fagin, and he'll try to make me steal. Please, Nancy, let me go. Mr. Brownlow is waiting for me.

NANCY (*Reluctantly*): There's no help for it. Now come along!

NARRATOR: As Oliver struggles to escape her and shouts for help, Bill Sikes suddenly runs up, seizes Oliver and claps his hand over the boy's mouth. Fagin, the Artful Dodger, and Charley join the group.

SIKES: Hold your noise, you young dog!

FAGIN: Ah, Sikes, you've caught him.

CHARLEY: Just look at him, Fagin!

DODGER: Fancy clothes and books. Nothing but a gentleman.

FAGIN: Delighted to see you looking so well, Oliver. And what fine books might these be?

OLIVER: Those books belong to Mr. Brownlow, who brought me into his house and took care of me. Please send them back to him. He'll think I stole them.

FAGIN (*Chuckling*): You're quite right, Oliver. He *will* think you've stolen them, and he won't ever want to see you again. It couldn't have happened better if we'd planned it!

OLIVER (*Shouting*): Police! Help! Help!

FAGIN (*Furiously*): So you wanted to get away, Oliver? Called for the police, did you? I'll cure you of that, my young master!

NANCY: No! I won't stand by and see it done, Fagin! Let him be!

FAGIN (*Surprised*): Come, come, my dear. It's for our own good.

NANCY: You villain! I robbed for you when I was only half as old as he is, and see the good it's done me!

FAGIN: Well, my dear, it's been your living ever since.

NANCY: Yes, and the cold dirty streets are my home, and the shadow of the gallows hangs over me every hour! You're the wretch that drove me to it, and you'll keep me there 'til I die!

FAGIN (*Fiercely*): I'll do you a mischief worse than that if you say much more.

SIKES: Keep quiet, Nancy! Who are you to be a friend to the boy? Go home and cool your temper!

NANCY: I wish I'd been struck dead before I lent a hand in bringing him back. He's a liar and a thief from this night on.

FAGIN: Temper! Passion! It's the worst of having to do with women, but we can't get on in our line without them. Dodger, Charley! Hold the boy! Are you set for the job next week, Bill?

SIKES: I need a boy, yet, a small one, to get through the window and unlock the door of the house from inside.

FAGIN: A small boy? Use Oliver!

SIKES: Him?

FAGIN: The other boys are too big, Bill. And he'll do everything you want, if you frighten him enough.

SIKES: Frighten him? Hah! If he makes one wrong turn, you won't see him again. Think of that before you send him on a job with me!

FAGIN: I have thought of it, Bill. I want to fill his mind with the idea that he's been a thief. Then he'll be ours forever, and he won't try to escape again.

NARRATOR: Fagin signals to Charley and the Dodger, who keep a firm grasp on Oliver. Then all except Nancy start off down the street. Oliver looks back pleadingly at her before he is dragged away.

NANCY (*Moved*): Oh, Oliver, if I could help you, I would! But I haven't the power. I . . . (*Thinks a moment, then seems resolved*) Perhaps there is something . . . but the danger in it! If I am discovered . . . Mr. Brownlow . . . he's the boy's last hope. If only I can find him!

SIKES (*Calling roughly*): Nancy!

NANCY (*Hastily*): I'm coming, Bill.

* * * * *

SCENE 7

NARRATOR: Nancy told no one about her plan to help Oliver, but a few days later, she approaches Mr. Brownlow and Rose, who are browsing at the bookstall . . .

NANCY (*Timidly*): Miss . . .

ROSE (*Kindly*): Yes? What is it?

NANCY: Forgive me, miss, but . . . is this gentleman Mr. Brownlow?

BROWNLOW: Yes, I am Mr. Brownlow. What do you want, young woman?

NANCY: Sir, I'm risking my life to come here, but I must speak to you. (*Nervously*) I am the girl who took Oliver away a few days ago, when you sent him here with your books.

ROSE: You? Oh, but where is he now? Is he safe?

NANCY: Yes, miss, as safe as he can be in a den of thieves.

ROSE: Thieves?

BROWNLOW: Then I'm sure the boy is quite at home!

NANCY: At home, sir? Why, the poor child is a prisoner, frightened and miserable!

ROSE: I knew he wouldn't leave us of his own will. I just can't believe what that gentleman told us this morning.

NANCY (*Nervously*): What gentleman, miss?

BROWNLOW: A certain Mr. Bumble came to us from the parish

workhouse where Oliver was born. He answered my newspaper advertisement about the boy. It seems that Oliver is a wicked and ungrateful child who ran away from the workhouse several weeks ago. He is also a young villain who has robbed me and run away, when I had thoughts of giving him a home. In short, I never want to hear of him again!

NANCY: Sir, please, listen to me! Oliver was taken from you by force. He speaks of you and this young lady with the greatest affection, and his only wish is to be safely back with you again.

BROWNLOW (*Hesitantly*): I would like to believe you, young woman. I became very fond of the boy, but . . .

NANCY: If he isn't rescued soon, he'll be forced to steal and forever after keep company with thieves. You are his only hope, sir!

ROSE: We must get him back, at once!

BROWNLOW (*Convinced*): Yes, yes, we must. Young woman, can you help us?

NANCY: I'll try. But I must not be watched or followed, now or any other time.

BROWNLOW: Very well.

NANCY: Sunday night at the stroke of twelve, meet me here. I'll bring Oliver if I can. But if I am discovered, you will never see either of us again.

BROWNLOW: We'll trust you to do what you can. And thank you!

NANCY: Until Sunday then.

* * * * *

SCENE 8

NARRATOR: The next Sunday, Mr. Brownlow and Rose reach the bookstall at the appointed time. At the sight of Oliver and Nancy coming up the street, Rose calls out with joy . . .

ROSE: Oliver!

OLIVER: Rose! Mr. Brownlow! I didn't think I would ever see you again.

BROWNLOW: My boy! Young woman, we shall always be grateful to you. Please tell me how I can help you.

NANCY (*Near tears*): I'm past all help. Take the boy and go quickly!

BROWNLOW: But you must let me do something for you. I can see you to a safe place, out of England if you like. You don't have to return to your old haunts.

OLIVER: Oh, yes, Nancy, please come with us. I'm afraid for you to go back.

NANCY (*Hesitating a moment*): No, I hate my life, but I cannot leave it. I must hurry back before I am missed. Goodbye, Oliver. You'll have a home now with these good people.

OLIVER: I shall never forget you, Nancy. Never!

NARRATOR: Nancy turns away quickly, sobbing. Mr. Brownlow watches her anxiously for a moment, then he and Rose take Oliver by the hand and they start for home. Nancy starts off down the street. Suddenly, Bill Sikes leaps out in front of her. He carries a club.

SIKES: Well, Nancy! It's a pretty piece of work you've been up to!

NANCY (*Terrified*): Bill! Bill, please, don't look at me like that!

SIKES: Keep quiet! You know what I have to do.

NANCY: No! Bill, please! I haven't betrayed anyone! I only saved the boy, that's all. I've been true to you and the others, Bill, upon my soul I have!

SIKES: You put the mark on us! Betrayed us all to that meddling old gentleman!

NARRATOR: Sikes hits Nancy with the club, and she screams as she falls to the ground and lies motionless. He backs away from her, stunned and horrified. Fagin, the Dodger and Charley appear, just as Mr. Brownlow hurries back.

MR. BROWNLOW: I heard a scream . . . Murder! Help, police!

NARRATOR: Sikes, Fagin and the boys start to scatter, but the

police swarm in and surround them. The constables hand-
cuff the thieves. Mr. Brownlow joins those trying to help
Nancy, but it is too late. He shakes his head sadly and walks
away slowly as the constables take away their prisoners.

CONSTABLE: All right! Let's go!

DODGER (*Cockily*): Watch how you handle me, my man. I'm
an Englishman as much as you, and I've got my privileges.

CONSTABLE: Hah! You're a young vagabond, and we've got
you now. Your old master, too. Come along!

* * * * *

SCENE 9

NARRATOR: A short time later, in Mr. Brownlow's parlor, he
and Mr. Grimwig tell Rose, Mrs. Bedwin, and Oliver what
they have learned about Oliver . . .

BROWNLOW: Now, Oliver, my boy, you are going to hear some
very astonishing things tonight. I have made some inquiries,
and I've learned that my old friend, Edwin Leeford, was your
father. He died ten years ago in Rome. But in his will, which
my lawyer friend, Mr. Grimwig, has in his hands, your father
left his property to you and your mother. Unfortunately,
your mother did not know about it before she died.

GRIMWIG: Your father's will reads that if you were a boy,
which you are, you would inherit a sizable sum of money, on
the condition that you did not stain your name with any public act of dishonor or wrong.

BROWNLOW: And since you have been an honest lad, Oliver,
the money is yours.

GRIMWIG: We also learned that when your mother died, she
left a gold locket with the old nurse who attended your birth.

OLIVER: Old Sally?

BROWNLOW: Yes. She has died, but she gave the locket to the
workhouse matron, Mrs. Corney, who sold it for her own

profit. Both she and Mr. Bumble are no longer in service at the workhouse. I saw to that!

GRIMWIG: The locket is gone forever, my boy, but we have learned that it contained your mother's wedding ring.

ROSE: You see, Oliver, the sweet lady in this picture was your mother. Your father painted it and left it with Mr. Brownlow before he went to Rome. You look very much like her.

OLIVER: My mother! I have always loved her, and dreamed of seeing her face.

ROSE: She was my older sister, Agnes. And that means, Oliver, that I am your aunt!

MRS. BEDWIN: And Oliver, my dear, you shall have a home here with us for as long as you like!

GRIMWIG: Ahem! Now that everything has turned out well, and I'm truly glad of it, my boy, perhaps you could persuade Mrs. Bedwin to bring out a plate of those excellent muffins? Otherwise, I shall be forced to eat my head!

MRS. BEDWIN: Oh, do come downstairs to tea, all of you!

THE END

How Much Land Does a Man Need?

This play is based on a short story by Leo Tolstoy, the famous author of *War and Peace* and other great books. It takes place in Russia many years ago, and it is about greed. There is an ironic answer to the question the title asks.

Read the play through silently, and then discuss the story of the play with your group. Do you understand the play? Talk about irony. Can you think of other examples?

After you have chosen your parts, read the play aloud, getting the proper feeling into all the speeches. How does Pahom treat his wife? How does he treat Widow Litzki? Does his character change as the play goes along? How do you show this with your voice?

The Devil is the narrator in this play; he is also a distinct character. How do you think the Devil should sound? Do you understand his part in the play?

Practice reading the play aloud until you have it word perfect.

When you feel you are ready, read the play for the entire class. You may want to have a discussion with the class about the play's meaning.

HOW MUCH LAND DOES A MAN NEED?

by Leo Tolstoy
adapted by Michael T. Leech

Characters

(5 boys, 3 girls)
DEVIL, *the narrator*
PAHOM, *a peasant*
NATASHA, *his wife*
KATYA, *her sister*
WIDOW LITZKI
THE DEALER
SERVANT
CHIEF OF THE BASHKIRS

SCENE 1

DEVIL: Ladies and gentlemen, we bring you a short drama on the subject of greed—with me, the Devil himself, providing the final answer. How much land does a man need? It's a very interesting question, isn't it? I answered the question most satisfactorily a few years ago, on one of my visits to Earth from my dominions—er—down below. I was passing through Russia when this adventure befell me. I had found a peasant's house and was lodged behind the stove to keep warm. The peasant, Pahom, was himself asleep on a mattress on the top of the stove. I was aroused by the peasant's wife, Natasha, as she chattered away to her sister.

NATASHA: What a dreadful journey you must have had, Katya darling.

KATYA: Yes, Natasha, it was hard—but it's good to see you again! (PAHOM *snores loudly*.) Who is that?

NATASHA: It's my husband, Pahom. He sleeps on top of the stove. It's the only warm place when the nights are cold.

KATYA: That peasant husband of yours—oh, yes, I remember. I don't know how you can live in the country, Natasha, when you could be as comfortable as I am in the town.

NATASHA: Tell me about life in town, Katya. Sometimes it does get dull in the country.

KATYA: I can imagine it. My little town of Yoghov may not be as grand as Moscow or Petersburg, but we don't lag behind them in fashions, I can tell you!

NATASHA: Oh?

KATYA: My poor little sister, I don't know how you can possibly exist out here in the country, married to a mere peasant.

NATASHA: Hush, Katya! Pahom will hear you. (*Pause*) He has been a good husband to me.

KATYA: But he's a *peasant*, Natasha.

NATASHA: I should remind you, Katya, that before you married this shopkeeper of yours, *you* were the daughter of a peasant.

KATYA (*Hurriedly*): Why don't you give up this country life and come back with me to Yoghov? In this miserable part of the world what can you know of the good things of life? What do you know of society?

NATASHA: Nothing, it's true. . . .

KATYA: Why, I go to the theater at least once a week, and in the summer there are promenades and entertainments. I tell you, we know how to live!

NATASHA: You may live grandly and we roughly, but at least we are free from anxiety. You and your husband may live in better style, and you may earn more than you need, but you could just as easily lose all you have!

KATYA: My husband is too wise a man for that.

NATASHA: Our work may be coarse, but it is sure! We bow to no one, and we have our land for security. In the town you are surrounded by temptations. Today all may go well, but tomorrow the Devil may tempt your husband. Then all will go to ruin. I hear such things happen frequently.

KATYA: I should like to see my husband tempted while I am alive! Ha, ha! That's a good one, my little Natasha!

NATASHA: Sh-h-h! You will wake Pahom. He is so irritable when someone wakes him.

KATYA: Let us walk a little and I will tell you about the dresses the women are wearing in Yoghov this summer.

DEVIL: With Natasha and her sister gone, let us see what Pahom himself has to say.

PAHOM: I must say, my wife is a sensible woman. As she says, we have no time to let nonsense settle in our heads—we're kept much too busy working the land! My only wish is for more of it. Why, just a few more acres, and I'd be well satisfied. Ah, if only I had more land, I shouldn't fear the Devil himself!

DEVIL: Did you hear that? If he had the land he wanted, he wouldn't even be afraid of me! Well, we'll see about *that*. I'll make a bargain with you, my little Pahom. You shall have the land you desire. I'll give you that land—and it will be the means of getting your soul into my hands.

* * * * *

SCENE 2

DEVIL: Now we will look ahead a month or two and see what is happening about Pahom's wish for a little more land.

PAHOM: Where are you, Natasha? Someone is at the door.

NATASHA: It's the Widow Litzki, Pahom.

PAHOM: Well, let her in. But don't offer her any of our food, mind you. She's probably come for another installment of money for her land. She drives a hard bargain. I don't want her to have more than I need give her.

NATASHA: Pahom, you got a good bargain on her land.

PAHOM: *You* may think so—I don't like to pay more than is

absolutely necessary. Well, what are you waiting for? Let her in! (*Pause*)

WIDOW LITZKI: Good day to you, friend Pahom.

PAHOM: Good day, Widow Litzki. What can I do for you?

WIDOW: I've come for the payment on the forty acres of land you bought from me, Pahom. One more payment and you'll be all settled up.

PAHOM: I can't wait for the day when it's all mine.

WIDOW: It's a good piece of land.

PAHOM: It's all right, I suppose.

WIDOW: You were lucky to get it. If you remember, I had almost sold it to the innkeeper—and then the Commune offered to buy.

PAHOM: Yes, I remember. The Devil himself must have sown discord among the men of the Commune, for they couldn't agree to save their lives! So we smallholders bought it up in pieces.

WIDOW: And a good bargain I gave you.

PAHOM (*Rudely*): That's a matter of opinion, old woman. Here, I have your money for you. Take it, take it.

WIDOW: Now, there's no need to hurry business! I'm quite thirsty from climbing that long hill.

PAHOM: Then you'll be wanting to get home for a glass of tea. Good day to you.

WIDOW (*Annoyed*): Good day to you both.

NATASHA (*Reproachfully*): We might have offered her something, Pahom.

PAHOM: What ever for? That was the last payment, and I don't ever again have to listen to her telling me what a bargain it was. Imagine it, Natasha—forty acres and it's all our own!

NATASHA: It's a very good thing that the harvest fetched a high price.

PAHOM (*Expansively*): Yes—we've done very well, very well. Our cows are fat, we have fine pigs, and our fields are as rich and productive as any for miles around.

NATASHA: Yes, that is so. We should be well satisfied.

PAHOM: You know, when I passed this land before, it appeared just the same as any other land, but *now*, now that we own it, somehow it's a different story.

* * * *

SCENE 3

DEVIL: Now let us see what life is like for Pahom a year later. What is this? Pahom in a rich coat, Natasha in an expensive shawl. Surely Pahom now has plenty of money, and all the land he needs . . .

PAHOM (*Angrily*): You know, Natasha, it isn't easy being a landowner. Ever since we paid the Widow Litzki her last payment a year ago, there's been nothing but trouble. It's only a small piece of land, yet we are used hard by trespassers and thieves. You'd think they'd respect a man's land—but do they? I ask you, do they?

NATASHA (*Nervously*): No, Pahom, they don't.

PAHOM: They let their cows into *my* meadows, they run their horses into *my* corn. They even chop down *my* trees—and when, at long last, I prosecute, what happens? The judges acquit the offenders!

NATASHA: Life is sometimes very difficult. Our neighbors are uttering all sorts of threats against us since you quarreled with them and insulted the judges. You know, Pahom, I think it would be rather nice if we moved away from here.

PAHOM (*Suspiciously*): But where should we go? And why should we leave our land?

NATASHA: I've heard there's a peasant passing through the village who says that where he's settled, beyond the Volga, land is going begging. He says they *need* people to farm it. Several people are leaving these parts and going there.

PAHOM: So much the better for us. If others go, then we shall have more room to move and I shall be able to get more land. It's too cramped to be comfortable as it is.

NATASHA (*Persisting*): The peasant says that every man who goes there is granted twenty-five acres free by the Commune. With our four sons and yourself that would mean a great deal of land.

PAHOM (*Getting interested*): Twenty-five acres to every man? That would mean a hundred and twenty-five acres for us.

NATASHA: The land is good, too, for he tells of rye growing as high as a horse.

PAHOM: Where did you hear all this?

NATASHA: From old Fedor; the man from the Volga is staying with him.

PAHOM: I think I'll take a stroll into the village and find out a little more about all this.

NATASHA: He told Fedor he came back here only to fetch his wife and children to share in his good fortune. He says he went there with nothing but his bare hands and now he has horses, cows, and much land of his own.

PAHOM: Much land, eh? He has done well, very well. But not as well as *I* could do. I think it might be worthwhile to find out a little more about this. I'll be back in time for supper—after I've found out what I want to know.

* * * * *

SCENE 4

DEVIL: You see? Pahom can't resist it. He's greedy for land—more and more and more of it. He has moved his family beyond the Volga, and now he has one hundred and twenty-five acres. One hundred and twenty-five acres is a lot of land. But will little Pahom be satisfied? We shall see. I am very patient. Three years slip quickly by, and Pahom and his family are settled in their new home.

PAHOM (*In a fury*): Natasha! Natasha!

NATASHA: Yes, Pahom—here I am.

PAHOM: Do you know what has happened? Can you guess the trick the wretched landlord has played on me?

NATASHA (*Nervously*): No, I can't guess.

PAHOM: Of course you can't—you're just a foolish woman. I've just spent two whole days plowing up the extra land I rent from him, and what does he do? He waits until I've finished and then he tells me he's not going to let me have it! I was a fool not to demand a contract from him before I began. Oh!

NATASHA: Why do we have to rent more land when you already have one hundred and twenty-five acres?

PAHOM: We have been three years on this farm and now some of the land must be allowed to lie fallow before it can be used again. There isn't room here to swing a cat. There's only one thing to do—I must have more land.

NATASHA: But do you know anyone with land to sell? Can't we make do with what we have, Pahom?

PAHOM: I must have more. I'm tired of haggling over rent and having all this trouble when some little fool changes his mind. There's an old man in the village who has a piece to sell. It's not a lot, about thirteen hundred acres, but it's freehold.

NATASHA (*Aghast*): Thirteen hundred acres!

PAHOM: Yes, not very much, but I understand he's in difficulties, and I'm sure I could beat him down.

NATASHA: It seems such a lot. I wish you could be content with what you have already.

PAHOM (*Irritated*): Content with *this?* Ha, don't be more of a fool than you are already. Look—if I bargain cleverly I think I can get the whole lot, all thirteen hundred good acres, for 1,500 roubles.

NATASHA: That's a very fair price.

PAHOM: Fair? I tell you, woman, for this land that's a steal! It won't be easy to raise the money, but if I sell the young colt, and maybe some of the bees—and perhaps hire out young

Yasha as a laborer and take his wages in advance. . . . Hm, that won't be enough, but if your brother Pavel will lend us something . . . Hmm. I hear someone at the door. See who it is, Natasha. I'm busy.

NATASHA: It's a dealer, Pahom. He asks for feed for his horses.

PAHOM: Tell him to come in. Where is he traveling from?

NATASHA: He didn't say.

PAHOM (*To himself*): Oh, never mind. We shall be treated to some gossip, I suppose—wherever he comes from. (*Calling*) Oh, Natasha, tell Yasha to look after the horses—but not to feed them too well! We can't afford to be generous to other people's beasts!

NATASHA: Hush, Pahom!

PAHOM (*Angrily*): I don't care who hears me. (PAHOM *changes his tone.*) Come in! Welcome to my house! Sit down. My son will take care of your horses. Have you traveled far?

DEALER: Some long distance, I can tell you. I've come from the land of the Bashkirs!

PAHOM (*Curiously*): The Bashkirs? Who are they?

DEALER: They're a strange tribe. They live by a river on a great fertile plain which stretches as far as the eye can see. They don't cultivate it—they merely graze their flocks.

PAHOM (*Incredulous*): They don't cultivate it? Why not?

DEALER: They don't work more than they have to. The men are all stout and jolly. They sit at the entrances to their tents and play their pipes all day!

PAHOM: A strange life. They have much land then, these Bashkirs?

DEALER: Oh, very much. I myself have bought thirteen thousand acres.

NATASHA: Thirteen thousand acres!

DEALER: That is so. But can you imagine how much those fools of Bashkirs charged me for it?

PAHOM (*Greedily*): No—how much?

DEALER (*Laughing*): Ah, my friend, it was a mere trifle. I

bought all that rich land for the sum of one thousand roubles!

PAHOM (*Astounded*): One thousand roubles? Is that *all?* How did you do it?

DEALER: All that was necessary was to make friends with them and their chief. I gave them presents—dressing gowns, carpets, tea—and I bought the land for less than two cents an acre! It was easy.

PAHOM: Less than two cents an acre! Did you hear that, Natasha?

NATASHA: Yes—but, Pahom, we don't need to move again. Not for *more* land. What would we do with thirteen thousand acres?

PAHOM: Aha—what *wouldn't* I do? And at such a price.

DEALER: It's as easy as stealing from a child.

PAHOM: It's unbelievable! Er—is it possible, do you think, that they might sell some to me? They seem to have a great deal.

DEALER: There is more land there than you can cover if you walked for a year. It all belongs to the Bashkirs. As I told you, they are as simple as their sheep, and land can be had for almost nothing!

PAHOM: Well, well, well. You certainly came at the right time, my friend. If it had been a week from now I might have spent a thousand roubles for only thirteen *hundred* acres—and a debt into the bargain! (*To himself*) Now, if I left Natasha here to look after the homestead, I could take my money and get ten times as much there as here. (*Loudly*) You know, I think it would be an excellent idea if I went to see those foolish Bashkirs.

NATASHA (*Wailing*): But, Pahom, what is the sense?

PAHOM: Silence, woman! (*In a friendly tone*) Tell me, my good man, just how does one get to the country of the Bashkirs?

* * * * *

SCENE 5

DEVIL: Well, well, well. Thirteen hundred acres isn't enough for Pahom! How much land does he need? Will thirteen *thousand* acres be enough? Ha! We shall see. We shall see, for Pahom set out at once with his servant for the country of the Bashkirs.

SERVANT: Is it much farther, master? (*Plaintively*) We've been walking for six whole days now!

PAHOM: You're younger than I, and your legs should be stronger. Come on, we'll see the Bashkirs' tents soon.

SERVANT: I hope so. I'm getting very tired.

PAHOM (*Ignoring him; gleefully*): What good land we're passing through! And see how much of it there is! The dealer was right. If those Bashkirs are as stupid as he says, we should have no trouble at all.

SERVANT (*Shouting*): Look—there are tents ahead, master!

PAHOM: So there are.

SERVANT: Some people are coming out to meet us.

PAHOM: Quick—get some of the presents from the sack! We'd best make sure that they're friendly.

SERVANT: They *seem* very friendly. They're waving and laughing.

PAHOM: You never know. I don't want to be robbed of my money. (*Raising his voice*) Do any of you speak Russian? Is there someone who can talk with me? (*Louder*) Is there anyone who can talk with me?

CHIEF: I am the chief of the Bashkirs. What do you want with us?

PAHOM (*Aside*): Quick, numskull! Fetch me some tea and the best dressing gown we have brought with us.

SERVANT: Yes—oh, yes. At once, master, at once.

PAHOM (*In a flattering voice*): Sir, I bring you gifts. Here are some tea and a fine silk gown.

CHIEF: Hm. Very handsome. But what do *you* want?

PAHOM: I—er—nothing, sir. Er—that is, something that can only be nothing to you, since you have so much of it.

CHIEF: What is that? You give us presents and it is our custom to do all we can to repay our guests.

PAHOM: I would very much like some of your land, sir. At home, my land is crowded and the soil is exhausted, but you have lots of land and it is good! I never saw the like of it before. I should like to buy some of it from you.

CHIEF: My people wish to tell you that in return for your presents, they will gladly give you as much land as you want. You have only to point it out with your hand and it is yours.

PAHOM (*Puzzled*): Just like that?

CHIEF: Choose whichever piece of land you like. We have plenty of it!

PAHOM (*Aside, whispering*): How can I take as much as I like?

SERVANT (*Whispering*): Ask for a deed to make it secure, master. Otherwise they can take it from you as easily as they gave it.

PAHOM (*Whispering*): True. (*Louder*) Thank you for your kind words. You have much land, and I only want a very small part. But I should like to be sure which piece is mine. Could it not be measured and made over to me? Without a deed for my land, your children may wish to take it away from me even though you gave it yourselves.

CHIEF: You are quite right. We will make it over to you.

PAHOM (*Boldly*): I heard that a dealer came here once and that you gave him a little land, too, and signed title deeds.

CHIEF: Oh, yes, it can be done quite easily. We have a scribe here. We will draw up the deed and then go to town with you to have it properly sealed.

PAHOM (*Greedily*): What will be the price?

CHIEF: Our price is always the same—one thousand roubles a day.

PAHOM (*Taken aback*): One thousand roubles a *day*? What

sort of a measurement is that? How many acres would that be?

CHIEF: We do not know how to reckon it out—such things do not interest the Bashkirs. We sell it by the day. As much land as you can walk around in a day is yours—and the price is one thousand roubles a day.

PAHOM: As much as you can walk round in a day! But in a day you can walk round a large piece of land!

CHIEF (*Laughing*): It will be all yours! There is only one condition. If you don't return to the spot where you started before the sun sets, then your money is lost.

PAHOM: That's easy! How shall I mark the way I have gone?

CHIEF: You will take a spade with you. You will start from this spot in the morning and make your round, digging a hole whenever you think it is necessary to make a mark. We shall be able to see you from here, since this hill commands a wide view. When you have returned we shall go round with a plow from hole to hole. You may make as big a circuit as you wish, but before sunset you must return to the place you started from. All the land you have walked around will be yours!

PAHOM: Why, that is wonderful!

CHIEF: You agree with everything?

PAHOM: Agree with everything? I'd be crazy not to! Of course! Yes, yes.

CHIEF: Good. Now, let us eat and drink. Tomorrow we shall assemble at daybreak and ride out to this hilltop. You will begin to walk at sunrise.

* * * * *

SCENE 6

PAHOM: Soon it will be sunrise and I shall start to walk around my land! What a great piece of luck this is! Such a wonderful bargain. Imagine how much land I shall have by the end of this day—I feel as if I could walk for hundreds of miles! What fools these Bashkirs are. Brr-r-r! It's cold. Oh, what a terrible dream I had last night! I dreamt I was a corpse at the feet of the Devil. Thank goodness it's getting light and the dawn is breaking—it's time to go! Where's that servant of mine? Where are those lazy Bashkirs? Hey, there! Wake up! It's time to start!

SERVANT: Here I am, master!

PAHOM: Good. You have the spade?

SERVANT: Yes, master.

PAHOM (*Impatient to start*): The sun will be up in a minute! *Where* are the Bashkirs?

CHIEF: Here we are. There's plenty of time. What a blue sky —it's going to be a hot day.

SERVANT: You'll not need your coat, master.

PAHOM (*Brusquely*): I'll keep it, thank you. I trust nobody.

CHIEF: Are you ready to start? My men and I will stay here and watch you. All this land, as far as the eye can see, is ours. You can have any part of it you like.

PAHOM: It is marvelous land! As flat as the palm of my hand— and as black as the seed of a poppy!

CHIEF: I shall place my hat on the ground. There! You will start from here and come back to this point. My hat shall be our mark.

PAHOM: Here is my money—one thousand roubles. Now I am ready.

CHIEF: Which way will you start?

PAHOM: Towards the rising sun. In a moment it will be above the horizon. There! There it is!

CHIEF: Off you go. Walk well, my little Pahom. Walk well!

DEVIL: Looks as if Pahom will have all that his heart desires, doesn't it? After all, you would think that all the land he can walk around in a whole day should be as much as even he needs. There he is. He's walking well, pausing only to make a mark with his spade. After three hours he's in good shape.

Now he's turning. It's getting to be a hot day. I feel quite at home.

CHIEF: It's a splendid piece of land he's carving out for himself, but is it worth the price? (*He laughs loudly*)

SERVANT: He's so far away he can hardly be seen!

CHIEF: He still hasn't turned round, and it's past midday. Ah, I see. He can't resist taking that extra piece of sweet meadow at the end of the line. He has made his first sides too long.

SERVANT: He's turning now.

DEVIL: He's beginning to walk much faster now. The sun is halfway to the horizon and he has a long way to walk before he gets back. Ah, he's started his fourth side—and not a moment too soon!

SERVANT: He can't keep up that pace. He'll never make it back!

DEVIL (*Slyly*): Pahom is beginning to worry. He's taken off his boots as well as his coat. He is beginning to get very tired. Pahom is getting desperate. There is not much time left.

CHIEF: He has tried for too much! *Now* we shall see if the Bashkirs are such fools!

DEVIL: He has thrown off coat, boots and water bottle. Can he win? The sun is blood red now and very close to the horizon.

PAHOM: I *must* get there! They will call me a fool if I do not. There is so much land. Oh, don't let me die! Let me reach the hill. (*Gasping*) The sun is setting—my labor has all been in vain! No, no! I can still get there! From the hilltop the sun has not yet set! If I make one last great effort, I shall surely do it! (*He takes a great breath*) It is not the Chief of the Bashkirs, for he has the face of the dealer—and look, he is the peasant from the Volga, too! I must be dreaming some horrible dream. It is *not* the Chief of the Bashkirs! It is the Devil himself. (*He gives a terrible cry.*)

CHIEF: Poor fellow, he could not quite reach my hat. I wonder if he has the land he needs now?

SERVANT: Master, master! Get up, master! There is blood coming from his mouth! My master is dead! Oh, my poor master!

DEVIL: Everyone was very sorry, but what could they do? Pahom had tried for too much land and the effort had killed him. His servant picked up the spade and began to dig a grave for his master to lie in. How much land did he need? Six feet, from his head to his heels, that was all he needed.

THE END

The Scarlet Pimpernel

This play is based on a famous novel about the French Revolution. You may want to have one of your group do a short report on the French Revolution before you work on the play so you will understand the historical events of the time.

Read the play through silently to yourself. There are difficult human relationships in this play, and it is important to understand them if you want to make the play exciting and interesting.

What is Marguerite like? What is the relationship between her and Chauvelin? Between her and her husband, Sir Percy? Marguerite, the Countess and Suzanne?

What sort of a person do you think Sir Percy is? He is different at the beginning of the play from the way he is at the end. How would you read his part?

Discuss what Chauvelin is like. How would you show that he is French? What tone of voice do you think he uses?

Choose parts and read the play aloud together, scene by scene. Work on any problems in each scene before going on to the next. Be sure you understand all the words, and pay attention to phrasing, punctuation, and meaning.

When the group feels it is doing the play well, arrange to read for another group, or a tape recorder.

Note to the teacher: Starred parts may be doubled.

THE SCARLET PIMPERNEL

by Baroness Orczy
adapted by Michael T. Leech

Characters

(12 boys, 5 girls, and a narrator)

NARRATOR
LADY MARGUERITE BLAKENEY
SIR PERCY BLAKENEY, *her husband*
CHAUVELIN, *an agent of the French government*
CHAUVELIN'S COMPANION*
MR. JELLYBAND, *an English innkeeper**
SALLY, *his daughter**
MR. HEMPSEED, *a customer**
LORD ANTHONY DEWHURST
COUNTESS DE TOURNAY
SUZANNE, *her daughter*
VICOMTE, *her son*
SIR ANDREW FFOULKES
LORD GRENVILLE
BUTLER*
SERVANT, *a woman**
FRENCH INNKEEPER*
FRENCH OFFICER*

SCENE 1

NARRATOR: The Scarlet Pimpernel—a small red flower, and the name taken by a mysterious and daring man who aided the victims of the Reign of Terror after the French Revolution. The story of his adventures begins in the Fisherman's

Rest, an English inn on the coast. Mr. Jellyband, the inn-keeper, and his daughter, Sally, are serving the customers, among them a Frenchman named Chauvelin, his companion, and Mr. Hempseed, a friend of Jellyband's.

JELLYBAND: Bring in some more cider, Sally, there's a good girl. They're a thirsty lot tonight.

SALLY: All right, Father.

JELLYBAND: There you are, gentlemen. The best British cider from one of the best inns of old England!

COMPANION: That company you be having tonight—they coming over from France?

JELLYBAND: Yes, with Sir Andrew Ffoulkes. They'll be glad to see the lights of Dover, poor souls.

HEMPSEED: Terrible times they be having in France, what with their revolution and all.

JELLYBAND: Well, what do you expect of foreigners, Mr. Hempseed? What *can* you expect? Rising up and murdering their nobility as though they were cutting off the heads of cabbages. Why, three Royalist refugees from France are arriving at this inn tonight. Helped to their escape by the Scarlet Pimpernel.

ALL: The Scarlet Pimpernel!

HEMPSEED: They say he's like a shadow. No one knows who he is, except that he's English. He steals into Paris and rescues the prisoners from under the very knife of the guillotine!

JELLYBAND: I heard a story of him last week. It seems he led a duke and all his family safe out of France and across the sea to England.

HEMPSEED: Well I never! He's a clever man, whoever he is!

JELLYBAND: A toast! A toast, gentlemen, to that brave English-man, the Scarlet Pimpernel!

ALL: To the Scarlet Pimpernel!

CHAUVELIN: You seem very proud of the exploits of this gentleman, sir.

JELLYBAND (*Enthusiastically*): He's a true-blooded English-man. And being one myself, I'm proud of him!

CHAUVELIN: Does anybody—er—have any idea who he is?

HEMPSEED: Not a soul.

JELLYBAND: Ah, here is Lord Anthony!

LORD ANTHONY: Evening, Jellyband, old chap. Evening, Mr. Hempseed. Sally! You're growing prettier and prettier every time I see you!

SALLY: Oh, your lordship! Father, why don't you see if the wine is cooled for the company?

JELLYBAND: Certainly, my dear. Come along, Hempseed.

LORD ANTHONY (*Urgently*): Sally, will you do me a small favor?

SALLY: Why, of course!

LORD ANTHONY: Will you give Sir Andrew a message when he comes in? I haven't had a minute to see him alone. Tell him privately, mind you, that I'll meet him here in the coffee room at ten o'clock tonight on urgent business.

SALLY: You can rely on me.

LORD ANTHONY: I'm sure I can, Sally.

NARRATOR: Lord Anthony takes Sally aside. Chauvelin and his companion get up quietly and leave the room, followed shortly by Sally. Lord Anthony paces back and forth nervously, then Jellyband flings open the door and ushers in the Countess de Tournay and her grown children, Suzanne and the Vicomte, and their English friend, Sir Andrew Ffoulkes.

JELLYBAND: This way, Countess.

LORD ANTHONY: Welcome to old England, Countess. Mademoiselle Suzanne. Monsieur le Vicomte.

COUNTESS: Ah, messieurs, what can I say? I am so deeply grateful. I cannot believe we are safe at last. What a frightful journey!

SUZANNE: We were taken out of Paris in a filthy market cart full of vegetables.

VICOMTE: The cart was driven by a fearful old hag.

SUZANNE: She said her family had the plague, and the sergeant was so terrified that he let us through.

SIR ANDREW: Do you know who the old hag was, mademoiselle? The Scarlet Pimpernel!

SUZANNE: Is it true?

SIR ANDREW: I have it on excellent authority!

COUNTESS: Ah, what a hero—whoever he is!

SUZANNE: Why does he call himself the Scarlet Pimpernel?

SIR ANDREW (*Enthusiastically*): The Scarlet Pimpernel, mademoiselle, is the name of a humble English wayside flower, but it is also the name chosen to hide the identity of the best and bravest man in all the world!

SUZANNE (*Quietly*): We have heard that he has promised to save Father, who is still in hiding in France.

COUNTESS: I pray with all my heart that he succeeds.

LORD ANTHONY: So do we all. Tell me, Jellyband, old fellow, you have no one else staying here at the inn, have you?

MR. JELLYBAND: No, milord—leastways . . .

LORD ANTHONY: Yes?

MR. JELLYBAND: No one your lordship would object to. Sir Percy and Lady Blakeney will be here presently, but they won't stay.

LORD ANTHONY: Ah, yes—Lady Blakeney's brother Armand crosses to France tomorrow.

COUNTESS: Lady Blakeney? Was she not once Marguerite St. Just—an actress at the Comedie Française?

LORD ANTHONY: She was indeed, madame. A more beautiful and witty woman it would be hard to find! And she is married to the country's richest and most elegant man, Sir Percy Blakeney.

COUNTESS (*Coldly*): I know her. She sent my cousin's family to the guillotine.

SUZANNE (*Vehemently*): Marguerite and I were at school together in Paris. She is one of my dearest friends—how can she be so wicked?

COUNTESS: Suzanne! That woman's brother is an enemy to the Royalist cause. (*Coldly*) I pray that while I remain in England I never meet that accursed Marguerite St. Just! (*There is a cold silence.*)

SIR ANDREW (*In a stage whisper*): Mr. Jellyband, when do you expect Lady Blakeney to arrive?

MR. JELLYBAND (*Uncomfortably*): At any moment, Sir Andrew.

SALLY (*Excited*): Sir Percy and Lady Blakeney are here!

COUNTESS: I will not see her! I will *not*!

SIR ANDREW: Let us go in to dinner

NARRATOR: Before anyone can move, Lady Marguerite sweeps into the room, brushing by Lord Anthony on her way to the fire.

MARGUERITE (*Teasing*): Lord Tony, are you trying to keep me from the fire? I'm perished with cold! (*Delighted*) Suzanne! What are doing here? How good to see you! And your mama, too!

COUNTESS (*Sternly*): Suzanne, I forbid you to talk to that woman!

MARGUERITE (*Amazed, then rapidly regaining control*): Hoity-toity, Countess! What fly stings you, pray?

COUNTESS: We are in England now, madame, and I am at liberty to forbid my daughter to touch your hand in friendship. Come, Suzanne!

SUZANNE: Oh, Marguerite—

COUNTESS: Suzanne!

NARRATOR: The Countess sails past Marguerite toward the dining room. Suzanne gives Marguerite a last look and follows her mother out. Marguerite kisses her hand to Suzanne, then turns to Sir Andrew.

MARGUERITE: I hope little Suzanne doesn't grow old like that, eh, Sir Andrew?

SIR ANDREW: She is very lovely.

MARGUERITE (*Softly*): She is indeed. But, really, what an old dragon the Countess is! (*Mimicking her*) "Suzanne! I forbid you to talk to that woman!"

LORD ANTHONY: Lady Blakeney, how they must miss you at the Comedie! The Parisians must hate Sir Percy for taking you away!

MARGUERITE: Ah, but it would be hard to hate such a lazy love of a man! His wit would disarm even the Countess!

SIR PERCY: Odd's life—is some impudent person talking about me?

MARGUERITE: It's your wife, Percy, my dear. You have nothing to fear.

SIR PERCY: Nothing to fear? If it's my wife, I may have everything to fear! (*All laugh.*)

MARGUERITE: I don't know why I married you, Percy. Everyone tells me you're hopelessly dull!

SIR PERCY (*Laughing*): How do, Tony? How do, Ffoulkes? Did you ever see such a beastly day? Dreadful climate, this.

SIR ANDREW: Yes—it is—er—rainy. (*There is an awkward pause.*)

SIR PERCY: Bless my soul, what's got into you all?

MARGUERITE: Oh, it's nothing, Percy. Only an affront to your wife.

SIR PERCY: Who was the brave man who dared tackle you, my dear?

VICOMTE: Monsieur, it is my mother who has angered your wife. I cannot ask pardon for my mother. To me, she is right. But I am ready to challenge you to a duel.

SIR PERCY (*Unmoved*): Upon my life, it's marvelous. I vow I can't speak the French lingo like that!

MARGUERITE (*Dryly*): Whenever *I've* heard him speak French, he has had a British accent one could cut with a knife.

VICOMTE (*Choking with fury*): When do we fight, monsieur?

SIR PERCY: My good man, I never fight duels. Deuced uncomfortable things, duels, aren't they, Tony?

MARGUERITE: Play the peacemaker, I pray you, Lord Tony.

LORD ANTHONY: Sir Percy is right, Vicomte. It would hardly be fitting for you to start your stay in England with an illegal duel.

VICOMTE: If monsieur is satisfied, I withdraw.

SIR PERCY (*Aside to* LORD ANTHONY): Tony, if that's the sort you and your friends bring over from France, then I think you should drop 'em in the sea halfway over.

LORD ANTHONY: Come, Sir Percy, we'll go find Jellyband and forget the whole thing over some good hot food.

SIR PERCY: Good idea, Tony. Come along, Sir Andrew. Do join us, Vicomte. If you'll excuse us, my dear—

NARRATOR: Marguerite nods pleasantly and turns to the window as the men leave for the dining room. Sir Percy pauses at the door to look back at his wife before he leaves the room. Marguerite speaks her thoughts aloud while Chauvelin comes in quietly, unnoticed by her.

MARGUERITE: You don't seem to care, Percy, though I am still in love with *you*. You—the Countess—no one truly understands. . . . And tomorrow, when my brother has gone to France, then whom can I turn to?

CHAUVELIN: Ah! The beautiful Lady Blakeney!

MARGUERITE (*Suddenly*): Oh! How you startled me! Chauvelin—is it really you?

CHAUVELIN: Chauvelin himself, citizeness, at your service.

MARGUERITE: I am pleased to see you. But what brings you to the shores of England?

CHAUVELIN: I am the representative of the Revolutionary Government of France to King George's England.

MARGUERITE: Ah! You are climbing in the world.

CHAUVELIN: Thank you. And how is your brother Armand?

MARGUERITE: He leaves for France tomorrow.

CHAUVELIN: He is a good servant of the Republic, and of France, is he not?

MARGUERITE: What do you mean? Armand loves France.

CHAUVELIN: I do not doubt it. (*He pauses.*) You have heard, perhaps, of the Scarlet Pimpernel?

MARGUERITE (*With a gay laugh*): Heard of him? Faith, who has not heard of him? Why, we talk of nothing else.

CHAUVELIN (*Intensely*): If you have heard of him, then you must know that this person is one of France's bitterest enemies, and therefore the enemy of brave men like your brother Armand.

MARGUERITE: I daresay he is. France has many enemies these days.

CHAUVELIN: You are a daughter of France, Lady Blakeney. Now you have a chance to help your country.

MARGUERITE: I? But I don't see how, my little Chauvelin.

CHAUVELIN: As Lady Blakeney, you are the center of social London. You see and hear everything. . . .

MARGUERITE: You flatter me, Chauvelin.

CHAUVELIN: With your help I can unmask the Scarlet Pimpernel. *You* can help me find him.

MARGUERITE: It is only fair to tell you, Chauvelin, that although I am in full agreement with the revolutionary movement, I abhor its bloody murders. They are a blot on the name of France.

CHAUVELIN: Find the Scarlet Pimpernel for France, citizeness!

MARGUERITE: You are astonishing! Where can I find such an elusive creature—and I married to an English nobleman!

CHAUVELIN (*Insistent*): For the sake of France!

MARGUERITE: Besides, there is so little you could do even if you knew his identity. He is English.

CHAUVELIN: I would take a chance on that. He will go to the guillotine first, and we will apologize later.

MARGUERITE (*Shuddering*): You would send to the guillotine a brave man whose only crime is to save women and children, old and young men from a horrible death? I'll have none of your dirty work. And that's my last word.

CHAUVELIN (*With quiet emphasis*): Then you prefer to be insulted by every French aristocrat who escapes to this country? (*There is a pause.*)

SIR PERCY (*Calling*): Marguerite? Marguerite? (*Cheerfully*) Here you are, my dear. It's time to return home.

MARGUERITE: We've just been having a little chat, Percy.

SIR PERCY: Bless my soul, is that little Chauvelin from Paris with you? Good evening, little Chauvelin!

CHAUVELIN (*Coldly*): Good evening.

SIR PERCY: Marguerite, we must start back.

MARGUERITE: Goodbye, monsieur.

CHAUVELIN: That is *not* your last word, I trust. We meet in London?

NARRATOR: Chauvelin watches Marguerite sweep out, her head in the air, followed by Sir Percy. As they leave, the clock begins to strike ten. Chauvelin withdraws to a shadowy corner. Lord Anthony and Sir Andrew come in for their arranged meeting.

LORD ANTHONY: There, the place is deserted.

SIR ANDREW: I have the papers here—instructions from the Scarlet Pimpernel.

LORD ANTHONY: I understand there are special orders for me.

SIR ANDREW: Yes. Armand St. Just will be on his way to Paris tomorrow. There's a letter here from him. No one suspects Armand yet, but he warns us to watch out for a clever and dedicated man who is determined to find the Scarlet Pimpernel and to crush the League. Armand says the man is named Chauvelin . . .

NARRATOR: Sir Andrew and Lord Anthony pore over the letters. They do not notice Chauvelin's companion creep in behind them, and Chauvelin move silently from his hiding place. They sneak up on the Englishmen, and catching them unaware, knock them unconscious. Chauvelin holds up the papers triumphantly.

CHAUVELIN: Hm-m—Armand St. Just a traitor after all! Now,

my fair and haughty Lady Blakeney, I think you *will* help me find the Scarlet Pimpernel!

* * * *

SCENE 2

NARRATOR: Three days later, all the important figures in the story are attending a ball at the London home of Lord Grenville. As Lord Grenville greets his guests—Countess de Tournay, Suzanne and the Vicomte, Lord Anthony and Sir Andrew—Chauvelin, invited as a representative of the French Government, lurks in the background. Suzanne is telling Sir Andrew about her feelings . . .

SUZANNE: What a delightful ball! It's so good to be dancing again, though I wonder at my having such a gay time when poor Papa is in such danger!

SIR ANDREW: Dear Suzanne, if the Scarlet Pimpernel has sworn to effect his escape from France, then you have nothing to fear!

BUTLER (*Announcing*): Sir Percy and Lady Blakeney!

LORD ANTHONY: My dear Lady Blakeney, your beauty leaves us breathless.

MARGUERITE: My thanks for the compliment, Lord Tony.

CHAUVELIN (*Aside*): Lady Blakeney, a word with you, please.

COUNTESS (*Loudly*): You see, Suzanne, your dear Marguerite is already a faithful ally of revolutionary spies!

NARRATOR: Marguerite goes reluctantly to one side with Chauvelin while the Countess leaves the room in a huff. Suzanne and the other guests follow her, leaving Marguerite and Chauvelin alone.

CHAUVELIN: This is my only opportunity to talk to you. (*He pauses.*) I think you would be wise to listen.

MARGUERITE (*Calmly*): Is that a threat, monsieur?

CHAUVELIN: Just an arrow, shot in the air. (*He pauses again.*) Your brother is in deadly peril.

MARGUERITE: Come now! Armand in danger? I don't believe it!

CHAUVELIN: I have news of him. But first I would remind you that I asked your help for France three days ago, and you refused.

MARGUERITE (*Coldly*): The answer is still the same, Chauvelin.

CHAUVELIN: Perhaps now you will change your mind, citizeness. Recently, at that inn in Dover, some papers came into my hands. One was a letter from your brother Armand to Sir Andrew Ffoulkes.

MARGUERITE: Well? What of it?

CHAUVELIN (*Slowly*): That letter showed him to be the arch enemy of France. He is in league with that meddler, the Scarlet Pimpernel.

MARGUERITE (*Trying to hide her terror*): What a tale! Armand helping the aristocrats he so despises! The tale does credit to your imagination, Chauvelin!

CHAUVELIN: Armand is compromised beyond slightest hope of pardon, and I need hardly remind you that he is now in France. As soon as we catch him, it is goodbye to your dear Armand—unless . . . you help me. (*Harshly*) Find the Scarlet Pimpernel, Lady Blakeney, find him for me, and the compromising letter will be returned to you.

MARGUERITE: You would force me to spy for you in return for Armand's life—is that it?

CHAUVELIN: Citizeness, do not waste my time. Among the papers carried by Sir Andrew was a note indicating that the Scarlet Pimpernel himself would be at the ball tonight. Use your influence to find out who he is, and your work is done. Farewell—until later, citizeness!

MARGUERITE (*Desperately*): Wait—oh, wait! Oh, how can I do such a thing? I must betray a fearless man to save a life! What a choice! Yet if I do *not* do as Chauvelin wishes, my dear Armand will be—guillotined!

NARRATOR: Marguerite goes to join the others. After a moment,

Sir Percy leads in a group of gentlemen who are laughing gaily at his jests.

SIR PERCY: And we poor husbands, Grenville, have to stand by while the ladies worship a cursed shadow!

LORD GRENVILLE: A toast to the shadowy Pimpernel—whoever he is!

SIR PERCY: In his honor, devil take the man, I've made up a little verse.

LORD GRENVILLE: Let's hear it, Sir Percy!

LORD ANTHONY: Yes, come on, old chap, let's hear it.

SIR PERCY: Since you insist, gentlemen.
We seek him here, we seek him there.
Those Frenchies seek him everywhere.
Is he in Heaven? Is he in Hell?
That old elusive Pimpernel!

LORD ANTHONY: Hurrah for the poet!

LORD GRENVILLE: Come along, we must tell the others.

NARRATOR: The gentlemen all leave the room, reciting his verse about the Pimpernel. Sir Percy remains behind. He stretches out on a sofa, yawns, and settles down for a nap. As he sleeps, Chauvelin comes in quietly, followed a moment later by Marguerite, who seems upset. Chauvelin indicates the sleeping Sir Percy and, with his finger to his lips, draws her aside.

CHAUVELIN (*Whispering*): You have news for me?

MARGUERITE: Yes. (*Haltingly*) I stole a note from Sir Andrew.

CHAUVELIN (*Eagerly*): What was in it?

MARGUERITE: It was from the Pimpernel. It said, "I start for Calais tomorrow. If you wish to speak to me, I shall be in the supper room at one o'clock precisely."

CHAUVELIN: Good. It is almost one o'clock, and we are in the supper room now.

MARGUERITE: What will you do?

CHAUVELIN: When I find out who the Scarlet Pimpernel is, I shall have him followed. I myself will leave for France tomorrow. The papers I acquired spoke of a certain Blanchard's hut at Calais. I must find out where it is, and when I have caught him trying to help the Count de Tournay escape, I shall unmask the Scarlet Pimpernel—at last!

MARGUERITE: And Armand?

CHAUVELIN: Have I ever broken my word? I have already promised you I would return the letter, and I assure you, on the day I lay hands on the Scarlet Pimpernel, your precious Armand will be in England, safe with his charming sister.

NARRATOR: Marguerite withdraws, still upset. Chauvelin sits down and prepares to wait for the Scarlet Pimpernel to appear. The clock strikes one.

CHAUVELIN: It's one o'clock, and I'll soon know the secret of the Scarlet Pimpernel. (*Impatiently*) I wonder what can be keeping him.

NARRATOR: Chauvelin waits and Sir Percy snores loudly, asleep on his sofa. Chauvelin pays no attention to him, and does not notice, as he waits for someone who does not come, that Sir Percy seems to be smiling in his sleep.

* * * * *

SCENE 3

NARRATOR: A few hours later, Marguerite and Sir Percy return to their home at Richmond. Marguerite leads Sir Percy into the garden in the hope of having a quiet talk with him about Chauvelin and her brother's danger.

MARGUERITE (*Urgently*): Percy—I need you.

SIR PERCY: What can I do for you, madame?

MARGUERITE: Percy, Armand is in danger. He is so rash—and one of his letters, a very compromising one, has fallen into the hands of a fanatic. Armand may be guillotined.

SIR PERCY: So the murderous dog of a revolution is about to bite the very hands that fed it, eh? (*Gently*) Don't cry, m'dear. I never could bear to see a pretty woman cry.

MARGUERITE: Can you do anything?

THE SCARLET PIMPERNEL 313

SIR PERCY: Perhaps you should seek the help of Chauvelin.

MARGUERITE: I cannot ask him, Percy!

SIR PERCY: Faith, if it distresses you, we'll not talk of it. As for Armand, I pledge my word that he'll be safe. Now, have I your permission to go?

MARGUERITE: A little more time! I have something I have wanted to explain to you for a very long time.

SIR PERCY: The hour is late—

MARGUERITE: It is very important.

SIR PERCY (*Gently*): What do you wish to tell me?

MARGUERITE: It concerns us—and the Countess. (*Haltingly*) The Countess de Tournay believes I am responsible for sending her cousin and his family to the guillotine. I swear I am innocent, but so-called friends have told you, and the Countess, otherwise—and you have believed them. Until now, I have been too proud to tell you *my* story, since you listened to others first.

SIR PERCY (*Moved*): I have waited almost a year to hear the story from your own lips.

MARGUERITE: Up until the very morning the family were executed, I was doing all I could to save them—

NARRATOR: The pair moves from the garden toward the house, arm in arm, seemingly reconciled. Yet when Marguerite returns to the garden in the hours just after dawn, she is not easy in her mind.

MARGUERITE: Have I convinced him? He seemed so different in the hour we spent in the garden. Oh, I *do* love him.

NARRATOR: As Marguerite walks about the garden, Sir Percy returns, dressed for travel.

MARGUERITE: Percy! Where are you going?

SIR PERCY (*His old, distant self*): I have urgent business to attend to.

MARGUERITE: You will be back soon?

SIR PERCY (*More warmly*): Very soon.

MARGUERITE: Must you go today?

SIR PERCY: I must go to London. My business has to do with Armand.

MARGUERITE: Oh, Percy! You will run no danger? And you will come back soon?

SIR PERCY (*Tenderly*): Yes, I will come back very soon.

MARGUERITE: Farewell!

SERVANT: Madame, a young lady is here to see you.

MARGUERITE: It must be Suzanne! I had forgotten that I had invited her today. Ask her to come into the garden.

SERVANT: Yes, madame.

MARGUERITE: How furious the old Countess was when I invited Suzanne here!

SUZANNE: *Chérie!* Where are you? You did not expect me so soon?

MARGUERITE: My dear, dear Suzanne, you are welcome, early or late! It's good to have you here.

SUZANNE: How lovely it is here! How happy you must be!

MARGUERITE: Indeed, I should be happy, shouldn't I?

SUZANNE (*Suddenly*): Look—you've dropped something, Marguerite. It's a ring.

MARGUERITE: It must be Percy's—perhaps he dropped it last night. How very strange. . . .

SUZANNE: What is it?

MARGUERITE: Nothing, really—but it's odd. Percy *sets* the fashion as a rule. I didn't expect him to be following one!

SUZANNE: What do you mean?

MARGUERITE: I have several dresses in the style of the Scarlet Pimpernel. I even have a set of jewels with the device of that mysterious man. And here is my foolish husband with a ring bearing the same flower! See—a scarlet pimpernel! He is secretly jealous, no doubt, of that hero of the ladies! Tell me, Suzanne, what of you and Sir Andrew?

SUZANNE: I think Mama will consent, but of course nothing is to be thought of until Papa is safe in England.

MARGUERITE: Tell me—what is the latest news of your father?

SUZANNE: Oh, we have no fear now! Marguerite, the great and noble Scarlet Pimpernel himself has gone to save Papa. He is to be in London this morning—and Calais by tonight!

MARGUERITE (*Thoughtfully*): In London this morning? And then Calais? (*Suddenly*) Oh, no!

SUZANNE: What is it, Marguerite?

MARGUERITE (*Weakly*): It's nothing, nothing. You did say that the Scarlet Pimpernel has gone *today*?

SUZANNE: Yes, but what is wrong?

MARGUERITE: I must be alone for a moment. I may have to go away shortly.

SUZANNE: Whatever you say, Marguerite. I will leave you alone for a while.

MARGUERITE: How could I have been so blind! So blind and so *stupid*! The Scarlet Pimpernel—the Scarlet Pimpernel is Sir Percy Blakeney, my husband! Now I can understand everything. He played a part. He wore a mask of stupidity to throw dust in everyone's eyes. Oh, Percy, Percy, what a fool I've been! (*Suddenly*) I've betrayed him! I've betrayed my husband to Chauvelin! It was I who stole the Scarlet Pimpernel's note at the ball and gave it to Chauvelin. And now Percy has gone to Calais with that monster at his heels. Have I sent my own husband to his death?

SERVANT: A letter just arrived by special runner, your ladyship.

MARGUERITE: It is Armand's letter returned by Chauvelin! Heaven help me—that means he is on the track of the Scarlet Pimpernel! (*Calling*) *Suzanne!*

SUZANNE: Is it bad news, Marguerite? Can I do anything?

MARGUERITE: Yes—yes, Suzanne. I will come back to London with you. We must go immediately. I must see Sir Andrew, and then I must go to Calais! Come, Suzanne, I have not a moment to waste!

* * * *

SCENE 4

NARRATOR: By that evening, Marguerite managed to reach Calais, with the help of Sir Andrew. Now, at a small French inn, the innkeeper is showing them the one private room, which is divided from the common room by only a curtain.

INNKEEPER: This is the only private room I have, madame.

MARGUERITE: How dreadful it is! Are you sure this is the place, Sir Andrew?

SIR ANDREW: Aye, 'tis the place, all right. That will be all, innkeeper.

MARGUERITE: Oh, what a frightful journey! The delay in crossing from Dover was unbearable. Do you think Sir Percy crossed before us in his yacht?

SIR ANDREW: It is almost certain.

MARGUERITE: Oh, Sir Andrew, I'm terrified that Percy will walk straight into a trap, and I, his own wife, shall have betrayed him to his archenemy!

SIR ANDREW (*Gently*): But how could you have known, Lady Blakeney?

MARGUERITE: I just pray that we are not too late. You say Percy will be here for supper?

SIR ANDREW: That was the plan. Lady Blakeney, I do not wish to worry you, but Chauvelin and his men may be on the way here already. He followed our boat from Dover, less than an hour after we left. He knows of this inn, and I don't doubt that on reaching Calais he will make straight for it.

MARGUERITE: But we have an hour's start, and Sir Percy will be here soon. By the time Chauvelin arrives, we shall be at sea again with Sir Percy safe aboard.

SIR ANDREW: You are forgetting one thing—the Count de Tournay and your brother Armand are at Blanchard's hut waiting for the Scarlet Pimpernel. And I know he will not leave without them.

MARGUERITE: You are right. Heaven help me, I had forgotten!

THE SCARLET PIMPERNEL 317

Whatever the risk, he *must* save them. But he has to be told that Chauvelin is on his track. Do you think you can find Sir Percy before he comes here, and warn him? I could stay here . . .

SIR ANDREW: It's a good plan. You do not mind being here alone?

MARGUERITE: No, I don't mind. From here I can watch the main room without being seen myself.

SIR ANDREW: Very well. But I beg you, madam, do nothing rash. The place is infested with spies. If I do not find Sir Percy, and he comes here first, do not reveal yourself to him unless you are positive that you are alone.

MARGUERITE: I can promise that. Believe me, I would not jeopardize my husband's life more than I have already.

SIR ANDREW: Very well. Remain here, unseen if possible. I will return as fast as I can.

CHAUVELIN (*Calling*): Innkeeper! Innkeeper!

INNKEEPER: Ah, monsieur—

CHAUVELIN: Quick, get me some soup and something to drink. Then go!

INNKEEPER: At once, citizen!

MARGUERITE (*Aside*): Heaven help us! It is Chauvelin—Chauvelin here already! What can I do?

CHAUVELIN (*To himself*): *Eh bien*, my little Scarlet Pimpernel, at last I have you cornered. Every road is guarded, every corner watched! I shall soon find out where those fugitives are hidden—and then the tall stranger cannot possibly get away. With luck I shall get him alive! (*He laughs maliciously*.)

MARGUERITE: Every road guarded, every corner watched! Oh what can I do? What can I do? Percy, oh Percy, where are you? (*In the distance* SIR PERCY *is heard loudly singing* "God Save the King.") There he is! And he is walking straight into a trap.

NARRATOR: Marguerite peers from behind the curtain as Sir Percy strolls in, and stops singing as he sees Chauvelin.

SIR PERCY: Odd's fish, it's Monsieur—er—Chauvelin. I vow I never thought to find you here!

CHAUVELIN: My dear Sir Percy, what a pleasant surprise!

* * * * *

SCENE 5

NARRATOR: Unable to warn Sir Percy while Chauvelin is present, Marguerite leaves the inn shortly after Sir Percy—who has told Chauvelin he is traveling on to Paris—and struggles along the lonely cliffs toward Blanchard's hut.

MARGUERITE: Oh, I can't go on. I can't go any further. The road is so stony and my feet are cut. (*She pauses to regain her breath.*) But somehow I must get to Blanchard's hut to warn Sir Percy and the others before Chauvelin comes. What's that? Someone's coming.

NARRATOR: Marguerite ducks behind some bushes just as Chauvelin approaches with an old man.

CHAUVELIN (*Angrily*): The Pimpernel may have gotten the better of me at the inn, but I'll make him pay for it now! How much further do we have to go, old man?

OLD MAN (SIR PERCY *disguised; fearfully*): Not far, your honor, I promise you.

CHAUVELIN: You are sure of the road?

OLD MAN: As sure as I am of the presence of the gold pieces in your excellency's pocket.

FRENCH OFFICER: Citizen Chauvelin?

CHAUVELIN: Himself. What news? Have you seen the stranger?

OFFICER: No, but a few moments ago we saw two men, one old, the other young, go into a fisherman's hut just over the cliff from here. By creeping close to the hut I overheard them.

CHAUVELIN (*Eagerly*): Yes, yes.

OFFICER: There is no doubt that the old man is the Count de Tournay, and they are here to slip across the sea to England.

CHAUVELIN: Where is the hut?

OFFICER: Very close. You can see it if you look over the cliff top.

CHAUVELIN: Good. Where are your men from here?

OFFICER: All about. Every path is covered.

CHAUVELIN: Here are my orders. Your life may depend on your memory, so listen carefully. Creep up to the hut again to see if a tall Englishman has joined the other two. If he has, you will signal with a sharp whistle. The hut will be surrounded immediately, and the men inside taken prisoner. On no account is the tall man to be molested. I want him alive and unhurt, you understand?

OFFICER: I understand, Citizen.

CHAUVELIN: If the two men are still alone, we will wait for the arrival of the leader and your signal will then be the hoot of an owl. No one—*no one*—will move until the leader arrives. He is the one we *must* capture tonight!

OFFICER: Your orders shall be carried out exactly, Citizen.

CHAUVELIN (*Roughly*): Old man, you will stay here. We shall need you to carry back the wounded.

OLD MAN: But I am terrified of being alone in the dark, excellency. If I am alone, I might cry out in fear and warn the fugitives. . . .

CHAUVELIN: That's true. Go with the officer and keep quiet.

MARGUERITE (*Aside*): I must get to the hut to warn them.

NARRATOR: The Officer takes the old man away, and Marguerite stumbles off in the darkness to find the hut.

MARGUERITE (*Urgently; aside*): I must warn them. Somehow I must get to the hut to warn them. . . .

CHAUVELIN: If only the moon would stay out for a moment, I could see. That looks very much like a British schooner standing off there. It is—with all sails set! But I cannot see her boat.

NARRATOR: Suddenly the French officer returns with Marguerite, who is bound and gagged.

OFFICER: Look what I found by the cliff—this dainty little creature. I bound and gagged her before she could make a sound.

CHAUVELIN: A woman! By all the saints in the calendar, who can it be? I wonder now . . . Dear me, Lady Blakeney, this *is* a pleasant surprise! Before I remove this handkerchief from your charming mouth, it is only fair to warn you that the slightest hint of a shout or scream from you that might warn the fugitives in the hut, and my men will seize the Count and your dear brother and shoot them before your eyes.

MARGUERITE (*Faintly*): What do you wish me to do?

CHAUVELIN: You will remain here, still and silent, until I give you leave to speak. Believe me, your brother will be quite safe if you make no sound. It is the Pimpernel I am after and his time has almost run out. (*Hoot of an owl is heard.*) Ah, the owl signal. Very well, we must sit here and wait until the Scarlet Pimpernel arrives!

NARRATOR: Chauvelin bows to Marguerite and withdraws to one side to wait. Ten minutes, twenty, then an hour pass, and the Pimpernel does not come. Suddenly, Sir Percy is heard singing "God Save the King," somewhere nearby. Chauvelin slowly draws a pistol from his belt, cocks it, and takes aim. As he does so, Marguerite rushes toward the voice, screaming.

MARGUERITE: Armand, Armand! For God's sake, fire! Your leader is near—he is betrayed! Fire!

CHAUVELIN (*Calling*): One of you men stop that woman's screaming. (*To himself*) Now, into the hut, and not a one of them shall escape alive. After them then!

NARRATOR: Chauvelin disappears into the woods, only to return with Marguerite and the French officer. Marguerite collapses on the ground as Chauvelin turns angrily to the officer.

CHAUVELIN: You fool! You and all the rest of them—stupid

fools! You let them get away! You and your men will pay for this blunder with your lives!

OFFICER: But you ordered us not to move until the Englishman arrived.

CHAUVELIN: I ordered you to let no one escape!

OFFICER: Then men in the hut had been gone some time . . .

CHAUVELIN: You mean—you *let* them go?

OFFICER: You ordered us to wait, and not to move, on pain of death. We waited. The men had left long before the woman screamed.

CHAUVELIN: Which way did they go?

OFFICER: I could not tell. They descended the cliff and then vanished.

CHAUVELIN: Hush—what's that sound?

OFFICER: It must be the schooner's boat, way out to sea.

CHAUVELIN (*Furious*): With the fugitives aboard! (*Suddenly*) Yet wait a minute! I don't believe in the supernatural, and this Scarlet Pimpernel, despite his tricks, must be human. We heard his own voice only a few moments ago. He has contrived to send the fugitives ahead, but he himself cannot have gotten away. Was there anything left in the hut?

OFFICER: Just this note, dropped in a corner, Citizen.

CHAUVELIN: Give it to me! Fetch a lantern! Aha! Instructions to the fugitives, signed with the device of the Pimpernel! Here, hold the lantern close! "When you receive this, wait for two minutes and then creep out of the hut one by one. Keep to the left. A mile away a boat awaits you." Aha. (*Reading again*) "Tell my men to send the boat back to the creek at Calais, the one in a direct line from the Inn of the Chat Gris. I shall be there." This is good news. Perhaps the enigmatic Pimpernel is going to pay for this adventure after all! We must go at once.

OFFICER: What about the woman?

CHAUVELIN: Leave her. (*Suddenly*) Where's that sniveling old fool who brought me here?

OFFICER: I think he is nearby, Citoyen.

CHAUVELIN: Have your men give him a good beating. But don't kill him!

NARRATOR: The officer hurries to execute Chauvelin's orders, and Chauvelin listens unmoved to the old man's screams and moans. Chauvelin goes to Marguerite and raises her limp hand to his lips.

CHAUVELIN: I much regret, fair lady, to leave you here. No doubt our old friend will prove a gallant defender. *Au revoir*, Lady Blakeney. Shall we meet again in London? No? Ah well, remember me to Sir Percy! Farewell.

MARGUERITE (*Tearfully*): Oh, what have I done? What has happened? Oh, Percy, my dear husband, where are you?

SIR PERCY (*Weakly*): Odd's life, but I'm weak as a mouse. I wish those fellows had not hit quite so hard. I can hardly walk.

MARGUERITE: Percy! Percy, is that you? Come to me, Percy!

SIR PERCY: Bless my soul, m'dear, where are you?

MARGUERITE: Percy, it *is* you! You, disguised as the old man! Oh, Percy, Percy!

SIR PERCY: There, there, m'dear. It's all right.

MARGUERITE: Oh, Percy, how could I have treated you so badly? If you only knew—

SIR PERCY (*Gently*): I know, dear—everything.

MARGUERITE: And can you forgive. . . .

SIR PERCY: I have nothing to forgive, dearest. Your heroism and devotion have more than atoned for that episode at the ball.

MARGUERITE: Then you knew, all the time?

SIR PERCY: All the time. Had I but known what a noble heart yours was, Marguerite, I would have trusted you as you deserved.

MARGUERITE (*Suddenly remembering*): Is Armand safe?

SIR PERCY: Safe with the Count de Tournay and Sir Andrew aboard the yacht.

MARGUERITE: How did they get there?

SIR PERCY: I'll tell you the whole story. Back at the inn, I shook off Chauvelin by offering him a pinch of snuff. Only I gave him a whiff of pepper instead, and while he went into a regular fit of sneezing, I made my escape. I went to an old friend in Calais and borrowed this disguise. Then I offered to help friend Chauvelin find the hut. . . .

MARGUERITE: But if Chauvelin had discovered . . . he is so sharp!

SIR PERCY: I had to take the risk.

MARGUERITE: Percy, how daring of you!

SIR PERCY: Fortunately I was able, by being very cautious, to creep up to the hut in the dark and leave a note for Armand and the Count. The soldiers paid no attention to the dirty old man from Calais! They were terrified of Chauvelin. I waited until I was sure my friends had escaped, and then I gave the signal!

MARGUERITE: And no one suspected you. Least of all your own wife! (*Suddenly*) But, Percy, we are lost! The note you left at the hut with orders for the boat to return—Chauvelin found it! He has gone to surround the creek!

SIR PERCY (*Laughing merrily*): Have no fear. Along with the first note I sent a second, a fake one, to be left in the hut. Our friend Chauvelin will wait for hours, but no boat from the yacht will go to Calais! Armand has the real instructions.

MARGUERITE: You are so clever!

SIR PERCY: Come, sweetheart, I shall not be happy till you are safe in England again!

MARGUERITE: With you, dear Percy, to look after me!

THE END

Tom Sawyer, Pirate

This play is one episode from Mark Twain's famous book about Tom Sawyer. It is about an adventure that turns out to be sad for some people, but ends up happily.

There is a misunderstanding in this play. Read the play through silently and discuss what it is with the group.

Answer these questions about the characters:

What is the difference between Tom and his cousin Sid?
What is Alfred Temple like? How would you read his part?
Does Tom change his ways during the play?
How does Becky feel about Tom at the beginning of the play and at the end?

Choose your parts and read Scene 1. Most of the characters appear in this scene. You can practice it several times to be sure you know all the words. If there are any that give you trouble, talk them over with the group.

When you feel Scene 1 is just right, go on to the others.

After you have read the play through together and think you are all reading well, arrange for an audience to hear you. Ask them to criticize and evaluate your performance.

TOM SAWYER, PIRATE

by Mark Twain
adapted by Adele Thane

Characters

(6 boys, 6 girls, and a narrator)
NARRATOR
AUNT POLLY
SID SAWYER
TOM SAWYER
BECKY THATCHER
ALFRED TEMPLE
JOE HARPER
HUCK FINN
MRS. HARPER
BEN ROGERS
AMY LAWRENCE
GRACIE MILLER
WIDOW DOUGLAS

SCENE 1

NARRATOR: On an afternoon in September, in 1847, in Hannibal, Missouri, Aunt Polly is sitting on a stool in her back yard, paring potatoes. Sid Sawyer comes up the street and into the yard, carrying his schoolbooks in a leather strap.

SID: Hello, Aunty.

AUNT POLLY: Why, Sid! Is school out already?

SID: It's after four o'clock.

AUNT POLLY: Land sakes! I'd better get these potatoes on to boil right away.

SID (*With pride*): I got one hundred in arithmetic today, Aunty!

AUNT POLLY (*Suitably impressed*): My! You don't say! (*Changing her tone*) What did Tom get?

SID: He wasn't there.

AUNT POLLY: He wasn't there? Why, where was he?

SID: I don't know, Aunty. He wasn't in school all afternoon.

AUNT POLLY: Humph! Playin' hooky, like as not. Oh, that child! Well, you just wait till I lay my hands on *him!*

SID (*Gleefully*): Here comes Tom now!

NARRATOR: Tom Sawyer comes up the street, whistling a merry tune. He comes into the yard, barefoot, but wearing his jacket, which is buttoned, for once.

TOM: Hello, Aunt Polly.

NARRATOR: Aunt Polly looks at Tom severely, and he casts a suspicious glance at Sid. Suddenly he reaches for the pan of potato peelings.

TOM: Why, Aunty, I'll throw away the peelin's for you.

AUNT POLLY: Just a minute, Tom Sawyer. It was powerful warm in school, wasn't it?

TOM (*Warily*): Yes'm.

AUNT POLLY: Didn't you want to go swimmin'?

TOM (*Uneasily*): No'm—well, not very much.

AUNT POLLY: But you're not too warm now, though.

TOM: Some of us pumped water on our heads. Mine's damp yet. See?

AUNT POLLY: Tom, you didn't have to undo your shirt collar where I sewed it, to pump water on your head, did you? Unbutton your jacket. Bother! Your collar's still sewn on. I was sure you'd played hooky and been a-swimmin'.

SID (*With feigned innocence*): Well, now, Aunty, I thought you sewed his collar with *white* thread this mornin'. That thread is black.

AUNT POLLY: Why, I *did* sew it with white. Tom!

NARRATOR: But Tom has bolted out of the yard.

AUNT POLLY: Tom Sawyer, come back here! (*Sighing*) I never did see the likes of that boy! Well, I'll just have to put him to work sawin' wood to punish him. He hates work more'n anythin' else. Come on to the house, Siddy. You can get the fire started for me.

NARRATOR: Aunt Polly and Sid gather up the pans of potatoes and peelings and go into the house. Tom comes back and crouches by a large rain barrel in the yard and looks after them.

TOM (*Muttering*): She'd never have noticed the thread if Sid hadn't mentioned it. Sometimes she sews my collar with white and sometimes with black. I wish she'd stick to one or the other. But I'll beat you up, Sid Sawyer. I'll fix you!

NARRATOR: As Tom thinks about what he'll do to Sid, Becky Thatcher and the very proper Alfred Temple come up the street and stop at the gate to the Thatchers' garden, next door.

BECKY (*Coyly*): Thank you for carrying my books, Alfred.

ALFRED: That's all right, Becky. I'll tell you some more about St. Louis tomorrow and show you the pictures. We can look at them during recess.

BECKY: Oh, that will be nice.

TOM (*Interrupting*): I can lick you, Alfred Temple!

ALFRED (*Calmly*): I'd like to see you try it.

BECKY: For shame, Tom Sawyer!

TOM: Well, I can do it. (BECKY *gives a little scream*)

ALFRED: No, you can't.

TOM: Yes, I can.

ALFRED: You can't.

TOM: Can!

ALFRED: Can't!

TOM: You think you're *somebody* now, *don't* you? I could lick you with one hand tied behind me.

ALFRED: Why don't you *do* it, then? Are you afraid?

TOM: I'm *not* afraid.

ALFRED: You are!

TOM: I am not!

ALFRED: You are!

TOM: Get away from here!

ALFRED: Go away yourself!

TOM: I won't!

ALFRED: I won't, either!

TOM (*Laughing*): Where did you get that hat?

ALFRED: I dare you to knock it off.

TOM: For two cents I *will!*

NARRATOR: Alfred takes two pennies from his pocket and holds them out. Tom strikes them to the ground, knocks Alfred's cap off. The two boys start to wrestle, while Becky dances around them, squealing and trying to separate them.

BECKY: Stop it, Tom! Don't, Alfred! Shame on you both! Please, *please* stop!

ALFRED (*Panting*): All right, Becky. I won't fight—for *your* sake.

BECKY (*Angrily*): You're a bad boy, Thomas Sawyer! Bad, bad, bad! Don't you ever speak to me again! I *hate* you! Come along, Alfred. Let's go in.

TOM (*Furiously*): Any other boy! Any boy in the whole town but that St. Louis smarty Alfred, who thinks he's so great. You just wait, mister, till I catch you! I'll just take you and . . . thrash you! Oh, you do, do you? You holler enough now, do you? Let that be a lesson to you, then!

NARRATOR: As Tom thrashes an imaginary Alfred, Huck Finn and Joe Harper stroll down the street and stop to watch him.

JOE: Say, Tom, whatcha doin'?

TOM: Huh? Oh, hullo, Joe, hullo, Huck.

HUCK: Who was that you were trouncin', Tom?

TOM: Nobody. (*Mournfully*) Joe . . . Huck . . . Don't you forget me. I'm goin' away. *She* will be sorry, then.

HUCK: What?

TOM: I'm goin' into the unknown countries beyond the seas—

TOM SAWYER, PIRATE 329

and never comin' back again. (*He sighs heavily.*) Nobody loves me.

JOE: Me, too, Tom! My mother just scolded me for drinkin' cream I never even tasted and don't know anythin' about.

TOM: I try to do the right thing and get along, but they won't let me. They won't be happy until I'm gone. All right, I'll go. When they find out what they've done to me, maybe they'll wish they'd treated me better.

JOE: It's plain my mother is tired of me. If she feels that way, I might just as well go along with you, Tom.

HUCK: Where you goin'?

TOM (*After a pause; excitedly*): I'm goin' to be a pirate, that's what!

HUCK: What do pirates do?

TOM: Oh, they just have a great time! They take ships and burn 'em and get heaps of money and bury it on an island.

HUCK: Do pirates always have an island?

TOM: Of course!

HUCK: Can I go along?

TOM: Sure. You just have to take the oath.

HUCK: How do I do that?

TOM: Put your hand on mine. Joe, you, too. Now. (*In a serious tone.*) We swear to stand by each other, and never separate from each other, till death ends this oath.

HUCK: That's perfect.

JOE: We have to have a countersign.

TOM: I know a good one—blood!

ALL (*In low and mysterious tones*): Blood!

HUCK: We have to have an island.

TOM: Jackson's Island is right handy. It isn't more than two miles down the river.

JOE: How will we get there?

TOM: We'll have to build a raft.

HUCK: I know where there's an old one that would do.

TOM: Could we capture it and be off by midnight?

Huck: I reckon so.

Joe: We'll each bring hooks and lines and somethin' to eat.

Tom: This is the life!

Huck: It's a whack!

Joe: It's the nuts!

Tom: Hucky, you're Huck Finn, the Red-Handed, and Joe, you're Joe Harper, the Terror of the Seas. And I am Tom Sawyer, the Avenger of the Spanish Main. Shove off, mates. We'll meet—at midnight!

Joe: On the dot!

Huck: At the raft!

All: B-L-O-O-D!

* * * * *

Scene 2

Narrator: The boys go their separate ways, to meet again at midnight and head for Jackson's Island and the life of pirates. Now, two days later, they have set up their pirates' camp on the island, complete with a homemade skull and crossbones flag stuck in a tree. Joe is busy feeding the campfire when Huck comes from the woods, carrying a string of small fish.

Huck: Tom hasn't turned up yet?

Joe: Nope.

Huck: You don't reckon he's given us the slip, do you?

Joe: No, Tom's true blue, Huck. He won't desert. He's up to somethin' or other.

Huck: I wonder what.

Joe: Put the fish in the hot ashes, Huck. We'll go ahead and eat if Tom isn't here before they're done.

Tom: Which he is!

Joe: Tom! What have you been up to?

Tom: Let me near the fire to dry my clothes and I'll tell you. Well, after you boys were asleep last night, I swam across to the other shore.

HUCK (*Alarmed*): What made you do that, Tom?

TOM: I got to wishin' Aunt Polly knew we hadn't drowned. So I wrote on this piece of bark here and thought I'd sneak into the house and put it where she'd find it.

JOE: What's it say?

TOM: It got pretty wet, but you can read it.

JOE: It says, "We haven't drowned. We're only off bein' pirates." Why didn't you leave it?

TOM: I got another idea. You just wait till you hear my idea! It's a whiz!

JOE: Well, tell it!

TOM: I'm not ready yet.

JOE: Aw, come on!

HUCK: Did you see anythin' over in town?

TOM: Well, when I got there, there was nobody on the streets. All the houses were dark. But when I turned up my street, I saw a light in my house. I looked in the window, and who do you think I saw?

JOE: Your aunt?

TOM: Yes, and someone else.

JOE: My mother?

TOM: Yes. They were sittin' close together and talkin' and cryin'. I heard 'em sayin' what noble boys we were and what comforts to them we were. I could hardly keep from rushin' right in and surprisin' them. And then I got my idea. Oh, will it be a winner! (*He laughs.*)

HUCK (*Impatiently*): Well, come on, tell us!

JOE: What is it?

TOM: I haven't got it all thought out yet. When I have, I'll tell you. Got anything to eat? I'm starved.

HUCK: There's fish. I don't know if it's done though.

TOM: Pirates eat things any sort of way. Let's eat.

JOE: Cracky! No fish ever tasted as good as this before.

TOM: This is the life for me! You don't have to get up

mornin's, and you don't have to go to school, and wash, and all that foolishness.

HUCK: What will we do when we're through eatin'?

TOM: We'll explore the island again. I'll bet there's been pirates here before. And then tomorrow, we'll have to go back, on account of my idea.

JOE: Go back!

HUCK: What *is* this idea, Tom? I wish you'd stop talking about it, or else tell us.

TOM: All right, I'll tell you. Well, when I was listenin' to Aunt Polly last night, I found somethin' out.

JOE *and* HUCK: What?

TOM: They're goin' to have a funeral for us tomorrow.

JOE: A funeral?

HUCK: For us?

TOM: Preachin' and everythin'! And when I heard 'em plannin' it, I got the idea to go back, all three of us, and listen to Reverend Kellerman preach our funeral sermon.

JOE: Whoopee!

TOM: And in the middle of it, we'll march in among 'em!

HUCK: Hey! That's great!

* * * * *

SCENE 3

NARRATOR: With Tom leading the way, the boys march around the campfire, and then down the path to explore. The next afternoon, they leave the island and head for home. Aunt Polly's yard is empty when they creep stealthily from behind the fence. They hide behind the vine-covered arbor which divides the yard from the Thatchers' garden. They are just in time, for Ben Rogers, Amy Lawrence, Alfred Temple and Gracie Miller, all dressed in their best, and trying to look serious, come into the yard and stand about near the door, waiting for the funeral of Tom Sawyer, Huck Finn, and Joe Harper to start.

BEN: I reckon just about everybody in town will be here for the funeral.

AMY: My goodness, yes! Do you remember, Ben, the last time we saw Tom? He wanted to trade his white marble for your mouth-organ and you wouldn't do it. I'll bet you wish you had now.

ALFRED (*Boasting*): I guess I was the last one to see Tom alive. It was the afternoon before he went away. He licked me.

BEN: Aw, that's nothin'. Tom's licked every boy in town.

GRACIE: There's Becky and Mrs. Harper coming out of the Thatchers' house. My, I reckon Mrs. Harper feels badly about Joe.

AMY: I reckon Becky feels worse about Tom.

GRACIE: Yes, I heard they were engaged.

AMY (*Proudly*): Tom and *I* were engaged once.

GRACIE: It's Becky he was engaged to when he was drowned. Well, we'd best go in the house—Widow Douglas wants us to practice singing the hymn before the service begins.

WIDOW DOUGLAS (*Calling*): Come along in, children. Don't stand there gawking.

NARRATOR: The children shuffle into the house, as Becky and Mrs. Harper come into Aunt Polly's yard. Becky is crying and Mrs. Harper tries to comfort her, while sniffling into a handkerchief herself.

MRS. HARPER: Sh-h-h, Becky, dear.

BECKY: I can't help it, Mrs. Harper.

MRS. HARPER: Control yourself, child. There, there.

BECKY: Oh, Mrs. Harper, if I only hadn't said it.

MRS. HARPER: Said what, dear?

BECKY: What I said to Tom the last time I saw him. It was right out here, and that nasty Alfred Temple—(*She breaks into fresh sobs*) Oh, if I could have another chance, I wouldn't say it for the whole world. But he's gone now, and I'll never, never see him again.

MRS. HARPER (*Sympathetically*): I reckon Tom knows you are sorry, Becky.

BECKY: I'll never know if he does. He'll never come and ask me to make up again, never, never, never.

NARRATOR: Tom, deeply moved, starts to go to her, but Joe and Huck hold him back. He wipes his eyes on his shirt sleeve. Aunt Polly and Sid come from the house and Aunt Polly goes to greet Mrs. Harper.

AUNT POLLY (*Tearfully*): Oh, Mrs. Harper, I don't know how to give Tom up. He was such a comfort to me. He was full of mischief, but he never meant any harm, and he was the best-hearted boy that ever was.

MRS. HARPER: It was just so with my Joe. He was as unselfish and kind as he could be. And to think I whipped him for takin' that cream, never once recollectin' that I threw it out myself because it was sour—poor, poor abused boy.

SID: I hope Tom's better off where he is, but if he'd been better in some ways—

AUNT POLLY: Sid! Not a word against my Tom! God will take care of *him*, never you trouble *your*self, sir! (*Emotionally*) Oh, I wish Tom were alive again!

NARRATOR: Tom signals to the other boys and they come out from hiding. Aunt Polly is the first to see him, and her shout brings Widow Douglas and the children to the door.

AUNT POLLY: *Tom Sawyer!*

TOM: Ma'am?

MRS. HARPER: Joe Harper!

JOE: Yes'm?

AUNT POLLY: Tom! Is it really you? You're not dead and playin' tricks on me?

TOM: No, Aunt Polly. We were just off bein' pirates on Jackson's Island.

ALL: Pirates!

TOM: Somebody's got to be glad to see Huck, too.

WIDOW DOUGLAS: And so they shall. *I* am glad to see him, poor motherless thing, and I am going to take him straight home with me.

AUNT POLLY (*Teasing*): So you were off bein' pirates, were you?

TOM: Yes'm.

AUNT POLLY: I suppose you did a powerful lot of swimmin'.

TOM: Yes'm. Pirates always swim when they capture boats—with knives between their teeth.

AUNT POLLY: You don't say! Did pirates ever chop up kindling wood for the kitchen stove?

TOM: I reckon not, Aunt Polly. They mostly had campfires.

AUNT POLLY: Well, young man, here's one pirate who's goin' to chop kindling—right now.

TOM: But Aunt Polly!

AUNT POLLY: No arguing! There's the woodshed. March!

TOM: Aw, geeminy!

NARRATOR: Tom goes slowly in the direction of the woodshed, but as he nears it, he turns and dashes toward the street. As he passes Aunt Polly, she grabs him by the collar of his jacket, but Tom slips out of it quickly, leaving her holding an empty jacket.

AUNT POLLY: Drat that boy! (*Everyone bursts out laughing, and* AUNT POLLY *joins in good-naturedly.*) The best-hearted boy there ever was!

THE END

A Christmas Carol

This is one of the most famous Christmas stories ever written. You have probably heard the story before, but now you have the chance to read it aloud as a play.

There are many different kinds of characters in the play—old and young men, ghosts, children. Each one must sound just right.

After you have read the play through silently and have chosen your parts, discuss with the group these questions:

How does Scrooge change during the play? What causes him to change?

How are the three ghosts different? Would you read their parts differently? How?

What is Tiny Tim like? How should he sound?

Read the play aloud together. Are there any places that need more work? If so, practice them until they sound right.

Some of the language in the play is different from that used today. Are there any words you need help with? Are you paying attention to your tone of voice? Are you expressing the proper feelings when you read?

Work on the play until you can read it smoothly and meaningfully. When you think you are good enough, arrange to read it for the class. You might prefer to read it into a tape recorder and then play it back so that you can listen to yourselves along with the class.

Note to the teacher: The starred parts may be doubled if desired.

A CHRISTMAS CAROL

by Charles Dickens
adapted by Walter Hackett

Characters

(14 boys, 4 girls, and a narrator)
NARRATOR
EBENEZER SCROOGE
TWO BOYS*
FRED
BOB CRATCHIT
GENTLEMAN*
MARLEY
THREE GHOSTS
FAN
BELLE
MRS. CRATCHIT
TINY TIM
TWO MEN*
MARTHA
BOY*

NARRATOR: It is the afternoon before Christmas Day in the year of our Lord 1844. Despite the bitterly cold weather, all London is in a festive mood. As the clock strikes three, a group of young people caroling through the city pass by the offices of Ebenezer Scrooge . . .

SCROOGE (*Angrily*): Stop it! Stop it, I say. Away from here with all that noise! We'll have no singing around here! Do you understand that? No singing, I say.

1ST BOY: A Merry Christmas, sir.

2ND BOY: No need to wish '*im* a Merry Christmas. That's Old Scrooge.

NARRATOR: Yes, that's old Scrooge, all right—Ebenezer Scrooge. And there's no sign of happiness or festivity on his lined face. He closes the door and returns to his office. He looks around, glowers at his clerk, Bob Cratchit, snorts as he sees Cratchit bent over his desk hard at work. As he adjusts his spectacles and turns, without warning the door opens.

FRED: A Merry Christmas, Uncle. God save you!

SCROOGE (*Impatiently*): Bah! Humbug!

FRED: Christmas a humbug? Surely you don't mean that, Uncle?

SCROOGE: Merry Christmas, indeed! What right have you to be merry? You're poor enough.

FRED: What right have you to be dismal? You're rich enough.

SCROOGE: What's Christmas time to you but a time for paying bills without money; a time for finding yourself a year older, and not an hour richer? (*His voice rising*) If I had my way, every idiot who goes about with "Merry Christmas" on his lips would be boiled in his own pudding and buried with a stake of holly through his heart. You keep Christmas in your own way, and let me keep it in mine.

FRED (*Placatingly*): I came here to ask you to spend Christmas Day with Peg and me.

SCROOGE (*Flatly*): No! Certainly not!

FRED: We want nothing from you, Uncle, other than your company for Christmas Day. (*Pause*) Won't you change your mind and have dinner with us?

SCROOGE: You know my sentiments on Christmas. (*Firmly*) Good day, Fred.

FRED (*Glumly*): A Merry Christmas, Uncle.

SCROOGE (*Sternly*): Good afternoon.

FRED (*Pleasantly*): And a Happy New Year to you.

SCROOGE (*With annoyance*): Bah! Humbug!

CRATCHIT (*Interrupting, timidly*): Er-uh-pardon me, Mr. Scrooge . . .

SCROOGE (*Impatiently*): Well, what is it?

CRATCHIT: There is a gentleman here to see you.

SCROOGE: What about, Cratchit?

CRATCHIT: He didn't say, sir.

GENTLEMAN (*Smoothly*): Ah, good afternoon, sir. Have I the pleasure of addressing Mr. Scrooge or Mr. Marley?

SCROOGE: Mr. Marley, my former partner, has been dead these seven years. He died seven years ago, this very night.

GENTLEMAN: Then I have no doubt his liberality is well represented by his surviving partner.

SCROOGE (*Suspiciously*): What do you want?

GENTLEMAN: At this festive season, Mr. Scrooge, we try to make some slight provision for the poor and destitute. Many thousands are in want of common necessities.

SCROOGE (*Coldly*): Are there no prisons?

GENTLEMAN (*Trying to keep calm*): Oh, plenty of prisons.

SCROOGE: And the workhouses, are they still in operation?

GENTLEMAN (*Sighing*): I wish I could say they were not. (*Pause*) How much shall I put you down for, Mr. Scrooge?

SCROOGE (*Heatedly*): Nothing!

GENTLEMAN (*Puzzled*): Nothing?

SCROOGE: Exactly! Let these deserving people of yours go to the establishments I have mentioned.

GENTLEMAN: Most of them would rather die than do that, Mr. Scrooge.

SCROOGE (*Harshly*): Then let them do that, and help decrease the surplus population. I'm busy. Good afternoon to you.

GENTLEMAN (*Quietly*): Very good, Mr. Scrooge. Merry Christmas to you.

SCROOGE (*Grumbling*): Charity! Bah! Humbug!

CRATCHIT: Er—Mr. Scrooge, sir.

SCROOGE: Well, what is it, Cratchit?

CRATCHIT (*Timidly*): I was wondering—

SCROOGE: You were wondering if you could go home.

CRATCHIT: Yes, sir. It is getting late.

SCROOGE: Yes, go on. You'll want all day tomorrow, I suppose?

CRATCHIT: If it's quite convenient, sir.

SCROOGE: It's not convenient, and it's not fair!

CRATCHIT: It's only once a year, sir.

SCROOGE: A poor excuse for picking a man's pocket every twenty-fifth day of December. I suppose you must have the whole day, but be here all the earlier the next day. Understand?

CRATCHIT: Yes, sir. And Merry Christmas.

SCROOGE: Christmas! Humbug!

NARRATOR: A few minutes later Scrooge leaves his office and makes his way to his gloomy suite of rooms. By the light of a single flickering candle, he eats his cold supper. And then to save lighting his stove, Ebenezer Scrooge retires for the night. The minutes tick away. Scrooge sleeps uneasily, tossing from side to side—then he awakes with a start. Walking toward him, dragging a heavy chain, is a gray, dim figure, which stops at the foot of the bed.

SCROOGE (*Frightened*): Who are you? What do you want with me? (*Pause*) Who are you? Answer me!

MARLEY (*In a quivering voice*): Ask me who I *was*.

SCROOGE (*Terrified*): You are—you are—you can't be . . .

MARLEY: Yes, in life I was your partner, Jacob Marley.

SCROOGE (*Loudly*): But it cannot be so. You're dead.

MARLEY: You don't believe in me?

SCROOGE: No. (*With bravado*) You're nothing but an undigested bit of beef, a blot of mustard, a crumb of cheese.

MARLEY: You are wrong, Ebenezer. I am the ghost of Jacob Marley.

SCROOGE (*Frightened*): Why do you come to me?

MARLEY: It is required of every man that the spirit within him should walk abroad among his fellowmen and travel far and wide; and if that spirit goes not forth in life, it is condemned to do so after death.

SCROOGE: No, no, I don't believe it.

MARLEY: It is then doomed to wander through the world.

SCROOGE: You are chained, Jacob. Tell me why.

MARLEY: I wear the chain I forged in life. I made it link by link, and yard by yard. I wore it of my own free will. Is its pattern strange to you?

SCROOGE (*In a trembling voice*): I don't understand.

MARLEY: This chain I wear is as heavy as the one you are now forging.

SCROOGE (*Puzzled*): You talk strangely, Jacob.

MARLEY: For seven years I have been dead—traveling the whole time. (*Sighs deeply*) No rest, no peace. Only remorse.

SCROOGE: But you were always shrewd, Jacob.

MARLEY: Aye, too shrewd.

SCROOGE: A good man of business.

MARLEY: Business! Mankind was my business. The common welfare was my business; charity, mercy, forbearance and benevolence were all my business. But I heeded none of these. Instead, I thought only of money.

SCROOGE: And what is wrong with making money?

MARLEY: That is your weakness, Ebenezer, as it was mine. That is why I am here tonight, part of the reason for my penance. I am here to warn you . . . to help you escape my fate. You have one chance left.

SCROOGE (*Anxiously*): Tell me how this chance will come!

MARLEY: My time draws near. I must go. Tonight you will be haunted by three spirits. The first will appear when the bell strikes one; expect the second at the stroke of two, and the third as the bell tolls three.

SCROOGE: Couldn't they come all at once and have it over with?

MARLEY: No. And heed them well when they appear. (*Fading*) Remember, it is your last chance to escape my miserable fate.

NARRATOR: As Scrooge stares in frightened silence, the figure of his deceased partner, Marley, recedes into space. Then, exhausted by the ordeal, Scrooge drops off to sleep. In the distance, the steeple clock is heard striking one. The curtains of

Scrooge's bed are drawn aside, as if by invisible hands. Suddenly, there stands by the bed a strange figure with white hair, holding a sprig of fresh green holly. Scrooge stares and then speaks.

SCROOGE (*Nervously*): Are you the spirit whose coming was told me by Jacob Marley?

1ST GHOST (*In a gentle voice*): I am.

SCROOGE (*In agitation*): Who, and what are you?

1ST GHOST: I am the Ghost of Christmas Past.

SCROOGE: Long past?

1ST GHOST: No. Your past. Rise and walk with me.

SCROOGE: Where?

1ST GHOST: Out through the window.

SCROOGE (*Terrified*): But we are three stories above ground. I am only a mortal.

1ST GHOST: Bear but a touch of my hand upon your heart and you shall be upheld in more than this.

SCROOGE: What are we to do?

1ST GHOST: I am going to help redeem you. Come! Walk with me out into the night . . . into the past.

SCROOGE: Tell me, Ghost of Christmas Past, where are we?

1ST GHOST: Look down, Ebenezer, and think back to your youth. . . .

SCROOGE (*Amazed*): Why . . . why, of course. The river . . . the meadows . . . and—there's the old school where I went as a lad. But there is no one about.

1ST GHOST: It's the Christmas holiday. Look into this study hall. (*Pause*)

SCROOGE: Empty, except for a young boy sitting at a desk, his head in his hands. Left behind. He . . . he's crying. Poor chap! No place to go at Christmas. Ah, now he's looking up.

1ST GHOST: Do you recognize him?

SCROOGE (*Stunned*): Why, it's—it's—

1ST GHOST: What is his name?

SCROOGE (*Slowly*): Ebenezer Scrooge. (*Pause*) I wish (*Sighs*) —but it's too late now.

1ST GHOST: What is the matter?

SCROOGE: Nothing, nothing. (*Sadly*) There were some boys singing Christmas carols outside my office door yesterday afternoon, and I drove them away. (*Pause*)

1ST GHOST: Come. Let us look back on another Christmas a year later.

SCROOGE: Why, there's the school again. (*Hesitantly*) There is a boy pacing up and down in the school yard . . . I wonder who . . .

1ST GHOST: Do you recognize him?

SCROOGE: Yes, I see it is myself as a boy. . . . A coach is coming up the roadway. Now it has stopped, and a little girl gets out. Look, she is hugging me. It's my sister, Fan.

1ST GHOST: Listen to what she says.

FAN: I've come to bring you home, dear brother Ebenezer. Father's not mean anymore, and he says you're never coming back here, and from now on we'll always be together. (*Fading*) Just think, we're together for the first time in four years.

1ST GHOST: Your sister was a delicate creature . . . kind . . . soft-hearted.

SCROOGE (*Sighing*): So she was, so she was. She died comparatively young.

1ST GHOST: And left one child behind her.

SCROOGE: Yes—Fred, my nephew.

1ST GHOST (*Mildly*): He came to wish you a Merry Christmas yesterday.

SCROOGE: Yes, yes, he did! (*Pauses, then in agitation*) Please, please take me back!

1ST GHOST: Not yet. There is one more spirit for you to see.

SCROOGE (*Pleadingly*): No more, please. I do not wish to see it.

1ST GHOST: You must. Several years have passed. In the house below, there sits a young, very beautiful girl. . . .

SCROOGE (*Incredulously*): It's Belle.

1ST GHOST: The girl you were to marry. And there you sit next to her, a young man in your prime. Only now your face begins to show the signs of avarice. There is a greedy, restless motion in your eyes. Listen to what she is saying to you.

BELLE: It matters very little to you, Ebenezer. Another idol has displaced me, a golden one. You hold money more important than me—or anything else, for that matter. And I am going to grant your wish: free you from marrying me. (*Fading*) That is what you desire, Ebenezer. I feel sorry for you.

SCROOGE (*In anguish*): Spirit, show me no more.

1ST GHOST: Today, Belle is a happy woman, surrounded by her fine children. Those children might have been yours if you hadn't been so selfish.

SCROOGE: Take me back. (*Wildly*) Haunt me no more! I beg of you, cease.

NARRATOR (*After a pause*): The second hour of Christmas Day! Scrooge finds himself back in his bedroom. Slowly, his door, though bolted, swings open.

2ND GHOST (*In a booming voice*): Good morning, Ebenezer. I am the Ghost of Christmas Present. Look upon me.

SCROOGE (*Fearfully*): You're practically a giant. Yet you have a young face.

2ND GHOST: Have you never seen the like of me before?

SCROOGE: Never.

2ND GHOST: I have many brothers, over eighteen hundred of them, one for each Christmas since the very first.

SCROOGE (*Frightened*): And you are here to take me with you?

2ND GHOST: Yes. I trust you will profit by your journey. Touch my robe, Ebenezer. We have little time, and there is a place we must visit. It is a very poor house in a very poor section of London. This one directly below us.

SCROOGE: Indeed it is. Who, may I ask, lives here?

2ND GHOST: An underpaid clerk named Bob Cratchit.

SCROOGE: The Bob Cratchit who is employed by me?

2ND GHOST: The very same.

SCROOGE: That woman . . . those four children.

2ND GHOST: His wife and family.

SCROOGE: That's Cratchit coming up the stairs right now. He's carrying a young boy. . . .

2ND GHOST: His fifth child . . . Tiny Tim.

SCROOGE: The child carries a crutch.

2ND GHOST: Because he is crippled.

SCROOGE: But the doctors—

2ND GHOST: Cratchit cannot afford a doctor, not on fifteen shillings a week.

SCROOGE: But—

2ND GHOST: Sh-h-h! Listen!

CRATCHIT (*Heartily*): Good afternoon, everyone.

TIM: And a most Merry Christmas!

MRS. CRATCHIT: Father . . . Tiny Tim.

OTHER CRATCHITS (*Ad lib*): Merry Christmas! Welcome! Tiny Tim, sit next to me. Father, let me take your muffler. (*Etc.*)

MRS. CRATCHIT: And how did Tiny Tim behave at church?

CRATCHIT (*Affectionately*): As good as gold, and better.

TIM: I was glad to be able to go to church. That's because I wanted the people to see that I'm a cripple.

MRS. CRATCHIT: Now that's a peculiar thing to say, Tiny Tim.

TIM (*Eagerly*): No, it isn't. That's because I was in God's House, and it was God who made the blind able to see, and the lame able to walk. And when the people at church saw me and my crutch, I was hoping they would think of what God can do, and that they would say a prayer for me.

MRS. CRATCHIT (*Tearfully*): I . . . I'm certain they prayed for you.

TIM (*Cheerfully*): And one of these days I'm going to get well, and that'll mean I can throw away this crutch, and run and play like the other boys.

CRATCHIT (*Softly*): You will, Tim—one of these days. (*Heartily*) And now, Mother, the big question. When will dinner be ready?

MRS. CRATCHIT: It's ready now: just about the finest goose you have ever seen. Martha, you carry it in. Tom, you fetch the potatoes and turnips. Dick, Peter, set the chairs around the table.

TIM (*Happily*): And I'll sit between Father and Mother.

CRATCHIT: This is going to be the best Christmas dinner anyone could hope for. (*Fading*) And I'm the luckiest man in the world, having such a fine family.

SCROOGE: It isn't a very big goose, is it? I could eat the whole bird myself, I believe.

2ND GHOST: It is all Bob Cratchit can afford. His family doesn't complain. To them, that meager goose is a sumptuous banquet. But more important, much more important, Ebenezer—

SCROOGE: Yes?

2ND GHOST: They are a happy and united group. Look at their shining faces. Listen to them.

CRATCHIT (*Contentedly*): What a superb dinner we have had . . . the tempting meat, the delicious dressing.

TIM: And the plum pudding, Father. Don't forget that.

CRATCHIT: That pudding was the greatest success achieved by Mrs. Cratchit since her marriage. (*All laugh.*)

MRS. CRATCHIT (*Happily*): Thank you for the compliment. I must confess it was good.

CRATCHIT: And now for the crowning touch. The punch!

ALL (*Ad lib*): The punch! Good! Delicious, I'm sure! (*Etc.*)

CRATCHIT: Here we are. Get your glasses. You, Peter . . . Dick . . . Tom . . . Martha . . . Tiny Tim . . . and last, but far from least, you, Mother. And not to forget myself. (*With finality*) There!

TIM: A toast!

CRATCHIT (*Heartily*): First, to the founder of this feast, the man who has made it possible. I give you Mr. Scrooge.

MRS. CRATCHIT (*Bristling*): Mr. Scrooge, indeed! I wish I had him here! I'd give him a piece of my mind to feast upon, and I hope he'd have a good appetite for it.

CRATCHIT (*Warningly*): My dear, the children! Remember, this is Christmas Day.

MRS. CRATCHIT: He's a hard, stingy, unfeeling man. You know he is, Robert; you know better than anybody else.

CRATCHIT (*Mildly*): My dear. Remember, Christmas Day.

MRS. CRATCHIT: I'm sorry. (*Sighing*) Very well, I'll drink his health. Long life to him! A Merry Christmas to him! To Mr. Scrooge.

ALL: To Mr. Scrooge.

CRATCHIT: And now a toast to us: A Merry Christmas to us all. God bless us!

ALL: God bless us all.

TIM: God bless us every one!

SCROOGE: Spirit, tell me—will Tiny Tim live?

2ND GHOST: I see a vacant seat in the chimney corner, and a crutch without an owner, carefully preserved. If these shadows remain unaltered by the Future, the child will die.

SCROOGE: No, no. Oh, no, kind Spirit! Say he will live, that he will be spared.

2ND GHOST: Why concern yourself about him? (*Harshly*) Isn't it better that he die and decrease the surplus population?

SCROOGE (*Frantically*): But these poor people must be helped.

2ND GHOST (*Sarcastically*): Are there no prisons? And the workhouses, are they still in operation?

SCROOGE (*Disturbed*): Do not taunt me.

2ND GHOST (*Coldly*): Come. It is time for us to go.

SCROOGE: No, I wish to remain.

2ND GHOST: I can remain no longer. Touch my robe, and we shall go.

SCROOGE: No! No, I say! Spirit, don't desert me. I need your help.

NARRATOR: Ebenezer Scrooge shortly finds himself standing outside his lodgings. A heavy snow is falling, blanketing a sleeping London. The wind has died down. It is still early Christmas morning.

3RD GHOST (*Warningly*): Ebenezer . . . Ebenezer Scrooge.

SCROOGE: You are the third and last.

3RD GHOST: I am the Ghost of Christmas Yet to Come.

SCROOGE: You are about to show me shadows of the things that have not happened, but will happen in the time before us. Is that so, Spirit?

3RD GHOST: Yes, Ebenezer.

SCROOGE: I fear what I am to see.

3RD GHOST: Come, Ebenezer.

SCROOGE: Why do we stop here on this street corner, Spirit?

3RD GHOST: Those two men standing there, do you know them?

SCROOGE (*Uncomfortably*): Why, yes, I do business with them.

3RD GHOST: Their conversation is interesting.

1ST MAN: When did he die?

2ND MAN: Last night, I believe.

1ST MAN: I thought he'd never die.

2ND MAN: What has he done with his money?

1ST MAN: I haven't heard. Left it to his company, perhaps. Well, one thing is certain, he didn't leave it to charity.

2ND MAN: Are you going to his funeral?

1ST MAN: Not unless a free lunch is provided.

2ND MAN (*Fading*): A very good point. Can't say that I blame you.

SCROOGE: Spirit, this dead man they were discussing, who is he?

3RD GHOST: I will show you. There is a bed in front of you. On it lies a man—that is, the body of a man—the one those gentlemen on the street were talking about.

SCROOGE: And no one has come to claim this body?

3RD GHOST: No one, for he left not a friend behind him. Come closer and look into his face.

SCROOGE (*In horror*): No!

3RD GHOST: Look!

SCROOGE: Spirit, this is a fearful place.

3RD GHOST: Look at the face of this unclaimed man.

SCROOGE (*Terrified*): I would do it if I could. But I haven't the power. Let me see some tenderness connected with a death. If I don't, that lonely body in this dark room will ever haunt me.

3RD GHOST: Yes, I know of such a home, one where there is tenderness connected with death. Over here on this poor street and in this dismal house.

SCROOGE: But this house—Why, yes, I've been here before. Bob Cratchit, my clerk, lives here. There are Mrs. Cratchit and her oldest daughter, Martha.

MARTHA: Your eyes, Mother—you'll strain them working in this bad light.

MRS. CRATCHIT: I'll stop for a while. I wouldn't want to show red, tired eyes to your father when he comes home. It's time he was here.

MARTHA: Past it, rather. But these days he walks slower than he used to, Mother.

MRS. CRATCHIT: I have known him to walk with Tiny Tim upon his shoulder very fast, indeed. He was very light to carry and your father loved him so, it was no trouble. There is your father at the door now, Martha.

MARTHA: I'll let him in. Hello, Father. You look tired.

MRS. CRATCHIT: You are late tonight, Robert.

CRATCHIT (*Dispiritedly*): Yes, I am late.

MARTHA: I'll get some tea for you.

CRATCHIT: Thank you, Martha.

MRS. CRATCHIT: You went there today?

CRATCHIT: Yes. I wish you could have gone. It would have done you good to see how green a place it is.

MRS. CRATCHIT: I'll see it soon.

CRATCHIT: I promised him I would walk there every Sunday. My poor Tiny Tim. (*Sighing*) At last he is rid of his crutch.

MRS. CRATCHIT: Yes, at last. Our poor Tiny Tim.

SCROOGE: Tell me, Spirit, why did Tiny Tim have to die?

3RD GHOST: Come, there is still another place to visit. When you see the next place I am taking you, perhaps you will understand. Come.

SCROOGE (*Timidly*): Is this a graveyard? Why do we pause here?

3RD GHOST: Look at that tombstone . . . read the name on it.

SCROOGE: Before I do, answer me one question. Are these the shadows of the things that *will* be, or are they the shadows of things that *may* be?

3RD GHOST (*Ignoring him*): Read the inscription on the tombstone.

SCROOGE: It reads . . . (*Slowly*) "Ebenezer Scrooge." (*Screaming*) No, Spirit! Oh, no, no! Hear me! I am not the man I was! I will not be like the man you have just shown me! I will honor Christmas.

3RD GHOST: Are you certain of this?

SCROOGE: Oh, yes. (*Anxiously*) I will try to keep it alive all the year. I will live in the Past, the Present and the Future. I will not shut out the lesson that all three Spirits have taught me. Oh, tell me there is hope, that I may rub away the writing on this stone!

3RD GHOST: We shall soon see.

SCROOGE (*Moaning, as though coming out of a dream*): Tell me there is hope, that I may rub away the writing on this stone. (*Coming to*) Eh, what am I holding on to? The bedpost. I am in my own bed . . . home. Those bells! It must be Christmas Day—I wonder if it really is. I'll look out the window. (*Calls*) You, boy, down there.

BOY: Yes, did you call me, sir?

SCROOGE: What day is it today, lad?

BOY: Today! Why, Christmas Day.

SCROOGE: And to think the Spirits have done it all in one night.

BOY: What did you say, sir?

SCROOGE: Do you know the poulterer's in the next street?

BOY (*Happily*): I should say so!

SCROOGE: An intelligent boy! A remarkable boy! (*To* BOY) Do you know whether they've sold the prize turkey that was in the window?

BOY: The one as big as me?

SCROOGE (*Laughing*): A delightful boy. Yes, the one as big as you.

BOY: It's hanging there now.

SCROOGE: Go and buy it. I am in earnest. Here is the money. Catch. (*Pause*) Deliver it to Bob Cratchit, on Golden Street in Camden Town.

BOY (*Puzzled*): But, sir, there will be considerable change left over.

SCROOGE (*Chuckling*): Keep it, lad!

BOY (*Delighted*): Oh, thank you, sir.

SCROOGE (*Seriously*): Don't let Mr. Cratchit know who sent the turkey. It's a surprise. And, lad—

BOY: Yes, sir?

SCROOGE (*Cheerfully*): A very Merry Christmas to you.

NARRATOR: Scrooge quickly dons his hat and coat and makes his way through the city. He knocks timidly on Fred's door.

FRED: Who can that be at the door? (*Pause*) Why, bless my soul, Uncle!

SCROOGE (*Heartily*): Yes, yes, it is—your Uncle Scrooge. I've come for Christmas dinner. Now let me in. I have a present for your good wife. From now on I'm going to be one of your most persistent guests. I've changed, my boy; you'll see! (*Laughs.*)

NARRATOR: Scrooge was better than his word. He did everything he promised, and infinitely more. He became a regular visitor to his nephew's home, and even took Fred into business with him. He raised Bob Cratchit's salary to a figure that left the bewildered gentleman gasping; and to Tiny Tim, who did not die, he was a second father. He provided doctors for the little lad, and very soon Tiny Tim will have his wish; he will be able to throw away his crutch and run and play like the other boys. As for the three Spirits, Ebenezer Scrooge never saw them again. That was due to the unchallengeable fact that Scrooge, for the rest of his days, helped keep alive the spirit of Christmas. And so, as Tiny Tim observed, God bless us every one.

THE END